Visit us at

Kismet Hacking

Brad 'RenderMan' Haines
Michael J. Schearer
Frank Thornton

KEY	SERIAL NUMBER
001	HJIRTCV764
002	PO9873D5FG
003	829KM8NJH2
004	BAL923457U
005	CVPLQ6WQ23
006	VBP965T5T5
007	HJJJ863WD3E
008	2987GVTWMK
009	629MP5SDJT
010	IMWQ295T6T

PUBLISHED BY
Syngress Publishing, Inc.
Elsevier, Inc.
30 Corporate Drive
Burlington, MA 01803

Kismet Hacking

Printed and bound in the United Kingdom
Transferred to Digital Printing, 2010

ISBN 13: 978-1-59749-117-4

Page Layout and Art: SPi Publishing Services
Copy Editor: Judy Eby

For information on rights, translations, and bulk sales, contact Matt Pedersen, Commercial Sales Director and Rights, at Syngress Publishing; email m.pedersen@elsevier.com.

Contributing Authors

Brad 'RenderMan' Haines is one of the more visible and vocal members of the wardriving community, appearing in various media outlets and speaking at conferences several times a year. Render is usually near by on any wardriving and wireless security news, often causing it himself. His skills have been learned in the trenches working for various IT companies as well as his involvement through the years with the hacking community, sometimes to the attention of carious Canadian and American intelligence agencies. A firm believer in the hacker ethos and promoting responsible hacking and sharing of ideas, he wrote the 'Stumbler ethic' for beginning wardrivers and greatly enjoys speaking at corporate conferences to dissuade the negative image of hackers and wardrivers.

His work frequently borders on the absurd as his approach is usually one of ignoring conventional logic and just doing it. He can be found in Edmonton, Alberta, Canada, probably taking something apart.

Michael J. Schearer is an active-duty Naval Flight Officer and Electronic Countermeasures Officer with the U.S. Navy. He flew combat missions during Operations Enduring Freedom, Southern Watch, and Iraqi Freedom. He later took his electronic warfare specialty to Iraq, where he embedded on the ground with Army units to lead the counter-IED fight. He currently serves as an instructor of Naval Science at the Pennsylvania State University Naval Reserve Officer Training Corps Unit, University Park, PA.

Michael is an active member of the Church of WiFi and has spoken at Shmoocon, DEFCON, and Penn State's Security Day, as well as other forums. His work has been cited in Forbes, InfoWorld and Wired.

Michael is an alumnus of Bloomsburg University where he studied Political Science and Georgetown University where he obtained his degree in National Security Studies. While at Penn State, he is actively involved in IT issues. He is a licensed amateur radio operator, moderator of the Church of WiFi and Remote-Exploit Forums, and a regular on the DEFCON and NetStumbler forums.

Frank Thornton runs his own technology consulting firm, Blackthorn Systems, which specializes in wireless networks. His specialties include wireless network architecture, design, and implementation, as well as network troubleshooting and optimization. An interest in amateur radio helped him bridge the gap between computers and wireless networks. Having learned at a young age which end of the soldering iron was hot, he has even been known to repair hardware on occasion. In addition to his computer and wireless interests, Frank was a law enforcement officer for many years. As a detective and forensics expert he has investigated approximately one hundred homicides and thousands of other crime scenes. Combining both professional interests, he was a member of the workgroup that established ANSI Standard "ANSI/NIST-CSL 1-1993 Data Format for the Interchange of Fingerprint Information." He co-authored *RFID Security* (Syngress Publishing, ISBN: 1597490474), *WarDriving: Drive, Detect, and Defend: A Guide to Wireless Security* (Syngress, ISBN: 193183603), as well as contributed to *IT Ethics Handbook: Right and Wrong for IT Professionals* (Syngress, ISBN: 1931836140) and *Game Console Hacking: Xbox, PlayStation, Nintendo, Atari, & Gamepark 32* (ISBN: 1931836310). He resides in Vermont with his wife.

Contents

Chapter 1 Introduction to Wireless Networking, Wardriving, and Kismet 1

Exploring Past Discoveries That Led to Wireless 2
   Discovering Electromagnetism 2
   Exploring Conduction 3
   Inventing the Radio 4
   Mounting Radio-Telephones in Cars 5
   Inventing Computers and Networks 6
   Inventing Cell Phones. 7
Exploring Present Applications for Wireless 9
   Applying Wireless Technology to Vertical Markets. 10
      Using Wireless in Delivery Services. 10
      Using Wireless for Public Safety 10
      Using Wireless in the Financial World 11
      Using Wireless in the Retail World 11
      Using Wireless in Monitoring Applications 12
   Applying Wireless Technology to Horizontal Applications. 12
      Using Wireless in Messaging. 12
      Using Wireless for Mapping 12
      Using Wireless for Web Surfing. 13
      Using Bluetooth Wireless Devices. 13
Introduction to Wardriving. 14
   The Origins of Wardriving 14
   Definition 14
      The Terminology History of Wardriving. 15
   Wardriving Misconceptions. 15
   The Truth about Wardriving 16
      The Legality of Wardriving 17
Introduction to Wardriving with Linux 17
   Preparing Your System to Wardrive 17
   Preparing the Kernel 17
      Preparing the Kernel for Monitor Mode. 18
      Preparing the Kernel for a Global
         Positioning System 21

Installing the Proper Tools. 23
   Installing Kismet 23
   Installing GPSD. 24
Configuring Your System to Wardrive 24
Wardriving with Linux and Kismet. 29
Starting Kismet. 29
Using the Kismet Interface 31
   Understanding the Kismet Options. 32
   Using a Graphical Front End 35
Summary. 38

Chapter 2 Basic Installation **39**
Introduction 40
Kismet Prerequisites 41
Kismet Installation 43
   Choosing a Wireless Card Driver 50
   Wireless Card Driver Compiling
      and Installation 55
   Configuring Kismet (Editing kismet.conf) 56
      Run Kismet 60

Chapter 3 Operating Kismet. **63**
Introduction 64
The Kismet User Interface 64
   The Introductory Splash Screen 65
   Play Sounds. 66
Additional RF Equipment: Antennas and Cables 66
Pigtails. 70
Using a GPS Receiver with Kismet 71
Typical GPS Problems. 74
Putting It All together: The Complete Kismet Setup 78
Summary. 81

Chapter 4 Kismet Menus. **83**
Introduction 84
Main Display 85
Network List Panel. 86
   Sorting 87
   Columns 88
      Decay. 89
      Name. 89

Type 89
WEP 90
Channel 90
Packets 90
Flags 90
IP 91
Size 91
Colors 91
GPS 92
Information Panel 93
Status Panel 93
Pop-up Windows 94
Network Details 95
Client List 96
Columns 96
Decay 96
Type 97
Manufacturer 97
Data 98
Crypt 98
Size 98
IP Range 98
Sgn 98
Client Details 98
Packet rate 99
Packet Types 100
Statistics 102
Wireless Card Power 102
Network Location 103
Customizing the Panels Interface 104
Customizing the Network List Window 105
Customizing the Client List Window 106
Customizing Colors 107
Third Party Front-ends 108
gkismet 108
KisWin 109
dumb kismet client 110
Further information 111
Summary 112
Solutions Fast Track 112

Chapter 5 Configuring the Kismet Server 115

Introduction 116
The Kismet Config File 116
    Kismet Parameters 116
Kismet.conf 117
    Kismet Server Command Line 143
Summary 147

Chapter 6 Kismet Client Configuration File 149

Introduction 150
The Kismet Client Config File 150
    Kismet Parameters 150
Command-Line Switches 168
Summary 170

Chapter 7 Server.conf File Advanced
Configuration 171

Introduction 172
Asus eeePC Installation 172
    Installation and Updating 172
    Install Development Tools 173
Kismet on Windows 175
    Installation 176
    Troubleshooting 177
Wardriving in a Box 177
Monitor Installation 184
Summary 185

Chapter 8 Kismet Drones 187

Introduction 188
Drone Installation 188
    Linksys WRT54G 188
        Installation 190
    Whiterussian 191
    Server Configuration 194
        Troubleshooting 197
    Kamikaze 198
    Server Configuration 204
    Cross Compiling with OpenWRT-Buildroot 205
    Buildroot Installation 205
        Troubleshooting 211
PC Drone Setup 212

Kismet Drone Configuration File 214
Summary. 222

Chapter 9 Kismet and Mapping 223
Introduction 224
GPSMap/KisMap. 224
Patching GPSMap 225
KisMap 225
WiGLE 225
WiGLE Google Map 226
IGiGLE 227
GpsDrive 228
Installation 229
Install from Source. 230
Install from Package 230
MySQL 231
Kismet + GpsDrive + MySQL 233
Maps 234
Alternatives 235
Kismet Earth 235
OpenStreetMap 235
Summary. 236
Solutions Fast Track 236

Chapter 10 Wardriving with Kismet and BackTrack 239
Introduction 240
Obtaining BackTrack 240
Downloading BackTrack. 240
Burning BackTrack to CD 242
Configuring Kismet 243
Booting into BackTrack 243
Wireless Card Configuration. 243
kismet.conf 244
Command Line 245
Log File Configuration 245
Other Configuration Issues 245
Wardriving with Kismet 246
Wardriving 247
Managing Your Results. 250
WiGLE 250

Index 253

## Chapter 1

Introduction to Wireless Networking, Wardriving, and Kismet

Solutions in this chapter

- **Exploring Past Discoveries That Led to Wireless**

- **Exploring Present Applications for Wireless**

- **Introduction to Wardriving**

- **Introduction to Wardriving with Linux**

- **Wardriving with Linux and Kismet**

☑ **Summary**

Exploring Past Discoveries That Led to Wireless

Wireless technology is the method of delivering data from one point to another without using physical wires, and includes radio, cellular, infrared, and satellite. A historic perspective will provide you with a general understanding of the substantial evolution that has taken place in this area. The common wireless networks of today originated from many evolutionary stages of wireless communications and telegraph and radio applications. Although some discoveries occurred in the early 1800s, much of the evolution of wireless communication began with the emergence of the electrical age and was affected by modern economics as much as by discoveries in physics.

Because the current demand of wireless technology is a direct outgrowth of traditional wired 10-Base-T Ethernet networks, we will also briefly cover the advent of the computer and the evolution of computer networks. Physical networks, and their limitations, significantly impacted wireless technology. This section presents some of the aspects of traditional computer networks and how they relate to wireless networks. Another significant impact to wireless is the invention of the cell phone. This section will briefly explain significant strides in the area of cellular communication.

Discovering Electromagnetism

Early writings show that people were aware of magnetism for several centuries before the middle 1600s; however, people did not become aware of the correlation between magnetism and electricity until the 1800s. In 1820, Hans Christian Oersted, a Danish physicist and philosopher working at that time as a professor at the University of Copenhagen, attached a wire to a battery during a lecture; coincidentally, he just happened to do this near a compass and he noticed that the compass needle swung around. This is how he discovered that there was a relationship between electricity and magnetism. Oersted continued to explore this relationship, influencing the works of contemporaries Michael Faraday and Joseph Henry.

Michael Faraday, an English scientific lecturer and scholar, was engrossed in magnets and magnetic effects. In 1831, Michael Faraday theorized that a changing magnetic field is necessary to induce a current in a nearby circuit. This theory is actually the definition of *induction*. To test his theory, he made a coil by wrapping a paper cylinder with wire. He connected the coil to a device called a *galvanometer*, and then moved a magnet back and forth inside the cylinder. When the magnet was moved, the galvanometer needle moved, indicating that a current was induced in the coil. This proved that you must have a moving magnetic field for electromagnetic induction to occur. During this experiment, Faraday had not only discovered induction but also had created the world's first electric generator. Faraday's initial findings still serve as the basis of modern electromagnetic technology.

Around the same time that Faraday worked with electromagnetism, an American professor named Joseph Henry became the first person to transmit a practical electrical signal. As a watchmaker, he constructed batteries and experimented with magnets. Henry was the first to wind insulated wires around an iron core to make electromagnets. Henry worked on a theory known as *self-inductance*, the inertial characteristic of an electric current. If a current is flowing, it is kept flowing by the property of self-inductance. Henry found that the property of self-inductance is affected by how the circuit is configured, especially by the coiling of wire. Part of his experimentation involved simple signaling.

It turns out that Henry had also derived many of the same conclusions that Faraday had. Though Faraday won the race to publish those findings, Henry still is remembered for actually finding a way to communicate with electromagnetic waves. Although Henry never developed his work on electrical signaling on his own, he did help a man by the name of Samuel Morse. In 1832, Morse read about Faraday's findings regarding inductance, which inspired him to develop his ideas about an emerging technology called the telegraph. Henry actually helped Morse construct a repeater that allowed telegraphy to span long distances, eventually making his Morse Code a worldwide language in which to communicate. Morse introduced the repeater technology with his 1838 patent for a Morse Code telegraph. Like so many great inventions, the telegraph revolutionized the communications world by replacing nearly every other means of communication—including services such as the Pony Express.

Exploring Conduction

Samuel Morse spent a fair amount of time working on wireless technology, but he also chose to use mediums such as earth and water to pass signals. In 1842, he performed a spectacular demonstration for the public in which he attempted to pass electric current through a cable that was underwater. The ultimate result of the demonstration was wireless communication by *conduction*, although it was not what he first intended. Morse submerged a mile of insulated cable between Governor's Island and Castle Garden in New York to prove that a current could pass through wire laid in water. He transmitted a few characters successfully, but, much to his dismay, the communication suddenly halted—sailors on a ship between the islands, unseen to the spectators, raised their ship's anchor and accidentally pulled up the cable, and not knowing what it was for, proceeded to cut it. Morse faced considerable heckling from the spectators and immediately began modification to the experiment. He successfully retested his idea by transmitting a wireless signal between copper plates he placed in the Susquehanna River, spanning a distance of approximately one mile. In doing so, he became the first person to demonstrate wireless by conduction. Conduction is the flow of electricity charges through a substance (in this case, the water in the river) resulting from a difference in electric potential based on the substance.

Inventing the Radio

After the significant discoveries of induction and conduction, scientists began to test conduction with different mediums and apply electricity to machinery. The scholars and scientists of the day worked to apply these discoveries and explore the parameters of the properties. After the theory of conduction in water was proven, new theories were derived about conduction in the air. In 1887, a German named Heinrich Hertz became the first person to prove electricity travels in waves through the atmosphere. Hertz went on to show that electrical conductors reflect waves, whereas nonconductors simply let the waves pass through the medium. In addition, Hertz also proved that the velocity of light and radio waves are equal, as well as the fact that it is possible to detach electrical and magnetic waves from wires and radiate. Hertz served as inspiration to other researchers who scrambled to duplicate his results and further develop his findings. Inventors from all across the world easily validated Hertz's experiments, and the world prepared for a new era in *radio*, the wireless transmission of electromagnetic waves.

An Italian inventor called Guglielmo Marconi was particularly intrigued by Hertz's published results. Marconi was able to send wireless messages over a distance of ten miles with his patented radio equipment, and eventually across the English Channel. In late 1901, Marconi and his assistants built a wireless receiver in Newfoundland and intercepted the faint Morse code signaling of the letter "S" that had been sent across the Atlantic Ocean from a colleague in England. It was astounding proof that the wireless signal literally curved around the earth, past the horizon line—even Marconi could not explain *how* it happened, but he had successfully completed the world's first truly long-distance communication, and the communication world would never be the same.

Today we know that the sun's radiation forms a layer of ionized gas particles approximately one hundred miles above the earth's surface. This layer, the ionosphere, reflects radio waves back to the earth's surface, and the waves subsequently bounce back up to the ionosphere again. This process continues until the energy of the waves dissipates.

Another researcher by the name of Reginald Fessenden proceeded to further develop Marconi's achievements, and he became the first person to create a radio band wave of human speech. The importance of his results was felt worldwide, as radio was no longer limited to telegraph codes.

Mounting Radio-Telephones in Cars

In 1921, mobile radios began operating in the 2 MHz range, which is just above the Amplitude Modulation (AM) frequency range of current radios. These mobile radios were generally used for law enforcement activities only. They were not integrated with the existing wireline phone systems that were much more common at that time—since the technology was still so new, the equipment was considered experimental and not practical for mass distribution. In fact, people originally did not consider mobile radio as a technology for the public sector. Instead, the technology was developed for police and emergency services personnel, who really served as the pioneers in mobile radio.

It was not until 1924 that the voice-based wireless telephone had the ability to be bi-directional, or two-way. Bell Laboratories invented this breakthrough telephone. Not only could people now receive messages wirelessly, they could also respond to the message immediately, greatly increasing convenience and efficiency. This improved system was still not connected to landline telephone systems, but the evolution of wireless communication had taken one more major step. One issue that still plagued this early mobile radio system was the sheer size of the radio; it took up an entire trunk. Add to the size restriction, the cost of the radio system that was almost as expensive as the vehicle.

In 1935, Edwin Howard Armstrong introduced Frequency Modulation (FM). This technology not only increased the overall transmission quality of wireless radio but also drastically reduced the size of the equipment. The timing could not have been any better. World War II had begun, and the military quickly embraced FM technology to provide two-way mobile radio communication. Due to the war, companies immediately sensed the urgency to develop the FM technology rapidly, and companies such as Motorola and AT&T immediately began designing considerably smaller equipment. Many of these new inventions became possible due to the invention of the circuit board, which changed the world of electronic equipment of all types.

Inventing Computers and Networks

Though the beginning of the computer age is widely discussed, computer discoveries can be attributed to a long line of inventors throughout the 1800s, beginning with the Englishman Charles Babbage, who in 1822 created the first calculator called the "Difference Engine." Then came Herman Hollerith, who in 1887 produced a punch card reader to tabulate the American census for 1890. Later developments led to the creation of different punch card technologies, binary representation, and the use of vacuum tubes.

The war effort in the 1940s produced the first decoding machine, the Colossus, used in England to break German codes. This machine was slow, taking about 3 to 5 seconds per calculation. The next significant breakthrough was the creation of the Electronic Numerical Integrator and Computer (ENIAC) by Americans John Presper Eckert and John W. Mauchley. The ENIAC was the first general-purpose computer that computed at speeds 1000 times greater than the Colossus. However, this machine was a behemoth, consuming over 160 Kilowatts of power—when it ran; it dimmed lights in an entire section of Philadelphia. The main reason these machines were so huge was the vacuum tube technology. The invention of the transistor in 1948 changed the computer's development and began shrinking the machinery. In the next thirty years, the computers got significantly faster and smaller.

In 1981, IBM introduced the personal computer for the home, school, and business. The number of PCs more than doubled from 2 million in 1981 to 5.5 million in 1982; more than 65 million PCs were being used ten years later. With the surge of computer use in the workplace, more emphasis was being placed on how to harness their power and make them work together. As smaller computers became more powerful, it became necessary to find a way to link them together to share memory, software, and information, and to find a way for them to communicate together. Network technology to this point consisted of a mainframe that stored the information and performed the processes hooked to several "dumb terminals" that provided the input.

Ethernet was developed in the early 1970s and was used to link multiple PCs within a physical area to form what is known as a Local Area Network (LAN). A LAN connects network devices over a short distance. Common applications include offices, schools, and the home. Sometimes businesses are composed of several LANs that are connected together. Besides spanning a short distance, LANs have other distinctive attributes. LANs typically are controlled, owned, and operated by a single person or department. LANs also use specific technologies, including Ethernet and

Token Ring for connectivity. There are typically two basic components to the LAN configuration: a client and a server. The client is the node that makes a request, and the server is the node that fulfills that request. The client computer contains the client software that allows for access to shared resources on the server. Without the client software, the computer will not actively participate in either of the two network models.

Wide Area Networks (WANs) span a much wider physical distance. Usually a WAN is a widely dispersed collection of LANs. The WAN uses a router to connect the LANs physically. For example, a company may have LANs in New York, Los Angeles, Tokyo, and Sydney; this company would then implement a WAN to span the LANs and to enable communication throughout the company. WANs use different connectivity technology than LANs—typically, T1 or T3 lines, Asynchronous Transfer Mode (ATM) or Frame Relay circuits, microwave links, or higher speed Synchronous Optical Network (SONET) connections.

The largest WAN is the Internet. The Internet is basically a WAN that spans the entire globe. Home networks often implement LANs and WANs through cable modems and digital subscriber line (DSL) service. In these systems, a cable or DSL router links the home network to the provider's WAN and the provider's central gateway to reach the Internet.

A wireless local area network transmits over the air by means of base stations, or access points, that transmit a radio frequency; the base stations are connected to an Ethernet hub or server. Mobile end-users can be handed off between access points, as in the cellular phone system, though their range generally is limited to a couple hundred feet.

Inventing Cell Phones

Wireless technology is based on the car-mounted police radios of the 1920s. Mobile telephone service became available to private customers in the 1940s. In 1947, Southwestern Bell and AT&T launched the first commercial mobile phone service in St. Louis, Missouri, but the Federal Communications Commission (FCC) limited the amount of frequencies available, which made possible only 23 simultaneous phone conversations available within a service area (the mobile phones offered only six channels with a 60 kHz spacing between them). Unfortunately, that spacing schema led to very poor sound quality due to cross-channel interference, much like the cross talk on wireline phones. The original public wireless systems generally used single high-powered transmitters to cover the entire coverage area. In order to utilize the precious frequencies allotted to them, AT&T developed an idea to replace the single high-powered transmitter approach with several smaller and lower-powered transmitters strategically placed throughout the metropolitan area; calls would switch between transmitters as they needed a stronger signal. Although this method of handling calls certainly eased some of the problems, it did not eliminate the problem altogether. In fact, the problem of too few voice channels plagued the wireless phone industry for several years.

The problem was that demand always seemed to exceed supply. Since the FCC refused to allocate more frequencies for mobile wireless use, waiting lists became AT&T's temporary solution as the company strove for the technological advances necessary to accommodate everyone. For example, in 1976, there were less than 600 mobile phone customers in New York City, but there were over 3500 people on waiting lists. Across the United States at that time, there were nearly 45,000 subscribers, but there were still another 20,000 people on waiting lists as much as ten years long. Compare this situation to today's, in which providers give away free phones and thousands of minutes just to gain a subscriber.

Cellular technology has come a long way. The term *cellular* describes how each geographic region of coverage is broken up into *cells*. Within each of these cells is a radio transmitter and control equipment. Early cellular transmission operated at 800 MHz on analog signals, which are sent on a continuous wave. When a customer makes a call, the first signal sent identifies the caller as a customer, verifies that he or she is a customer of the service, and finds a free channel for the call. The mobile phone user has a wireless phone that in connection with the cellular tower and base station, handles the calls, their connection and handoff, and the control functions of the wireless phone.

Personal communications services (PCS), which operates at 1850 MHz, followed years later. PCS refers to the services that a given carrier has available to be bundled together for the user. Services like messaging, paging, and voicemail are all part of the PCS environment. Sprint is the major carrier that typically is associated with PCS. Some cellular providers began looking into digital technology (digital signals are basically encoded voice delivered by bit streams). Some providers are using digital signals to send not only voice, but also data. Other advantages include more power of the frequency or bandwidth, and less chance of corruption per call. Coverage is based on three technologies: Code Division Multiple Access (CDMA), Time Division Multiple Access (TDMA), and Global System for Mobile Communication (GSM).

Exploring Present Applications for Wireless

Many corporations and industries are jumping into the wireless arena. Two of the industries most committed to deploying wireless technologies are airports and hotels, for business travelers' communications needs. If they are traveling in a car, they use their wireless phones. When they are at work or home, they are able to use their computers and resources to again be productive. But when staying in a hotel for the night or even a week, there are few choices—a business traveler can look for the RJ-11 jack and connect to the Internet via 56-kilobit modem, not connect at all, or connect wirelessly. When a hotel provides the correct configuration information based on the provider, and a software configuration, a business traveler with wireless capabilities can connect to their network without worrying about connection speed or out-of-date modems.

Airports offer such services to increase travelers' productivity at a time when they would otherwise be isolated from business resources. The same configuration applies: set the configuration in the wireless client software and voilà, you are connected. This wireless technology allows users to get access to the Internet, e-mail, and even the corporate intranet sites utilizing a virtual private network (VPN) solution. Now, the work (or in some cases, gaming) can be done during what used to be known as idle time. This increase in productivity is very attractive to corporations who need their increasingly mobile workforce to stay connected. This scenario is accomplished using the following scheme:

- A wireless Internet service provider contracts with the airport or hotel to set up wireless access servers and access points.

- Access points are located in specific locations to provide wireless coverage throughout the hotel or airport.

Using this scenario, anyone with an account to that service provider can get access to the Internet by walking into the location where the service is offered with their laptop, Personal Digital Assistant (PDA), or other wireless device, such as a mobile phone with 802.11 capability. This access includes such applications as e-mail, Intranet connection via VPN solution, push content such as stock updates or email, and Web browsing. Not that this is not all work and no play–you can also set up online gaming and video-on-demand sessions. In fact, non-work scenarios open up the possible user base to children and families, multiplying the use and demand of this technology.

Applying Wireless Technology to Vertical Markets

There are several vertical markets in addition to airports and hotels that are realizing the benefits of utilizing wireless networks. Many of these markets, including delivery services, public safety, finance, retail, and monitoring applications, are still at the beginning of incorporating wireless networks, but as time passes and the demand and popularity grows, they will integrate wireless networking more deeply.

Using Wireless in Delivery Services

Delivery and courier services, which depend on mobility and speed, employ a wireless technology called Enhanced Specialized Mobile Radio (ESMR) for voice communication between the delivery vehicle and the office. This technology consists of a dispatcher in an office plotting out the day's events for a driver. When the driver arrives at his location, he radios the dispatcher and lets them know his location. The benefit of ESMR is its ability to act like a CB radio, allowing all users on one channel to listen, while still allowing two users to personally communicate. This arrangement allows the dispatcher to coordinate schedules for both pick-ups and deliveries and track the drivers' progress. Drivers with empty loads can be routed to assist backlogged drivers. Drivers that are on the road can be radioed if a customer cancels a delivery. This type of communication benefits delivery services in two major areas, saving time and increasing efficiency.

United Parcel Service (UPS) utilizes a similar wireless system for their business needs. Each driver carries a device that looks like a clipboard with a digital readout and an attached penlike instrument. The driver uses this instrument to record each delivery digitally. The driver also uses it to record digitally the signature of the person who accepts the package. This information is transmitted wirelessly back to a central location so that someone awaiting a delivery can log into the Web site and get accurate information regarding the status of a package.

Using Wireless for Public Safety

Public safety applications got their start with radio communications for maritime endeavors and other potentially hazardous activities in remote areas. Through the use of satellite communications and the coordination of the International Maritime Satellite Organization (INMARSAT), these communications provided the ships with information in harsh weather or provide them a mechanism to call for help. This type of application led to Global Positioning Systems (GPS), which are now standard on naval vessels. In many cases, a captain can use the 24 satellites circling the globe in conjunction with his ship's navigational system to determine his exact location and plot his course. GPS is also used for military applications, aviation, or for personal use when tracking or pinpointing the user's location could save his or her life.

Today, there are medical applications that use wireless technology such as ambulance and hospital monitoring links. Remote ambulatory units remain in contact with the hospital to improve medical care in the critical early moments. An emergency medical technician can provide care under a doctor's instruction during transport prior to arriving in the hospital's emergency room. Standard monitoring of critical statistics are transmitted wirelessly to the hospital.

Using Wireless in the Financial World

Wireless applications can keep an investor informed real-time of the ticker in the stock market, allowing trades and updates to be made on the go. No longer is the investor tied to his desk, forced to call into his broker to buy and sell. Now, an online investor has the opportunity to get real-time stock quotes from the Internet pushed to his wireless device. He can then make the needed transactions online and make decisions instantaneously in response to the market.

There are also services that allow you to sign up and get critical information about earmarked stocks. In this scenario, you can set an alarm threshold on a particular stock you are following. When the threshold is met, the service sends a page to you instantly. Again, this improves the efficiency of the investor.

Using Wireless in the Retail World

Wireless point-of-sale (POS) applications are extremely useful for both merchant and customer, and will revolutionize the way retail business transactions occur. Registers and printers are no longer fixed in place and can be used at remote locations. Wireless scanners can further assist checkout systems. Wireless technology is used for connecting multiple cash registers through an access point to a host computer that is connected to the WAN. This WAN link is used to send real-time data back to a corporate headquarters for accounting information.

Another type of wireless point-of-sale application is inventory control. A handheld scanner is used for multiple purposes. The operator can check inventory on a given product throughout the day and wirelessly transfer the data back to the main computer system. This increases efficiency in that the device is mobile and small, and the data is recorded without manually having to enter the information.

Using Wireless in Monitoring Applications

We have been using wireless technologies for monitoring for years. There are typically two types of monitoring: passive and active. Active monitoring is conducted by use of radio signals being transmitted, and any of a number of expected signals received. An example of this implementation is the use of radar guns in traffic control. In this case, the patrolman points the gun and pulls the trigger, and a specific reading of a specific target is displayed on the radar unit. Passive monitoring is a long-term implementation whereby a device listens to a transmitter and records the data. An example of this is when an animal is tagged with a transmitter and the signal is collected and data is gathered over a period of time to be interpreted at a later date.

Monitoring applications in use today include NASA listening to space for radio signals, and receiving pictures and data relayed from probes; weather satellites monitoring the weather patterns; geologists using radio waves to gather information on earthquakes.

Applying Wireless Technology to Horizontal Applications

Along with the many vertical markets and applications, you can apply wireless technologies to horizontal applications, meaning that delivery services, public safety, finance, retail, and monitoring can all use and benefit from them. The next section gives an overview of some of the more popular horizontal trends in wireless technology.

Using Wireless in Messaging

The new wave of messaging is the culmination of wireless phones and the Wireless Application Protocol (WAP) and Short Message Service (SMS). This service is similar to the America Online Instant Messaging service. The ability for two-way messaging, multiservice calling, and Web browsing in one device creates a powerful tool for consumers, while providing the vendors the ability to generate higher revenues. Look for wireless messaging services to be introduced in local applications, particularly within restaurants, to replace conventional wait lists.

Using Wireless for Mapping

Mapping in a wireless environment, of course, relates back to the GPS system; GPS not only assists the maritime industry with navigation, but also commercial vehicles and private cars for safety. In a few cars out today, a GPS receiver is placed on board to prevent drivers from becoming lost. It will also display a map of the surrounding area. The signal from the GPS satellites is fed into an onboard computer, which contains an application with software that contains a topographical map. The more current the software is, the more accurate the map will be. The coordinates of the receiver are placed on the topographical map in the program, usually in the form of a dot, and a display screen provides a visible picture of where in relation to the map someone is at that moment. This is updated live as the receiver moves.

Using Wireless for Web Surfing

In addition to the standard laptop computer connected to a wireless LAN with Internet connectivity, there has been an explosion of other wireless units that offer multiple voice and data applications integrated in one piece of equipment. Typically, personal organizer functionality and other standard calculation-type services are offered, but now, these devices are used with appropriate software to get access to the Internet. This brings the power of the Internet and the vast repository of information to the palm of the hand.

PDAs, Palm, Inc.'s handheld devices, and wireless phones with the appropriate hardware and software are now being used for Internet access at speeds of up to 56 Kbps. With new technologies such as Evolution Data Only (EVDO), some wireless phones now even offer speeds up 400-700 Kbps with maximum speeds of 2.4 Mbps. This is moving wireless into the realm of not only browsing the Internet, which is a big accomplishment in and of itself, but Internet gaming. As the interface of the wireless devices gets better and better, the gaming community will be able to offer high quality online games played on your PDA.

Using Bluetooth Wireless Devices

In recent years Bluetooth devices that also transmit in the 2.4 GHz frequency range have become increasingly popular. With the convenience of Bluetooth, it is now possible to wirelessly sync devices such as PDAs or smartphones with laptop computers. Bluetooth headsets that allow hands free, wireless communication with wireless phones can be seen almost everywhere. In fact, many new cars now come with Bluetooth capability so that wireless phones can be paired with the car stereo allowing hands free calls to be made and received without even requiring a headset.

As more organizations and corporations realize the convenience that Bluetooth devices offer the popularity of these devices will only continue to increase. In addition to headsets and syncing capabilities, some wireless phones that have Internet access allow tethering via Bluetooth. Tethering allows you to connect your phone to the Internet through your wireless phone and access the Internet through your laptop computer.

Introduction to Wardriving

In this section, we'll briefly introduce you to wardriving and Kismet. Before you begin wardriving, it is important to understand what it is and, more importantly, what it is not. It is also important to understand some of the terminology associated with wardriving. In order to successfully wardrive, you need certain hardware and software tools. Since there are hundreds of possible configurations that can be used for wardriving, some of the most popular are presented to help you decide what to buy for your own initial wardriving setup.

Many of the tools that a wardriver uses are the same tools that an attacker uses to gain unauthorized access to a wireless network. These are also the tools that you will use during your wireless penetration tests.

Wardriving has the potential to make a difference in the overall security posture of wireless networking. By understanding wardriving, obtaining the proper tools, and then using them ethically, you can make a difference in your overall security. First, let's look at where wardriving comes from and what it means. (See Mike Schearer's Chapter 9 for much more on wardriving.

The Origins of Wardriving

Wardriving is misunderstood by many people; both the general public and the news media. Because the name "Wardriving" sounds ominous, many people associate wardriving with criminal activity. Before discussing how to wardrive, you need to understand the history of wardriving and the origin of the name. The facts necessary to comprehend the truth about wardriving are also provided.

Definition

Wardriving is the act of moving around a specific area, mapping the population of wireless access points for statistical purposes. These statistics are then used to raise awareness of the security problems associated with these types of networks (typically wireless). The commonly accepted definition of wardriving is that it is not exclusive of surveillance and research by automobile. Wardriving is accomplished by anyone moving around a certain area looking for data, which includes: walking, which is often referred to as warwalking; flying, which is often referred to as warflying; bicycling, and so forth. Wardriving does not utilize the resources of any wireless access point or network that is discovered, without prior authorization of the owner.

The Terminology History of Wardriving

The term wardriving comes from "War dialing," a term that was introduced to the general public by Matthew Broderick's character, David Lightman, in the 1983 movie, *WarGames*. War dialing is the practice of using a modem attached to a computer to dial an entire exchange of telephone numbers sequentially (e.g., 555-1111, 555-1112, and so forth) to locate any computers with modems attached to them.

Essentially, Wardriving employs the same concept, although it is updated to a more current technology: wireless networks. A wardriver drives around an area, often after mapping out a route first, to determine all of the wireless access points in that area. Once these access points are discovered, a wardriver uses a software program or Web site to map the results of his or her efforts. Based on these results, a statistical analysis is performed. This statistical analysis can be of one drive, one area, or a general overview of all wireless networks.

The concept of driving around discovering wireless networks probably began the day after the first wireless access point was deployed. However, wardriving became more well-known when the process was automated by Peter Shipley, a computer security consultant in Berkeley, California. During the fall of 2000, Shipley conducted an 18-month survey of wireless networks in Berkeley, California and reported his results at the annual DefCon hacker conference in July 2001. This presentation, designed to raise awareness of the insecurity of wireless networks that were deployed at that time, laid the groundwork for the "true" wardriver.

Wardriving Misconceptions

Some people confuse the terms wardriver and *hacker*. The term "hacker" was originally used to describe a person that could modify a computer to suit his or her own purposes. However, over time and owing to the confusion of the masses and consistent media abuse, the term hacker is now commonly used to describe a criminal; someone that accesses a computer or network without owner authorization. The same situation can be applied to the term wardriver. Wardriver has been used to describe someone that accesses wireless networks without owner authorization. An individual that accesses a computer system (wired or wireless) without authorization is a criminal. Criminality has nothing to do with hacking or wardriving.

In an effort to generate ratings and increase viewership, the news media, has sensationalized wardriving. Almost every local television news outlet has done a story on "wireless hackers armed with laptops" or "drive-by hackers" that are reading your e-mail or using your wireless network to surf the Web. These stories are geared to propagate fear, uncertainty, and doubt (FUD). FUD stories are usually small risk, and attempt to elevate the seriousness of a situation in the minds of their audience. Stories that prey on fear are good for ratings, but they don't always depict an activity accurately.

An unfortunate side effect of these stories is that reporters invariably ask wardrivers to gather information that is being transmitted across a wireless network so that the "victim" can see all of the information that was collected. Again, this has nothing to do with wardriving, and while this activity (known as sniffing) in and of itself is not illegal, at a minimum it is unethical and is not a practice that wardrivers engage in.

These stories also tend to focus on gimmicky aspects of Wardriving such as the directional antenna that can be made using a Pringles can. While a functional antenna can be made from Pringles cans, coffee cans, soup cans, or pretty much anything cylindrical and hollow, the reality is that very few (if any) Wardrivers actually use these for Wardriving. Many of them make these antennas in an attempt to verify the original concept and improve upon it in some instances.

The Truth about Wardriving

The reality of wardriving is simple. Computer security professionals, hobbyists, and others are generally interested in providing information to the public about the security vulnerabilities that are present with "out-of-the-box" configurations of wireless access points. Wireless access points purchased at a local electronics or computer store are not geared toward security; they are designed so that a person with little or no understanding of networking can purchase a wireless access point, set it up, and use it.

Computers are a staple of everyday life. Technology that makes using computers easier and more fun needs to be available to everyone. Companies such as Linksys and D-Link have been very successful at making these new technologies easy for end users to set up and use. To do otherwise would alienate a large part of their target market. (See Chapter 10 for a step-by-step guide to enabling the built-in security features of these access points.)

The Legality of Wardriving

According to the Federal Bureau of Investigation (FBI), it is not illegal to scan access points; however, once a theft of service, a denial of service (DoS), or a theft of information occurs, it becomes a federal violation through 18USC 1030 (*www.usdoj.gov/ criminal/cybercrime/1030_new.html*). While this is good, general information, any questions about the legality of a specific act in the U.S. should be posed directly to either the local FBI field office, a cyber-crime attorney, or the U.S. Attorney's office. This information only applies to the U.S. Wardrivers are encouraged to investigate the local laws where they live to ensure that they aren't inadvertently violating them. Understanding the distinction between "scanning" and identifying wireless access points, and actually using the access point, is the same as understanding the difference between Wardriving (a legal activity) and theft, (an illegal activity).

Introduction to Wardriving with Linux

Linux is the most robust operating system for wardriving. Unlike Windows, Linux offers the ability to place your wireless card in monitor (rfmon) mode, which allows you to perform passive scanning to detect access points that are not broadcasting the Service Set Identifier (SSID) beacon. These are commonly referred to as *cloaked*, or *hidden* access points. This capability, along with the large amount of open source and freeware wireless programs that have been developed for Linux, has helped make Linux one of the most popular operating systems used by both wardrivers and penetration testers.

Preparing Your System to Wardrive

Before you can wardrive using Linux, you need to ensure that your operating system is properly configured to utilize the tools that are available. Specifically, you need a kernel that supports monitor mode and your specific Wireless Local Area Network (WLAN) card. After kernel configuration is complete, you need to install the proper wardriving tools and tailor their configurations to your preferences.

Preparing the Kernel

Configuring Linux to Wardrive used to be a very difficult process that involved both kernel configuration and driver patching. That is no longer the case. As of the

2.6.16 kernel revision, it is possible to build a Linux kernel with all of the support you need compiled into it. Depending on your personal preference, this can be done by either compiling support directly into the kernel or by building the appropriate kernel modules.

Preparing the Kernel for Monitor Mode

There are several ways to generate a new kernel configuration, the easiest of which is probably using the *menuconfig* option.

```
# cd /usr/src/linux
# make menuconfig
```

Once the menu configuration opens, enable Generic IEEE 802.11 Networking Stack, IEEE 802.11 Wireless Encryption Protocol (WEP) encryption (802.1x), IEEE 802.11i Counter-Mode/CBC-Mac Protocol (CCMP) support, and IEEE 802.11i Temporal Key Integrity Protocol (TKIP) encryption:

```
Networking --->
--- Networking support
      Networking options --->

<*>      Generic IEEE 802.11 Networking Stack
<*>        IEEE 802.11WEP encryption (802.1x)
<*>        IEEE 802.11i CCMP support
<*>        IEEE 802.11i TKIP encryption
```

The 802.11i CCMP and TKIP support are not necessary for monitor mode; however, they are required for penetration testing of WiFi Protected Access (WPA)-encrypted networks.

Next, you need to configure your kernel to support your Wireless Fidelity (WiFi) card. Regardless of your type of card, you need the following options:

```
Device Drivers --->
Network device support --->
[*] Network device support

    Wireless LAN (non-hamradio) --->
    [*] Wireless LAN drivers (non-hamradio) & Wireless Extensions
```

Next you need to compile in support for your specific card(s). First you need to decide if you want to compile your drivers into the kernel or install them as kernel modules. In many cases, this is a personal choice. For the purpose of this book, we'll compile the drivers as modules. Two of the most popular cards for Wardriving are the Hermes chipset-based Orinoco Gold Classic card and the Prism 2.5-based Senao NL 2511 EXT 2.

Adding support for these cards is simply a matter of telling the kernel to compile the module:

```
Device Drivers --->
Network device support --->
Wireless LAN (non-hamradio) --->
<M>     Hermes chipset 802.11b support (Orinoco/Prism2/Symbol)
...
<M>     IEEE 802.11 for Host AP (Prism2/2.5.3 and WEP/TKIP/CCMP)
[ ]       Support downloading firmware images with Host AP driver
<M>       Host AP driver for Prism2/2.5/3 in PLX9052 PCI adaptors
<M>       Host AP driver for Prism2.5 PCI adaptors
<M>       Host AP driver for Prism2/2.5/3 PC Cards
```

Compiling modules for all three of these gives you the ability to use both Personal Computer Memory Card International Association (PCMCIA)-based Prism2 cards and Mini-PCI cards. This can be useful when performing penetration testing tasks that require two cards.

NOTE

The Hermes driver also has support for Prism2 cards. If you plan to use the Host access point drivers (which you will for many penetration testing tasks) you should not compile in both Hermes support and Host access point support. The Hermes driver will generally load first; consequently, you will have to unload it and manually modprobe the Host access point drivers.

Once you have selected all of the modules you need to compile, you are ready to make your kernel. Exit out of the *menuconfig* and choose **<Yes>** when prompted to save your new kernel configuration (see Figure 1.1).

Figure 1.1 Saving the Kernel Configuration

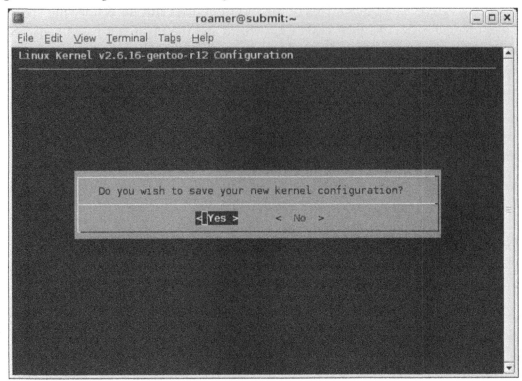

Next, compile the new kernel and the selected modules:

```
# make && make modules_install
```

Now copy the *bzImage* to *vmlinuz* in your boot partition:

```
# cp arch/i386/boot/bzImage /boot/linux/vmlinuz
```

If you use Grub for your bootloader, you do not need to make any configuration changes. If you use LILO, you need to rerun */sbin/lilo* to update the bootloader configuration.

Issuing the *lsmod* command allows you to verify that the proper drivers were loaded at boot (see Figure 1.2).

Figure 1.2 Host ACCESS POINT Drivers for a Mini-PCI Senao Card

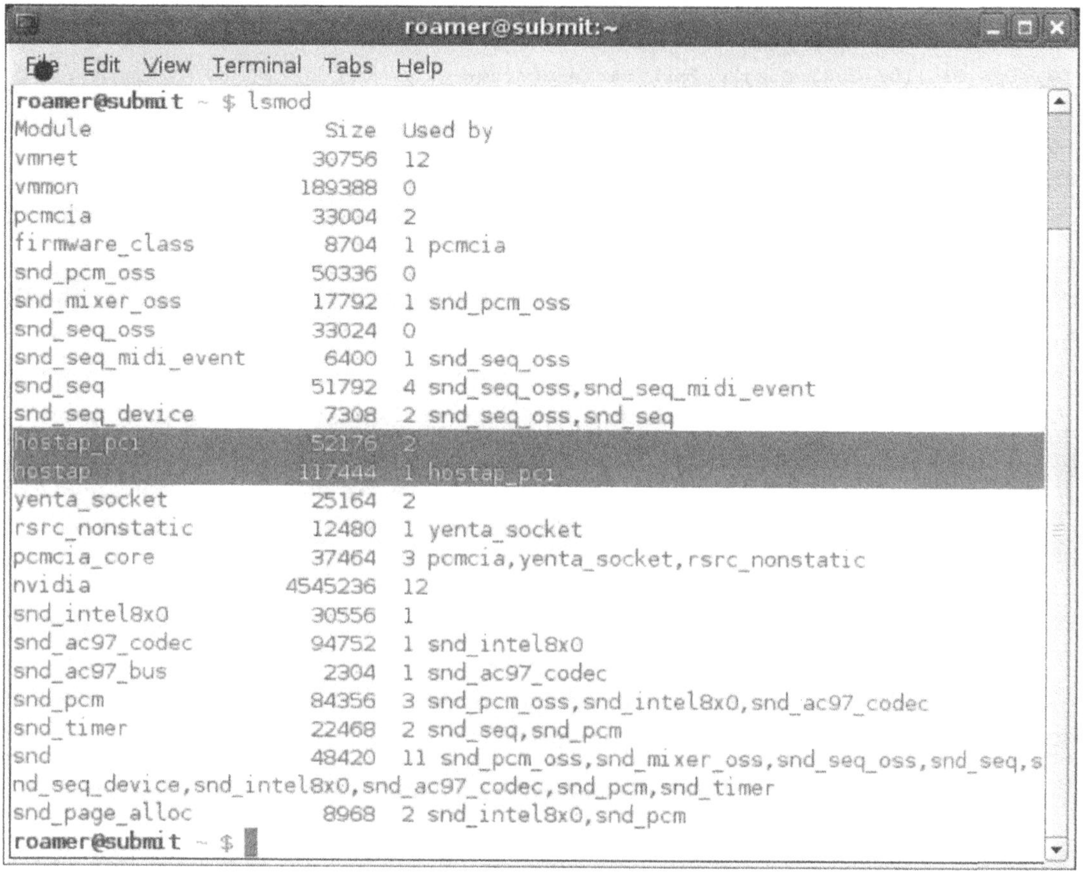

```
roamer@submit:~
File  Edit  View  Terminal  Tabs  Help
roamer@submit ~ $ lsmod
Module                Size  Used by
vmnet                30756  12
vmmon               189388  0
pcmcia               33004  2
firmware_class        8704  1 pcmcia
snd_pcm_oss          50336  0
snd_mixer_oss        17792  1 snd_pcm_oss
snd_seq_oss          33024  0
snd_seq_midi_event    6400  1 snd_seq_oss
snd_seq              51792  4 snd_seq_oss,snd_seq_midi_event
snd_seq_device        7308  2 snd_seq_oss,snd_seq
hostap_pci           52176  2
hostap              117444  1 hostap_pci
yenta_socket         25164  2
rsrc_nonstatic       12480  1 yenta_socket
pcmcia_core          37464  3 pcmcia,yenta_socket,rsrc_nonstatic
nvidia             4545236  12
snd_intel8x0         30556  1
snd_ac97_codec       94752  1 snd_intel8x0
snd_ac97_bus          2304  1 snd_ac97_codec
snd_pcm              84356  3 snd_pcm_oss,snd_intel8x0,snd_ac97_codec
snd_timer            22468  2 snd_seq,snd_pcm
snd                  48420  11 snd_pcm_oss,snd_mixer_oss,snd_seq_oss,snd_seq,s
nd_seq_device,snd_intel8x0,snd_ac97_codec,snd_pcm,snd_timer
snd_page_alloc        8968  2 snd_intel8x0,snd_pcm
roamer@submit ~ $
```

At this point, all of the drivers and kernel options you need are installed to run a WLAN scanning program in monitor mode.

Preparing the Kernel for a Global Positioning System

Discovering WLANs is a lot of fun if you can generate maps of your drives. In order to do that, you need to prepare your kernel to work with a Global Positioning System (GPS). Most GPS units come with a serial data cable; however, you can now purchase a unit that has a Universal Serial Bus (USB) cable. If you need to use a USB serial converter, you have to have support for your converter in the kernel.

Go to the */usr/src/linux* directory and issue the *make menuconfig* command. Then select the appropriate driver for your USB serial converter:

```
Device Drivers  --->
USB support  --->
```

```
USB Serial Converter support --->
<*> USB Serial Converter support
[*]    USB Generic Serial Driver
<*>    USB Prolific 2303 Single Port Serial Driver
```

The Prolific 2303 driver is a very common USB serial converter driver. You will need to ensure that you have compiled in support for your specific converter.

Next, exit out of the menuconfig, save your kernel configuration, compile your new kernel, move or copy the bzImage to your boot partition, and, if necessary, update your bootloader. After rebooting, insert your USB serial adapter. The system *dmesg* will show if the kernel correctly recognized your converter (see Figure 1.3).

NOTE

When you execute **make menuconfig**, it reads from the running kernel or from the kernel configuration file for the current kernel. This configuration has all of the changes that were previously made, therefore, they do not need to be repeated.

Figure 1.3 The Prolific USB Serial Converter

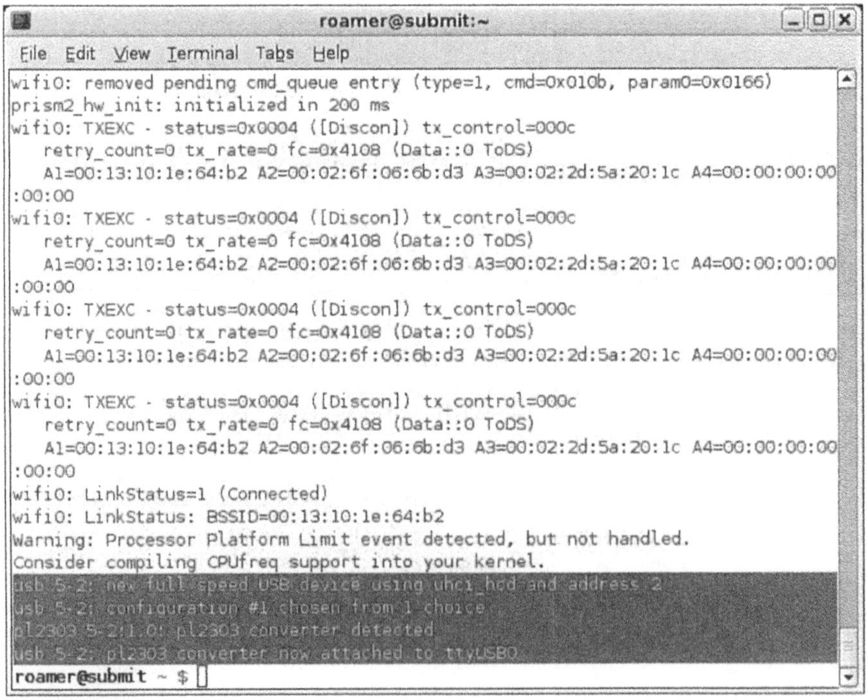

Now you have all of the kernel support you need to both wardrive and perform wireless penetration tests.

Installing the Proper Tools

Once you have generated a kernel to support monitor mode and have compiled the proper drivers, you are ready to install the necessary tools to perform a wardrive. There are two tools that you need to install in order to accomplish this: Kismet and GPSD (www.pygps.org/gspd/downloads).

Installing Kismet

In this section, we'll provide a brief introduction to installing Kismet. See Chapter 2 for complete installation instructions. Kismet installation is a very straightforward process. Simply download the latest release of Kismet from www.kismetwireless.net/download.shtml and save it in a directory of your choice. (Older versions of Kismet can be retrieved from www.kismetwireless.net/code.) Uncompress and untar the file and then change to the directory it created and issue the following commands:

```
# ./configure
# make
# make install
```

> **NOTE**
>
> These three commands are the standard way to configure and compile Linux programs from source. For the remainder of this chapter and unless otherwise noted, "compile the program" refers to these three steps.

This installs Kismet in the default directory (*/usr/local/bin/kismet*) and the Kismet configuration files in (*/usr/local/etc/kismet*).

Compiling from Source or Packages

The compilation examples in this chapter show how to compile programs from source by first obtaining the source from the developer's Web site and then manually compiling the program. This is only one way to compile and install programs. Most distributions have some sort of package management system that can be used to either install programs, or obtain and install them. Red Hat and Fedora use the Red Hat Package Manager (RPM) package management system, Gentoo uses emerge, and Slackware packages are in *.tgz* format. Sometimes it is beneficial to use your distribution's package management system to install programs; however, it should be noted that when you use a package manager to compile and install a program, it may place the binaries and configuration files in non-standard directories. This chapter assumes that you have compiled from source or that your package manager has placed the binaries and configuration files in the standard locations. If your package manager did not do this, you can search for the configuration files or binaries by using the *find* command:

```
# find / -name kismet.conf -print
```

This command searches the entire filesystem for the *kismet.conf* file and displays the results on the screen. The *–print* switch is rarely required on Linux systems; however, adding it doesn't change the functionality of the command.

Installing GPSD

GPSD is a program that interfaces with your GPS unit, which in turn passes data to Kismet to provide GPS coordinates of your location when an access point is discovered. The installation of GPSD is slightly different from the normal Linux installation procedure, because there is not a "make install" option. Issue the *./configure* and *make* commands, and then run either *gpsd* from the location where you compiled it, or copy the *gps* and *gpsd* files to a directory in your path such as */usr/bin* or */usr/local/bin*.

Configuring Your System to Wardrive

Once you have compiled and installed Kismet and GPSD, you need to edit the Kismet configuration files so that Kismet will function properly on your system. Unless you (or your package manager) have changed the location, the configuration files are put in */usr/local/etc.* There are two files you need to edit: *kismet.conf* and *kismet_ui.conf.*

The *kismet_ui.conf* file controls the user interface options of Kismet. For the most part, you can leave these options at their default, unless you want to tweak the appearance of the interface. Kismet does have a Welcome window that displays every time you start Kismet (see Figure 1.4).

Figure 1.4 The Kismet Welcome Window

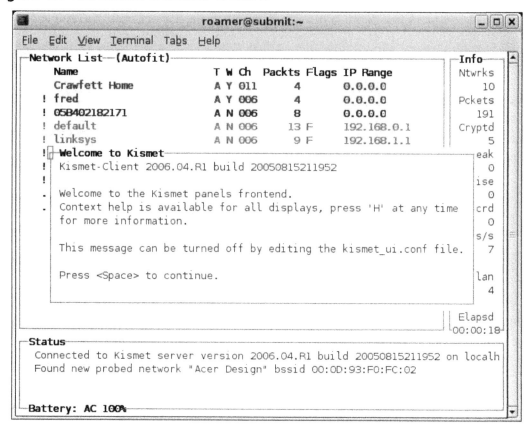

To get rid of the Welcome window when Kismet starts, change the *showintro* option to false:

```
# Do we show the intro window?
showintro=false
```

The *kismet.conf* file is where the important Kismet options are set. In order for Kismet to function properly, this file must be edited to reflect your environment and hardware. First, you need to edit the *suiduser* variable:

```
# User to setid to (should be your normal user)
suiduser=roamer
```

Next you need to set your *source* variable. This is the option that tells Kismet what type of driver and card you are using, as well as what interface your card is configured on. The following example tells Kismet to use the Host access point driver and that your card is configured as *wlan0*. The third option, *wlan*, can be set to any value.

```
source=hostap,wlan0,wlan
```

Here are some of the more common source options for different cards and drivers:

```
# Source line for Intel Pro Wireless 2100
source=ipw2100,eth0,ipw2100source
# Source line for wlan-ng Prism2 driver
source=prism2,wlan0,prism
# Source line for Cisco (dependent on Cisco driver used)
source=cisco,eth0,cisco
# Alternate Source line for Cisco (dependent on Cisco driver used)
source=cisco_cvs,eth1:wifi0,ciscocvs
# Source line for Hermes based cards (Orinoco)
source=orinoco,eth0,orinocosource
```

Unless you plan to enable multiple sources, you don't need to change the *enable-sources* variable, which is commented out unless it is changed.

By default, Kismet hops channels. This is what allows Kismet to detect access points that are operating on the different channels in the 2.4 GHz range. Unless you only want to detect access points on a specific channel, this should be left as is:

```
# Do we channelhop
channelhop=true
```

If you want to identify access points on a specific channel, disable channel hopping and set the initial channel in your source variable. For instance, to identify access points on channel 8 only:

```
source=hostap,wlan0,wlan,8
channelhop=false
```

The next option to tweak is the channel velocity. This controls how many channels Kismet should cycle through per second. By default, this is set to three channels per second. This is an acceptable, if conservative, option. To increase the speed that Kismet hops channels, increase this number. To decrease the speed, decrease this number:

```
# How many channels per second do we hop? (1-10)
# The following option scans each channel for 1/5 of a second
channelvelocity=5
# The following option scans each channel for ½ of a second
channelvelocity=2
```

The options between channel hopping and the GPS configuration are set correctly by default and do not usually need to be edited. The GPS configuration options should be set if you are using a GPS unit to capture report coordinates. Unless you change the port, GPSD listens on port 2947; therefore, the *kismet.conf* options for GPS should be set to reflect this:

```
# Do we have a GPS?
gps=true
# Host:port that GPSD is running on. This can be localhost OR remote!
gpshost=localhost:2947
```

The next option you need to look at is the interval that the log files are written. The default setting is to write the logs every 5 minutes. For a casual wardrive, this is probably acceptable; however, for professionals, it is a good idea to write the logs regularly in case of a system or program crash (every minute is a safe option):

```
# How often (in seconds) do we write all our data files (0 to disable)
writeinterval=60
```

Kismet produces a very comprehensive set of log files as shown in Table 1.1.

Table 1.1 The Kismet Log Filetypes

Dump	A raw packet dump that can be opened in Ethereal of other packet analyzers.
Network	A text file listing the networks that have been detected.
CSV	A comma-separated listing of networks detected
XML	An eXtensible Markup Language (XML) formatted log of networks detected. This is useful for importing into other applications.
Weak	The weak Initialization Vector (IV) packets detected in AirSnort format.
Cisco	A log of Cisco Discovery Protocol (CDP) broadcasts produced by Cisco equipment.
GPS	The log of GPS coordinates of access points detected.

The *logtypes* variable tells Kismet which types of log files you want it to generate. The default options are acceptable (*dump, network, csv, xml, weak, cisco,* and *gps*); however, you may not need all of these. The bare minimum that you should ensure are generated are the *dump, network* and *gps* logs:

```
logtypes=dump,network,gps
```

The *logdefault* variable specifies what text should be prepended to the log file name. Kismet writes the files in the format *[logdefault]-[date]-[sequence-number].[filetype].* For instance, if the *logdefault* is set to Roamer, then the *gps* log of the third wardriving session of the day would be named Roamer-Oct-14-2006-3.gps. This option can be helpful for sorting results if you are wardriving multiple areas in the same day:

```
# Default log title
logdefault=MyCustomer
```

The final option that you may want to change in the *kismet.conf* file is the *logtemplate*. This option controls both the location that the logs are created and stored in and the format of the log files. If no changes are made to this variable, the logs will be created in the default format, with the default title, in the directory that Kismet is launched from. However, it can be beneficial to store all of your logs in one location, or to store the different types of logs in different directories. There are seven variables that can be set in relation to the logtemplate:

- %n is the title set in logdefault
- %d is the current date in the format *Month-Day-Year (Mon-DD-YYYY)*
- %D is the current date in the format *YYYYMMDD*
- %t is the time that the log started
- %i is the increment number of the log (i.e., 1 for first log of the day, 2 for second, and so forth)
- %l is the log type
- %h is the home directory

For example, if you wanted to have your logs generated in different directories by filetype, and created in the wardrives directory, you would have the following *logtemplate*:

```
logtemplate=WarDrives/%l/%n-%d-%i
```

Assuming you set the logtypes variable to *dump*, *network*, and *gps*, you would need to create the wardrives directory with three sub-directories: *dump*, *network*, and *gps*.

After you have made any changes, save the file and you are ready to wardrive with Kismet.

Wardriving with Linux and Kismet

There are a lot of reasons to use Kismet to wardrive. The exceptional range of log files you can generate make it very attractive. Unlike some other wardriving software, Kismet doesn't just detect the access points, but also saves a complete log of all of the packets it sees. These dumps can be opened with other packet analyzers and can be fed into penetration test programs. Monitor mode allows you to identify access points that are cloaked (not broadcast via the SSID). Additionally, since the SSID is sent in cleartext when a client authenticates to the network, Kismet can often determine the SSID of these cloaked networks.

Now that we have tweaked the Kismet configuration files to our liking, we are ready to start wardriving with Kismet. In this section, you will learn how to start Kismet and how to use the Kismet interface once you have it running. We look at the different options that Kismet provides and, how to use a graphical front end for Kismet.

Starting Kismet

Starting Kismet is relatively simple. Assuming Kismet is in your path, type *kismet* at the command line as shown in Figure 1.5.

Figure 1.5 Starting Kismet...Something is Wrong Here

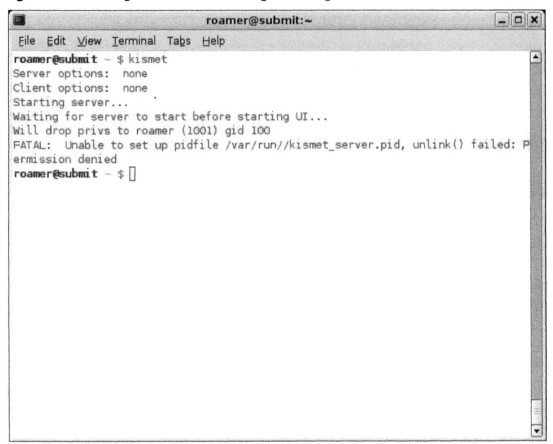

The process ID file (*pidfile*) could not be set. This is because you don't have permission to write to */var/run*. There are two ways to fix this. You can change the location where the *pidfile* is written in the *kismet.conf*:

```
# Where do we store the pid file of the server?
piddir=/home/roamer
```

Changing the location of the *pidfile* is one option, but because you have already set a *suiduser* in your *kismet.conf*, it is probably easier to *su* to root and then run kismet. Root has permission to write the *pidfile*, but after it has performed that action, Kismet drops the privilege down to the *suiduser*, avoiding the potential security risks of running as root.

Figure 1.6 Kismet Starts Successfully

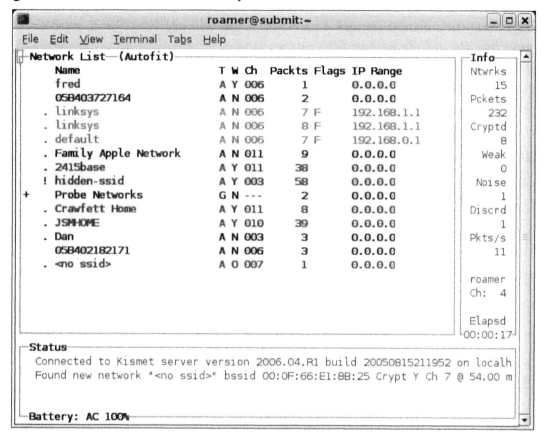

Using the Kismet Interface

In this section, we'll provide you with an introduction to the Kismet interface. See Chapter 4 for a complete discussion of the Kismet menus and functionality. In addition to its ability to identify access points, Kismet has a very powerful user interface. You can find a large amount of information about each access point you have identified by examining the Kismet options in the user interface. Obvious information (e.g., the SSID) is available to you immediately, whether or not an access point is encrypted. For a casual wardrive, this may be all of the information that you need. However, if you want to understand more about the networks you have discovered, you need to be familiar with the different options available to you.

Understanding the Kismet Options

When using the different options with Kismet, you will need to change your *sort* option first. By default, Kismet is in *autofit sort mode*. Unfortunately, in this mode you can't obtain a lot of information about the different access points beyond the information displayed in the default view. To change the sort mode, press the **s** key to bring up a menu of the sort options (see Figure 1.7).

Figure 1.7 Kismet Sort Options

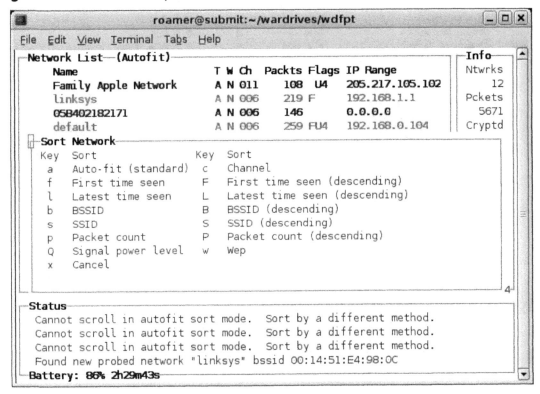

At this point, you have 14 different *sort* options to choose from. Choose the option that best suits your needs. For instance, if you are only interested in access points with a specific SSID, you would choose **s** to have the access points sorted by SSID and then scroll down to the desired SSID.

Once you have chosen your sort method, you can start to find out additional information about each network. Using the arrow keys, highlight the access point you are interested in and press **Enter** to get the Network Details (see Figure 1.8).

Figure 1.8 Network Details

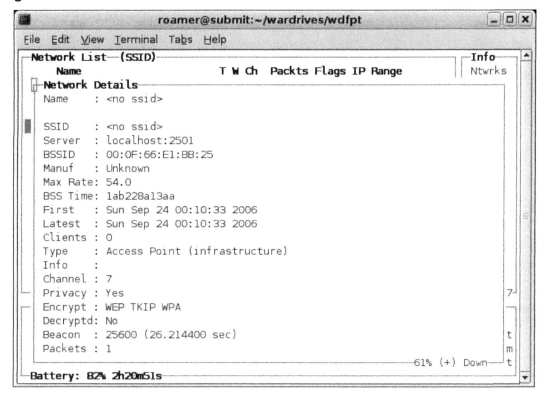

You now know the MAC address (Basic Service Set Identifier [BSSID]) of the access point. Because the access point has a max rate of 54.0, you know that it is an 802.11 g access point operating in infrastructure mode. Although the main screen said that the network was using encryption, you can now identify WPA as the encryption mechanism in place. Once you are satisfied with the information, press the **q** key to close the details and return to the main view.

You may want to know what clients are connected to a network. By highlighting the access point and pressing the **c** key, you are presented with a list of any clients associated with the network (see Figure 1.9).

Figure 1.9 The Client List

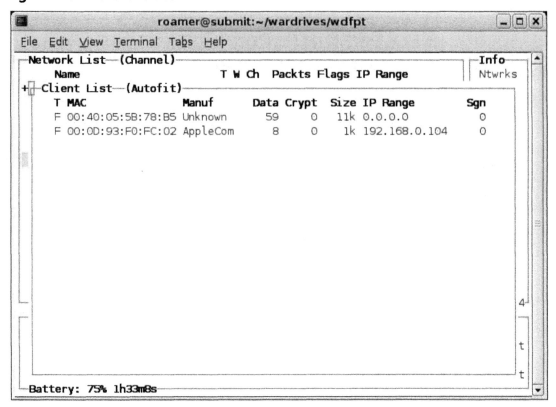

In client view, you can determine the MAC address of any clients associated with the access point. Additionally, in some cases, you can determine what type of card it is. The number of data packets that Kismet has seen and the number of those packets that are encrypted are identified. Once Kismet determines the Internet Protocol (IP) address of a specific client it is noted as well as the strength of the signal. Again, when you are finished looking at the client list, press **q** to return to the Network List.

There will be times where you are only interested in collecting information about access points on a specific channel. To disable channel hopping and collect data only on one channel, highlight an access point on that channel and press the **Shift+L** key to lock on that channel.

To resume channel hopping, press **Shift+H**.

Kismet also has a robust help panel. If you are unsure of an option, press **h** to display the Help menu (see Figure 1.10).

Figure 1.10 Kismet Help Interface

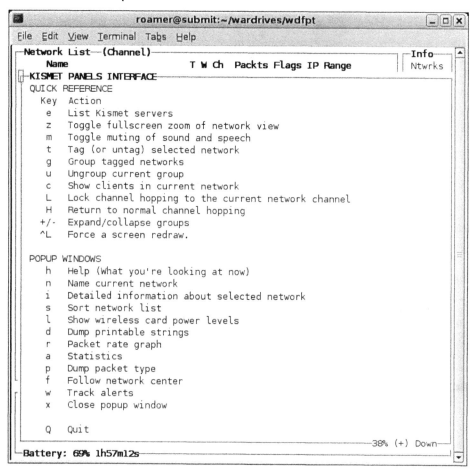

Using a Graphical Front End

In addition to the standard Kismet interface, you can also use a graphical front end with Kismet. Gkismet (http://gkismet.sourceforge.net) is a front-end interface that works with Kismet. Once you have downloaded, compiled, and installed gkismet, you need to start the Kismet server:

```
# /usr/bin/kismet_server
```

Next, start gkismet:

```
# /usr/bin/gkismet
```

This opens the gkismet interface and prompts for the *kismet_server* information (see Figure 1.11). In most cases, you will be connecting to *localhost* (127.0.0.1) on default port 2501.

Figure 1.11 Connecting to the Kismet Server

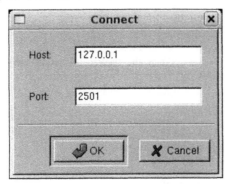

Once you have entered your server information, gkismet connects to the Kismet server and you receive a display of the access points Kismet has discovered (see Figure 1.12).

Figure 1.12 Gkismet in Action

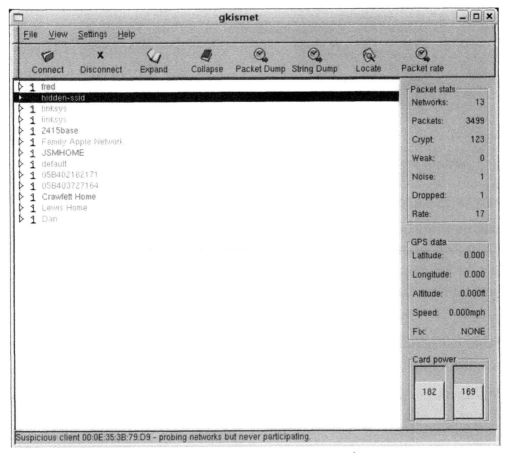

There are several advantages to using a graphical front end. For instance, the card power is displayed on the main screen. This can be very beneficial for direction finding and walking down rogue access points. Additionally, you can easily examine the information on each access point by double-clicking on the access point you want information on.

Additionally, the sort options can be accessed by right-clicking on the SSID of the access point and choosing how you want the information sorted.

Summary

In this chapter we have explored some of the history of how wireless technology evolved into what it is today. Wireless technology has been around a long time, considering the decades of development in radio and cellular telephone technology. These technologies have been quietly developing in the background while PDAs, Palm Pilots, and other handheld wireless devices have been gaining notoriety. Other uses such as GPS and satellite communications to the home have also been developing for mainstream applications. These applications offer consumers many advantages over wireline counterparts, including flexibility, mobility, and increased efficiency and timeliness.

Kismet is a very powerful tool for both wardriving and penetration testing. One of the biggest advantages of using Kismet is the ability to use monitor or rfmon mode. This allows you to identify wireless networks that are not broadcasting the SSID in the beacon frame and sets Kismet apart from it's Windows counterpart NetStumbler.

It is important to understand the many features of Kismet in order to maximize its effectiveness. You can edit the kismet.conf file to customize Kismet to your specific needs. The Kismet panel interface provides many different user options for sorting and viewing information about the networks you discover. Additionally, graphical front end programs like gkismet can make viewing data a bit easier on the eyes.

Kismet is also a great tool for a penetration tester that needs to perform WLAN discovery to identify a target network. Although not always 100% accurate, Kismet can be used to identify the type of encryption used on a network. For complete accuracy you can open your Kismet.dump file, which is a pcap formatted packet capture with a packet analyzer like Ethereal or Wireshark to get an accurate reading of the encryption level. Once you have identified your target and the encryption level there are several open source tools available to continue the penetration test. Tools like SirMacsAlot can spoof the MAC address and bypass MAC Address filtering. The Aircrack suite provides a rich set of tools for collecting packets, injecting packets and cracking WEP. CoWPAtty is a great tool for breaking WPA-PSK when used with a good dictionary file.

Performing a penetration test on a wireless network is often a way to get an initial foothold into the network. While always remembering to stay within scope, you can then begin your normal penetration test process for the internal network with your entry vector into the wireless network providing you with an excellent jumping off point.

## Chapter 2

Basic Installation

Solutions in this chapter:

- Introduction

- Kismet Perquisites

- Kismet installation

- Compiling and installing Kismet on a Linux laptop

- Choosing a wireless card driver

- Wireless card driver compiling and installation

- Editing the Kismet configuration file for a basic Kismet installation

- Run Kismet

Introduction

This chapter will introduce you to the basic installation of Kismet. A basic installation is one in which the server and the client portions of Kismet are on the same laptop. This is the installation that most people will be interested in, at least initially. Advanced installations for separate servers and clients, as well as remote and drone machines, will be covered in Chapters 7 and 8.

Here we'll be focusing on a "typical Kismet install" on a "typical Linux system." For those who don't know, Linux (formally known "GNU/Linux") is a UNIX-like operating system (OS), created in 1991 by Linus Tourvolds. Kismet can be installed on most "Unix-like" OS, including Linux, Debain, Berkeley Software Distribution (BSD), Apple OSX/Darwin, and Linux virtual machines running under Microsoft Windows. However, since Linux is the "native" operating system for Kismet, and is what most users will be using for running Kismet, it's going to be the basis for our initial "typical Kismet install."

While Kismet will run on almost any personal computer in which Linux is installed, it is assumed here that most people who are using a basic Kismet setup will be doing so on a wireless networking-enabled laptop. Therefore, throughout this chapter the terms "computer," "personal computer," "PC," and "laptop" are used interchangeably.

Also, as Linux systems tend to be almost as individualistic as their owners, the word "typical" is used here with a grain of salt. The installation covered here will be as generic as possible, but please understand that variations in how Linux has been installed on your laptop may render some of the following information useless. It will be impossible to cover all possible departures from the norm, although we will try to cover some common variations.

Going into this chapter, you will need to have some Linux distribution (or "distro" in Linux jargon) already installed on you laptop, and at least a passing familiarity with Linux's command-line interface (CLI) and how to do things in Linux such as downloading files.

Notes from the Underground

Live Distros

If you are brand new to Linux and the idea of learning a new OS seems overwhelming, you can still try Kismet and Linux without a huge investment of time, effort, or money. Many variations of complete Linux distributions, known as "Live Distros," are available on bootable read-only Compact Disks (CD-ROMs). To try a live distro, you simply download the CD-ROM image (called an International Organization for Standardization [ISO] file) from a creator's Web site, and burn it to a blank CD-ROM. When the computer is then booted off the new CD-ROM, it will start up in Linux. Most Live distros are based on standard distros such as Slackware.

To return to your original operating system, simply remove the CD-ROM and boot off the hard disk as you would normally.

One of the most popular live distros is Knoppix, available from www.knoppix.de and www.knopper.net. Knoppix runs with a Graphic User Interface (GUI) to make it easier for the novice Linux user to navigate. It has Kismet pre-installed along with a number of drivers for many popular cards.

Another popular live distro is Backtrack (www.remote-exploit.org). Backtrack is designed to be used by Information Security (InfoSec) professionals for system and network security audits, and as such has a plethora of security tools in addition to Kismet. It also has a number of popular wireless card drivers pre-installed. As of this writing, Backtrack 2 has been out for well over a year, and Backtrack 3 is in Beta Release.

Running Kismet in Backtrack is covered in detail in Chapter 10.

To keep the beginning as simple as possible, we'll discuss the basic installation of Kismet and its use with a common wireless card, but we aren't going to discuss things like antennas or using Kismet with a Global Positioning System (GPS) receiver until the next chapter. We will be installing Kismet as the user "root" for this initial installation. In Unix-type systems such as Linus, "root" is the administrator-level user.

Kismet Prerequisites

Depending on how you installed Linux on your machine, you may need some additional software before you install Kismet. Kismet is written in the C++ computer programming language. At a minimum, you will need the development package that contains a C++ language complier. Since Kismet is a wireless network program, the Linux networking package will also be required. If you haven't installed the development or networking packages on your Linux machine, it is recommended that you get them working on your PC before you go any further. It will be difficult, if not downright impossible, to get Kismet working on your laptop without these packages being installed ahead of time.

A package called SOMElib is also needed for Kismet to properly compile. SOMElib is used in conjunction with the C++ language. However, some Linux distributions split their SOMElib library packages into two, named the "SOMElib" and "SOMElib-devel" packages. If you have a distribution where the SOMElib is split, you will need to have both of these packages installed in order for Kismet to compile.

The LibPcap package is a Packet Capture library, and is required for the packet capturing portions of Kismet to compile properly. It provides the common capturing systems that Kismet uses to capture data packets on the wireless card interfaces. LibPcap 0.9.8 is the current version, and any version over 0.9 is preferred.

Tools & Traps

Application Installations in Linux

Kismet is installed from "source code," as is most software under Unix-like operating systems. Source code is simply a list of instructions of how a program should run, and what it should do as it runs, although this code will not function or execute as a program itself. In order to do that, you need to construct or "compile" the source code into an instruction set that the PC can understand. The resulting machine-capable instruction set can be executed by the laptop directly.

If you are familiar with the standard cycle of compiling and installing software on Linux, then installing Kismet shouldn't pose any great obstacle. However, if you're only accustomed to Windows, in which 99.999 percent of software is distributed as pre-compiled binary executable "EXE" programs, then the first time that you build your own software under Linux can be daunting, if not downright confusing and intimidating. Some Linux distros

Continued

such as Red Hat's Fedora also make their software available in pre-compiled binary formats. Since they were originally made for use with the Red Hat Package Manager, these packages are called RPM files. Users of such distributions may also be unfamiliar with how to compile and install under a "standard" distro. For those of you who are new to the compiling and installation cycle, here is a brief overview of installing Linux programs from source code and cover the needed commands.

The standard way to compile source code into an executable program is done via a series of three main commands: configure, make, and make install. Briefly, these commands tell the compiler, a program that constructs other programs, how to go about building the desired software package.

- **Configure** This command, usually run as *./configure* due to the way Linux is normally set up, tells the compiler what options are needed for the next step, and where to find the various sources of information that are needed to build the desired program. It is not uncommon to add your own options to the configure command.

- **Make** The *make* command is the step where the various options are used to actually create the executable binary program. Typically, *make* is the longest part of the creation cycle.

- **Make Install** The *make install* command is used to install all the various parts of the software into the appropriate directory locations on the laptop.

Some other steps such as *make dep* in which dependant programs are created, may be required for installation of some software packages. Such steps may be intermediary to the configure, make, and make install commands.

If you are having trouble getting a program to install and run under any Unix-like OS, the first place you should look is within the uncompressed source code directory. Most programmers will include what is known as a "README" file, usually named "README.TXT" or something very similar. Most README's will tell you what needs to be done to install a program, including some of the more common procedures that need to be completed prior to installation.

Kismet Installation

Kismet is installed from "source code." Source code is text files that tell the compiler program how to build the actual Kismet program itself. To get started on the installation, you need to log into your laptop as the root user. Then, download the latest source code from www.kismetwireless.net. Follow the links to the download page, and get the latest "Stable Source Release." (See Figure 2.1.)

Figure 2.1 The Kismet Home Page. www.kismetwireless.net

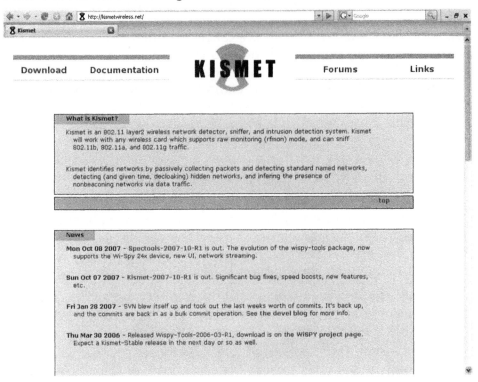

As of this writing, the latest stable release is kismet-2007-10-R1. It was issued on Monday, October 8, 2007. Kismet's release version follows a naming convention of:

```
kismet-yyyy-mm-Rn.tar.gz
```

where:

Yyyy = year

Mm = month

Rn is the revision number.

You should make sure that you download the latest stable release, as it will have the most up-to-date code and bug fixes.

For those new to Linux, the file extension of *tar.gz* indicates that the file is a type known as a "tar" or Tape ARchive (from an old name convention, when tapes were commonplace for storing archives), and that it is compressed using the GNU Zip compression utility.

We recommend that you place the downloaded file into the directory */usr/src*, which is the normal folder to place Linux source code files. To get to the */usr/src* folder, enter this command at the CLI:

```
cd /usr/src
```

Next we'll extract the Kismet source code files. This is done using the command:

```
tar -zxvf kismet-2007-10-R1.tar.gz
```

This command tells the tar program to pull the component files from the archive file. Specifically, the *z* tells tar that the component files were compressed using gzip. The *x* tells it to perform the extract function, while the *v* means that tar is to be verbose, or give information to the user about what it is doing as it performs the file extraction. Finally, *f* is used to force overwriting, which means that if a file was already extracted with that name, tar will write over it with the new file from the archive.

Once this command is entered on the command line, the tar program creates a new sub-directory following the same naming convention. In this case, the sub-directory name will be *kismet-2007-10-R1*. Following that, the program quickly extracts over 150 files and 8 additional folders into the newly created Kismet source code folder. Figure 2.2 shows the archive being extracted into the source code directory

Figure 2.2 Uncompressing Kismet Into Its Directory

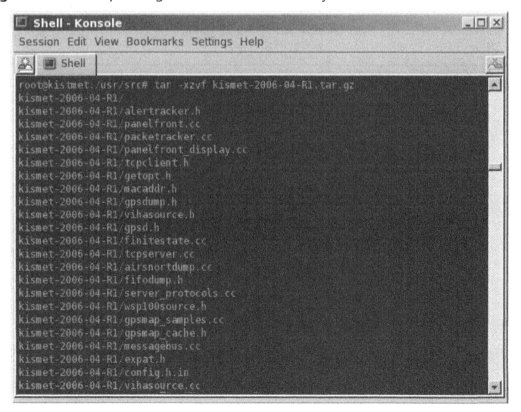

Change to the new sub-directory. It will have the same naming convention as the source code *tar.gz* file, and it will have the name */usr/src/kismet-yyyy-mm-Rn* based on the year, month, and revision number.

```
cd /usr/src/kismet-2007-10-R1
```

The next step is to run the configure command. This is run by typing:

```
./configure
```

Note the "./" in front of the command. If you're new to Linux, make sure you type the period and the forward slash in front of this command. It has to be there due to the way the command functions and where it is located in the Linux directory paths.

At this point, you should watch the output scrolling by on the screen. You don't have to pay rapt attention to it, as it may be too fast to follow. However, if Kismet runs into any problems, such as not finding the libraries or other development packages that it needs to run, this is where the error messages will appear. In Figure 2.3 you can see the configure command being run, and how the output will appear.

Figure 2.3 Running *configxure*

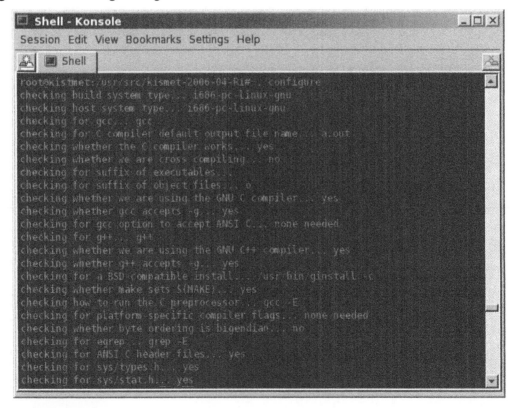

When it finishes, the configure command will give a summary of how it ran, and what libraries were installed. A typical summary is illustrated in Figure 2.4. If additional libraries are missing from your computer, you will most likely see error messages listed here saying which libraries are missing. Missing file libraries are a common cause of *make* failures. If any libraries are missing, you will need to download and install them, and then run the *configure* command again.

Figure 2.4 Configure Completes and Gives a Summary

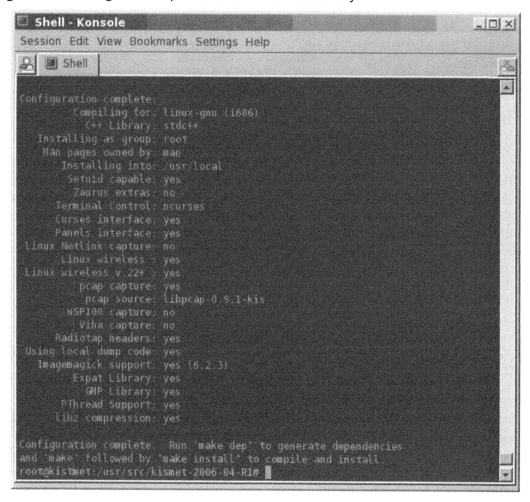

Now you need to execute three commands in succession. They are *make dep, make,* and *make install.* All three are run from the CLI. Run them one at time, letting the output from each one complete before executing the next command.

```
make dep

make

make install
```

Each one of these commands will produce some output on the screen. The output for each command will all differ to some extent, but they will look similar to the output screen in Figure 2.5.

Damage & Defense

The "make suidinstall" Option

Kismet needs root access to configure the wireless card to use the Radio Frequency Monitor mode (known as rfmon). It also needs root access to start the packet capture. The final *make install* command can also be run as *make suidinstall*. Running this option allows Kismet to run with root user privileges from any regular user account. This is potentially a big security problem on multiuser systems, as it makes your laptop vulnerable to misuse if you have users that you do not want to have full administrative privileges. Users who have full administrative privileges, have the ability to impact the entire system, and this can be very bad for those people who are malicious or simply don't know what they are doing.

If you have no other users on the machine besides the root account and trusted accounts, you can install Kismet using *make suidinstall*. This will allow you to run Kismet from any regular user account without changing to the root account.

If you have other, unprivileged users on the computer, you should install Kismet normally, which will only allow it to be run from the root account. When you want to run Kismet from any normal account, you would then use the superuser command *su* to access the root account, and start Kismet from there. The *sudo* command may also be used. There is a slight difference between this *su* and the *sudo* commands. The *su* command switches you to the root user until such time as you type "exit", which will drop to your normal user status. On the other hand, the *sudo* command allows you to execute a single command as the root user, and then instantly drop back to the normal user state, but it must be typed prior to each command. If you are going to run more than a few commands as the root user, then you probably would prefer to use the *su* command, as it will save you some time while typing.

Figure 2.5 The *make install* Command

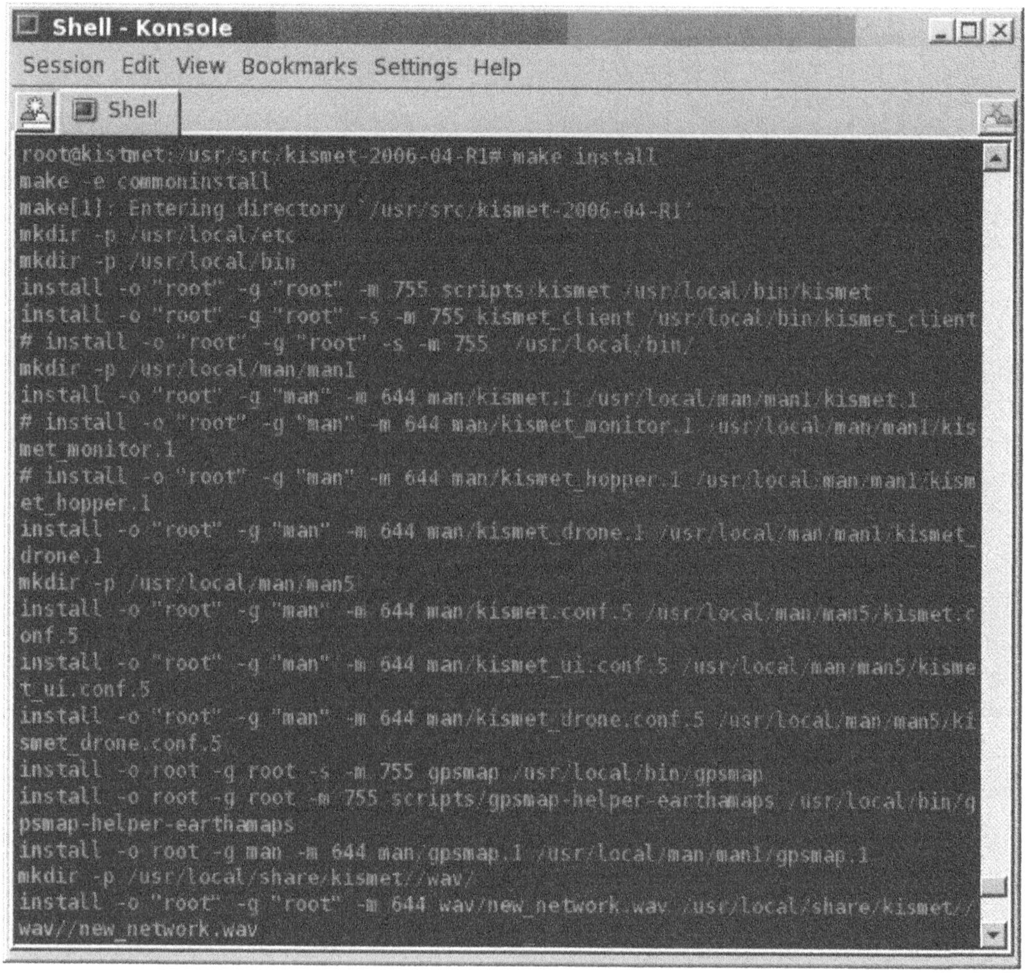

Once the *make install* command has finished, Kismet is installed on the laptop, but it's not quite ready to run. We have to make sure drivers are installed to work with the wireless card, and then edit some options to make the card work with Kismet.

Tools & Traps

Advance Packaging Tool

One other type of install is worth mentioning here. Some Linux distributions use the Advance Packaging Tool (APT), which is designed to greatly simplify the installation of software. The most notable of these distributions is Debian and its popular derivative, Ubuntu. To install Kismet using APT, the *apt-get* command is used. Since the root user is rarely used, the *sudo* command must prefix the *apt-get* command, or the user must switch to the root user using the *su* command as previously mentioned.

```
sudo apt-get install kismet
```

Running the *apt-get* command in this way will install Kismet in any system using the APT, and eliminates having to download and uncompress the source code, and then compile and install the program using the *configure, make* and *make install* commands.

Choosing a Wireless Card Driver

In order to use Kismet, you obviously need to have some wireless information being sent to the server portion of the program, which then passes it on to the client. Usually this is accomplished by a wireless card talking to the server. What may not be quite as obvious is that the wireless card needs a special program called a *driver* to allow it to talk to the server program in the first place. For those of you who don't often delve into the realm of hardware, a driver is nothing more than a small program that translates low-level electronic signals from a particular piece of hardware into information which can be easily used by a higher level program or the operating system itself. In this case, the hardware is your wireless card and the higher level program is Kismet.

Since around 2001, when 802.11b wireless equipment became common consumer items, the electronics marketplace has exploded with any number of different brands of wireless card. Due to this flood of wireless cards, you need to ask the question "Which wireless card am I going to use with Kismet?" In order to answer that question, we need to look at the available drivers for cards, and make sure that the card that we want to use has a driver that will work with Kismet.

To determine which card will work under Linux and with Kismet, we first need to find out what chipset the wireless card is based upon. Chipsets are exactly what the name implies, a collection or set of integrated circuit chips that are designed to work together and produce a specific end function. In the case of wireless cards, most tend to be based on one of several chipsets.

To confuse matters further, many cards are actually the same unit, made by the same manufacturer, but sold under a different brand name label or "badge." These "rebadged" cards will typically use the same driver as the manufacturer named card. The real trick in many cases is to figure out which card was made by what manufacturer, and then determine what chipset was used to make the card's hardware.

Some manufacturers will change chipsets, but will not change model names or numbers. Sometimes the manufacturer's name changes, as in the case of a buy-out or corporate takeover, but the model names remain the same.

Finally, you will need to find out what kernel your particular Linux distro is using. The kernel is the core of a given OS. Although many drivers will work with most Linux distribution, some drivers will work differently with different Linux kernels. For example, with the introduction of kernel version 2.6.13, Linux has a new way that the drivers are able to talk to the kernel, called the "hotplug mechanism." Some distros will have kernels below that number, while other distros will have that or a higher kernel. Some drivers will work with the hotplug mechanism, and some will not.

For example, version 0.13e-SN-9 of the ORiNOCO driver works closely with the hotplug mechanism, while the version 0.13e-SN-8 does not. Therefore, version 0.13e-SN-9 should be used with any kernel 2.6.13 or higher, where 0.13e-SN-8 card would need to be used with any Linux kernel 2.6.12 or below.

If you don't know which kernel you have currently installed, the Linux command *uname -r* will return the kernel version if entered at a CLI. The CLI is usually reached by a terminal or console session, or via an alternate login. For example, on one of the author's machines, typing the command *uname −r* returns the result "2.4.33.3," indicating that the kernel version is 2.4.33.3.

```
uname -r
2.4.33.3
```

The command *uname −a* will show all available system information.

```
uname -a
Linux ghost 2.4.33.3 #1 Fri Sep 1 01:48:52 CDI 2006 i686 pentium3 i386 GNU/Linux
```

For further information, typing *uname −help* will give a list of all available options for the command.

Once you have the kernel version, the next step is to determine the chipset used in the card. To help you figure out which cards and chipsets will work with some common wireless cards, their chipsets and their drivers are listed in Table 2.1. If your card isn't listed here, our suggestion is that you perform a search using your favorite World Wide Web (WWW) search engine. For example, if you have an ORiNOCO Gold 11b/g Card, you would search for "ORiNOCO gold 11b/g chipset." Adding the words "Linux "and "driver" to the search string may help you find sites where you may download a driver that will work with your particular card.

In addition, the Kismet README file has a list of known drivers and chipsets. The README file comes with the source files and is also available as a Web page at the http://www.kismetwireless.net Web site.

Table 2.1 Wireless Cards Chipsets and Linux Drivers

Chipset	Driver
ADMTek	ADMTek
Aironet 340, 350	Kernel 2.4.10–2.4.19, Kernel 2.4.20+, CVS
Atheros	Kernel/Madwifi
Atheros	madwifi; madwifi-ng
Atheros 802.11a	vtar5k
Atmel-USB	Berlios-Atmel
Broadcom	BCM43XX
Intel/Centrino	ipw2100-0.44+; ipw2200-1.0.4+; ipw3945; ipw2200/3945; iwl3945; iwl4965
Lucent, Orinoco	Patched orinoco_cs; Orinoco 0.14+
Nokia/TI	Nokies/TI
Prism/2	HostAP 0.4;wlan-ng 0.1.3 and earlier; wlan-ng 0.1.4–0.1.9; wlan-ng 0.2.0+
PrismGT	prism54
Ralink 2400 11b	rt2400-gpl, rt2500-gpl, rt73-gpl-cvs
Realtek 8180 11b	rtl8180-sa2400
TI ACX100	ACX100
ZyDAS USB	zd1211

The same procedure can be applied to any other OS that you might be running Kismet under. Table 2.2 gives a similar listing of chipset and drivers for use with several different OSes.

Table 2.2 Wireless Card Chipsets, Other OSes and Drivers

Cards	OS	Driver
Airpcap USB	cygwin	CACE Tech
Airport	OSX	viha
OSX native cards	OSX/Darwin	OSX
Prism/2	OpenBSD	Kernel
Radiotap	BSD	Kernel

There are two chipsets that are known not to work with Kismet, under any circumstances; the Atmel and Hermes II chipsets. Additionally, a special driver used for many wireless cards is the *ndiswrapper* driver. The ndisdriver is used to allow some cards which only have Microsoft Windows drivers to function somewhat under Linux. Unfortunately, due to the way that the ndiswrapper works, it is not compatible with Kismet.

For our working example, we're going to use a common and popular card, the ORiNOCO Gold 11b/g Card, Model 8470-FC, manufactured by Proxim. Following the steps above, and from looking at the chart, we know that this particular ORiNOCO card uses the Atheros chipset, and can be run using the Madwifi driver. (See Figures 2.6 and 2.7.)

Figure 2.6 Proxim ORiNOCO 802.11b/g Wireless Card, front

Figure 2.7 Proxim ORiNOCO 802.11b/g Wireless Card, back

Wireless Card Driver Compiling and Installation

Just like building and installing Kismet itself, the Madwifi driver has to be down-loaded as source code, then compiled and installed. So the first thing we have to do is download the source files from madwifi.org. (See Figure 2.8.)

Figure 2.8 MadWifi.orgWebsite

By following the download link, you will receive the latest version of the MadWifi driver in a compressed *tar.gz* file. Again, we change to the source code directory and decompress the source code.

```
cd /usr/src
tar -zxvf madwifi-0.9.4.tar.gz
```

Following that, we will change to the newly created sub-directory, and then run the commands *configure,make,* and *make install.*

```
cd /usr/src/madwifi-0.9.4
./configure
make
make install
```

When the *configure, make*, and *make install* commands have completed, the MadWifi driver has been installed. The installation process should be similar for any other wireless card driver.

Configuring Kismet (Editing kismet.conf)

At this point, we have successfully installed both Kismet and a wireless card driver. We've almost completed the process, but there is still one more task we have to complete before we can successfully run Kismet on the laptop. Kismet has to be told two pieces of information. The first piece of information is the name of the user who will be running Kismet, and the second is what wireless card will be receiving the wireless data, and passing that on to Kismet itself.

To accomplish this, we have to tell the *kismet.conf* file, which controls the Kismet configuration, which wireless card is running and send the wireless data to Kismet. This will be a brief introduction to editing the *kisment.conf*, enough to get this basic installation running. Editing *kismet.conf* will be fully covered in Chapter 6.

To set up the *kismet.conf* file, open it in a text editor. If using the CLI, then editor such as vi or nano will be perfect. The *kismet.conf* file is usually located in the */usr/local/etc/* directory.

```
vi /usr/local/etc/kismet.conf
```

Alternatively, you may use the GUI, and then pick a test editor which can be selected from a menu. The screenshots here were done in KWrite, which is a text editor under the KDE GUI.

First find the line that begins with *suiduser*. In the initial state, this line should read *suiduser=your_user_here*. (See Figure 2.9.)

Figure 2.9 Find the Line Beginning with *suiduse*

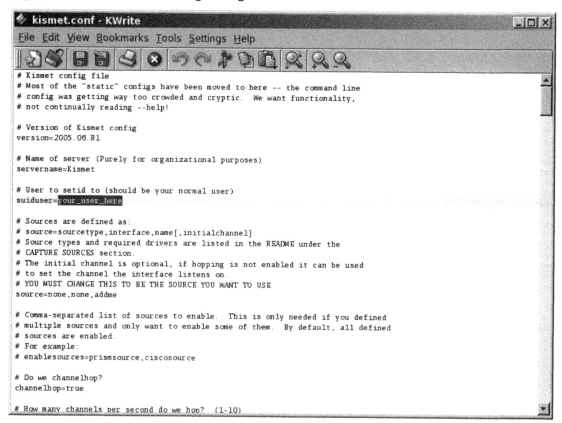

The *your_user_here* needs to be changed to the name of the user who will be running Kismet. Since we are installing Kismet as the user "root," this is the name that we want to type on this line. (See Figure 2.10.)

Figure 2.10 Edit the Line to Show the User Name*r*

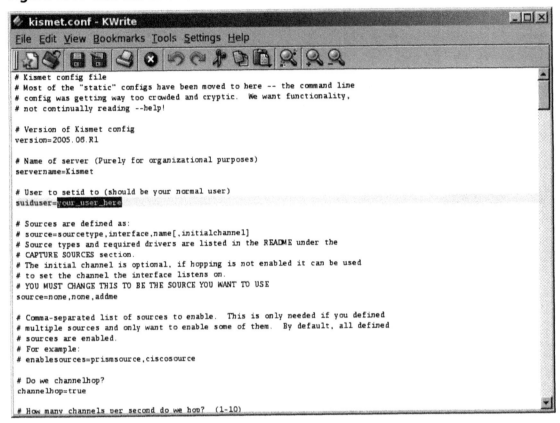

Next we need to find the line that says *source=none.none.addme.* This line tells Kismet which card is the "capture source," in other words, what card will be sending Kismet the wireless data. (See Figure 2.11.)

Figure 2.11 Locate the Line Beginning with *source*

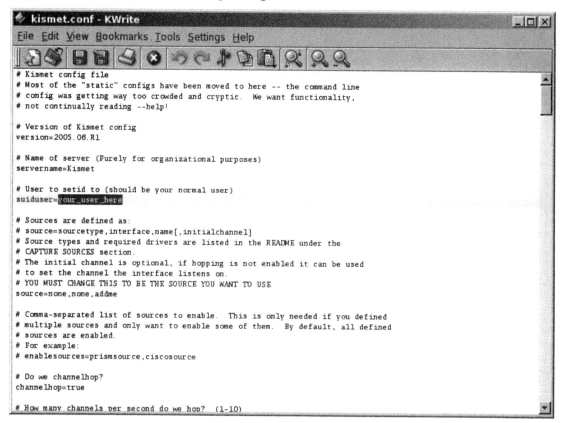

We need this line to show the card driver, the card physical name, and a reference name. In this case we are changing this line so that it says *source=madwifi_g, wifi0,ProximBG*. This line tells Kismet that the capture source is using the *madwifi_g* driver on physical card *wifi0*. The card's reference name is simply the brand name, "Proxim" and "BG," since the card is the type that uses both the 802.11b and 802.11g protocols. (See Figure 2.12.)

Figure 2.12 Change the *source* Line to the Appropriate Driver and Physical Card

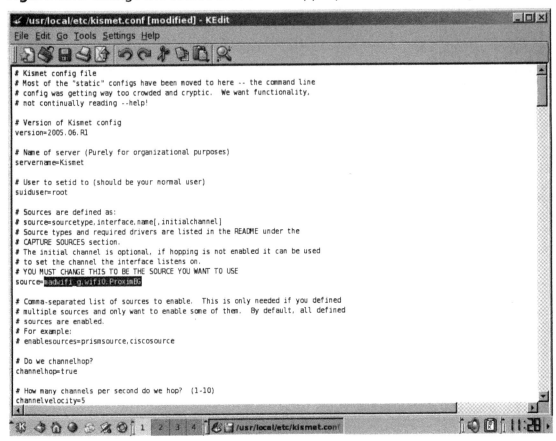

Run Kismet

Finally, we're done with the installation and ready to run Kismet. From the CLI, you should now be able to type "kismet" and the program will start. Initially, you will see a list of file names where Kismet will be saving the data files. These files will be in the directory of the user that is logged in and running Linux. If you've followed the directions in this chapter so far, then these files should be located in the root user's home directory.

```
kismet
```

A number of lines of text will scroll by as Kismet loads its needed files and parameters. After several seconds, the main Kismet screen will open. Kismet should begin to detect any wireless networks within range of the wireless card almost immediately. Figure 2.13 shows Kismet running.

Figure 2.13 Running the Basic Install of Kismet

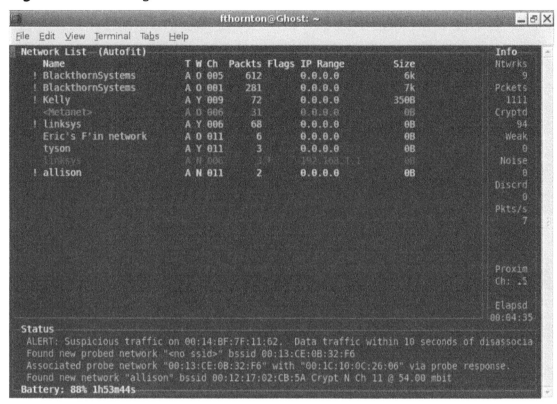

This completes the basic installation of Kismet. You should now have Kismet up and running on your laptop, and it should be able to detect wireless networks in your immediate vicinity.

To quit Kismet, press **Shift-Q** on the keyboard.

In the next chapter, we'll begin adding on to this basic installation, thus giving us the means to use Kismet as a true wireless security tool.

## Chapter 3

Operating Kismet

Solutions in this chapter:

- **Introduction**

- **The Kismet User Interface**

- **Additional RF Equipment: Antennas and Cables**

- **Using a Global Position System receiver with Kismet**

- **Putting It All Together: The Complete Kismet Setup**

☑ **Summary**

Introduction

In Chapter 2, our focus was to get Kismet installed and running in a minimal configuration. So far we have discussed the very basics needed to get it to operate on a laptop. Now, we are going to expand on that basic installation, and take the first steps to turning the Kismet laptop into a true wireless analysis tool.

Kismet has several configuration files that control its functions, most notably the *kismet_ui.conf* and *kismet.conf* files contained in the */etc/kismet* directory. We briefly mentioned editing the *kismet.conf* file in Chapter 2. In order to make Kismet more functional, this time we'll be performing editing to both the *kismet_ui.conf* and *kismet. conf* files to get Kismet running for everyday use.

The *kismet_ui.conf* and *kismet.conf* files are fully detailed in Chapters 5 and 6, but the changes noted in this chapter are those that are likely to be the most useful for those who are new to Kismet.

In addition to editing those files to make Kismet more functional and useful, we'll also discuss adding several pieces of equipment that will help you get the most out of the computer that you are using to run Kismet. Many users have an expectation that they can immediately use Kismet with little more than a laptop and a wireless network card. However, to obtain the best possible results, most users quickly find that they must add some extra Radio Frequency (RF) equipment in the form of external antennas and associated cables, and a Global Positioning Satellite (GPS) receiver. In addition to the GPS receiver, the *gpsd* software package will need to be added to the basic Kismet installation so that Kismet will work with the GPS receiver.

The Kismet User Interface

The first thing we should do is edit the *kismet_ui.conf* file, which controls how the user interface presents itself to the user. The user interface is the client portion of Kismet that the user sees when running the application.

The *kismet_ui.conf* file is a simple text file that can be edited by any text editor. Two common text editors under Linux are *vi* and *nano*, which are used on the command-line interface (CLI). Most window managers that run under Linux, such as KDE and Gnome, also have graphic text editors that are suitable for editing *kismet_ui.conf*.

To use a text-based editor such as *vi*, you would enter the editor name followed by the file name that you to edit on the CLI.

```
vi /etc/kismet_ui.conf
```

The Introductory Splash Screen

When Kismet is first run, a small splash screen opens up over the main window. The splash screen, entitled "Welcome to Kismet" tells you what Kismet client you're running, including the version and build number. It welcomes you to the Kismet panel's front end and advises you that you can press **h** at any time to get help information. It also tells you that you can turn off of the message by editing the *kismet_ui.conf* file. Pressing the space bar will get rid of the splash screen. This splash screen is shown in Figure 3.1.

Figure 3.1 Welcome to Kismet

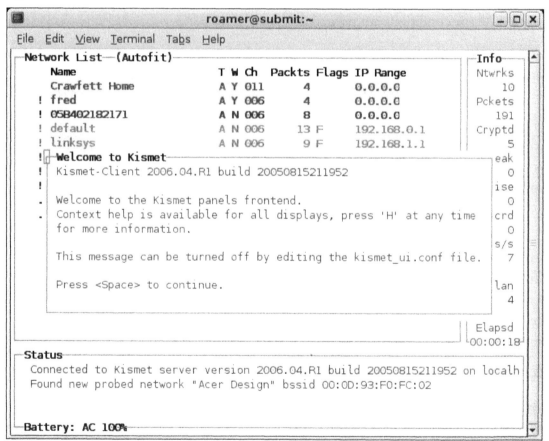

Now we want to get rid of the splash screen, so that it doesn't open whenever Kismet is run. To do this, edit the line *showintro=true* to and change it to *showintro=false*.

Save the file and restart Kismet. Kismet will now start up without the splash screen. Remember, press the **h** key to open a Help screen. The Help screen is further discussed in Chapter 4.

Play Sounds

Kismet, by default, plays sounds when certain events happen or are detected. Those events are when:

- A new network is detected
- Traffic is seen on a detected network
- Junk traffic is seen on a detected network
- Alarm conditions are triggered

Four sound files for these functions are installed in the */usr/share/kismet/wav* directory when Kismet is installed. Playing sounds can be turned on or off by setting the sound value to true or false. By default, the sound is on, and can be found on this line:

```
sound=true
```

The sound application that comes as part of most Linux installations is *play*, and by default, Kismet uses *play* to present those sounds to the user. This can be seen from this line:

```
soundplay=/usr/bin/play
```

However, some Linux distributions come with different sound applications. If *play* is not the sound application on your laptop, then you will have to change the *soundplay=/usr/bin/play* line to reflect the sound player that is installed. For example, *aplay* is the sound player application that comes with Ubuntu Linux version 8.04. If you are using Ubuntu v.8.04, you have to change the line to *soundplay=/usr/bin/aplay*, so that the *aplay* application is used to play the sound files.

Additional RF Equipment: Antennas and Cables

Most people using Kismet for the first time will use it for the activity known as "war driving," or locating Wireless Local Area Networks (WLANs) while driving through a given area. The steel and aluminum body panels in most auto bodies block radio signals very effectively, and because of this, an antenna is usually one of the first accessories purchased to be added to the Kismet laptop. An external antenna for WLAN uses functions in the same way as the AM/FM radio antenna on your car. It allows a weak signal, which otherwise might not penetrate the car body, to be brought in where the receiver—or in the case of Kismet, the wireless networking card—is located.

To help you understand antennas and how they work, here are some basic terms you should know when determining what type of antenna you want to use while running Kismet:

- **Gain** Gain describes how well an antenna performs. The units used to describe gain are the *decibels*.

- **Decibel (dB)** A decibel is the unit of measure for power ratios describing loss or increase of apparent radio frequency power, normally expressed in watts. A decibel is not an absolute value—it is the measurement of power gained or lost between two communicating devices. These units are usually given in terms of the logarithm to Base 10 of a ratio.

- **dBi value**. This is the ratio of the gain of an antenna as compared to an *isotropic antenna*. The greater the dBi value, the higher the gain. If the gain is high, the angle of coverage will be more acute.

- **Isotropic Antenna** An isotropic antenna is a theoretical antenna that radiates its signal to cover the area in a perfect sphere. It is used as the starting point to describe the performance and gain of a real antenna.

Generally, an antenna capable of transmitting and receiving the signal equally in all directions is preferred. These antennae are known as "omni-directional" or "omni" for short. Most war drivers use an omni antenna in the 3 dBi to 8 dBi range, as these give the best compromise on signal gain and pattern. Commonly, this type of omni-directional antenna has a magnetic base that sticks readily to a steel car body roof. Such "mag mount" antennas allow the antenna to be transferred between different vehicles without a complicated installation. Two small omni-directional antennas along with a wireless card can be seen in Figure 3.2. The antenna on the left is approximately 6 inches in height and has a magnetic base that allows it to be easily mounted on a car body. The antenna on the right is made for use on tabletop. Both have a gain of approximately 5 dBi.

Figure 3.2 3dBi Omni-Directional Antenna with Magnetic Mount Base

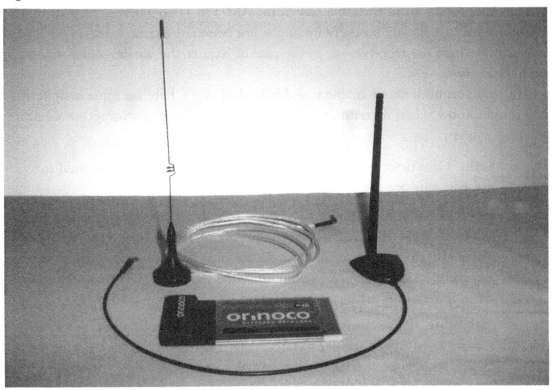

One common misconception is that the higher the gain of the antenna, the better your results will be when using Kismet. This is not true. The important thing to understand from the preceding definition of dBi value is the last sentence: "If the gain is high, the angle of coverage will be more acute."

The signal coverage area of an omni-directional antenna is shaped roughly like a donut. The higher (or larger) the gain, the "shorter" the donut. The opposite is true as well. A smaller gain antenna has a "taller" donut. Figure 3.3 shows the signal donut of a 5 dBi gain omni-directional antenna compared to that of an 8 dBi gain omni-directional antenna. The signal donut of the 5 dBi is taller than the signal donut of an 8 dBi gain omni-directional antenna. This is illustrated in the side view. What this means is that although it has a "weaker" signal, as indicated in the overhead view, a 5 dBi gain omni-directional antenna is likely to provide better results in a neighborhood with tall buildings, such as an urban downtown area. Also, because these antennas rely on line-of-sight communication, a 5 dBi gain antenna works well in residential areas where homes and other buildings provide obstructions between your antenna and any wireless access points (APs).

Figure 3.3 Omni-directional Antenna Patterns with Different Gain Levels

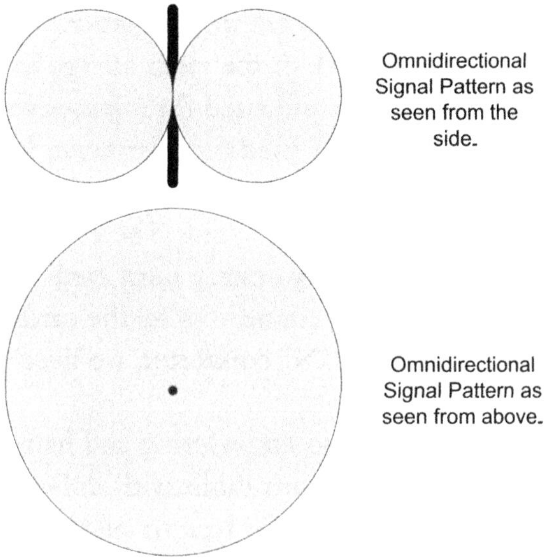

Omnidirectional Signal Pattern as seen from the side.

Omnidirectional Signal Pattern as seen from above.

Antennas of this type usually come with an attached cable, 10 to 20 feet in length. This cable allows the signal to be received easily inside a car or truck. The cable end opposite the antenna usually terminates in a "Type N-Male" connector. If the attached cable is too short or absent, a cable of the appropriate length will have to be purchased.

In addition to an omni-directional antenna, directional antennas of different types are available from a wide variety of sources. A directional antenna is confined to sending and receiving in a single direction, as the name implies. Directional antennas also come in different gain levels, and usually are described as having a particular "beam width" in degrees. Think of it like a flashlight beam of light. The beam width on a directional antenna is the area the antenna will send and pick up radio signals.

Due to the narrow focus of the beam, directional antennas are of limited use for general war driving, since the signal is confined to sending and receiving in one area only. Most times while war driving, you are attempting to find as many APs as possible, in all directions. However, for those people who are using Kismet for purposes such as security auditing of a WLAN, a directional is a must, especially if you are attempting to locate a specific AP. For example, when attempting to locate an unauthorized or "rogue" AP on a company network, a directional antenna is an indispensable tool.

Pigtails

The frequencies used by 802.11 WLANS fall into the microwave area of the radio spectrum. In order not to lose too much of the radio energy in the connectors, the connectors must be of the proper type and rated for microwave use. The "N" type connector is one of the most commonly used for microwave RF communications, and is seen on many brands of antennas and cables. Unfortunately, an "N" connector is huge in comparison to the average WLAN cards. The combined weight of the cable and the connector would almost certainly destroy most cards in short order. For this reason, the card manufacturers use tiny connectors on the cards. To convert from the tiny connector used on the card to an "N" connector, we need what is known as a "pigtail" cable.

The term "pigtail" comes from radio engineering and ham radios. A pigtail is nothing more than a short piece of antenna cable, with different connectors on each end. They are used to convert one connector type to another. Usually, the cable used for a pigtail is a smaller diameter and type than the main cable, but this is not always true. The exact origins of the term seem to be lost, but since most small diameter coaxial cables curl rather tightly after being unwound from a cable spool, it seems reasonable that the name came from the fact that a small length of cable might resemble the curled tail of a pig.

Two common pigtails used for WLAN antenna connections are the Orinoco proprietary connector (Type MC) to a Type N-Female connector, which is a reflection of the popularity of the ORiNOCO card and the Type MMCX connector to a Type N-Female connector. When purchasing a pigtail, you must determine the connectors that you need on each end of the cable. This will depend on the brand and model of your card, and the connector on the antenna cable. If you have more than one card that you will be using with you Kismet laptop, most likely you will need more than one pigtail. Most pigtails are about 12 to 18 inches (30 to 45 cm) in length. Longer pigtails may be found, but are generally best avoided. This is because the thin cables have a high signal loss, and the longer the cable, the more signal is lost before it gets to the radio card. Figure 3.4 shows an 802.11b WiFi card and its pigtail. The connector on the left joins to a standard antenna cable, and the connector on the right attaches directly to the card itself.

Figure 3.4 Pigtail (Type N to Type MC)

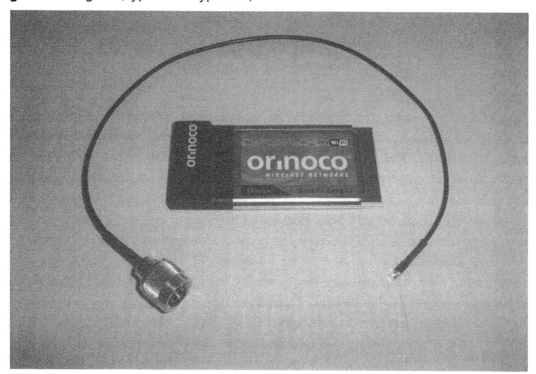

Using a GPS Receiver with Kismet

In order to physically locate a WLAN AP or to map WLAN locations, you have to know where you are when the AP is detected. So how do you track where you are when a WLAN is detected? You could take notes, writing down your exact location every time Kismet finds an AP. But this could be rather difficult because getting a precise location might involve taking measurements along with detailed notes. For instance, "Thirty-five feet north of the 'No Parking' sign in front of 23 Main St.; five feet from the edge of the sidewalk." Using such a technique might be rather tedious, and you would proceed at a snail's pace.

However, there is a much easier way to do this, with a level of precision within approximately 25 feet. By attaching a GPS satellite receiver to your computer, Kismet will automatically log your location every time it receives an 802.11 frame.

GPS units are radio receivers that measure a signal from several different global position satellites. By using triangulation, the receiver calculates its location on the surface of the Earth using those signals. The location is reported in terms of the latitude, longitude, altitude, and other data. Most GPS units continuously update their location information. The unit then sends out this position data over a serial data link, typically about once every second. In turn, Kismet reads the data via another program called *gpsd*, and then records the longitude and latitude from the GPS whenever it monitors an 802.11 packet or frame. Because of this ease of use in recording the location of a detected WLAN, a GPS is the second accessory that most users will add to their Kismet laptop.

Features of GPS receivers vary, but generally they fall into two categories: those that have an integral display and those that have no display. Those that are without a display are generally referred to as "mouse" or "puck" styles, since they tend to resemble either a computer mouse or a hockey puck. Mouse or puck GPS receivers without a display are generally less expensive, but they need to be connected to a computer (or some other device) to work properly. Those with displays can function in a standalone mode. If you plan on using your GPS solely for use with Kismet, a mouse or puck style may be fine. However, if you plan on using the GPS for other activities such as hiking, then you will want to buy one with a display. Figure 3.5 shows three common GPS units. The two on either end have a built-in Liquid Crystal Display (LCD), while the center one is a "puck" without a display.

Figure 3.5 Typical GPS Receiver Models

In addition to the GPS receiver itself, an additional software package known as *gpsd* is needed. The *gpsd* program collects the serial data from the GPS receiver and makes it available to be queried by Kismet and other programs on Transmission Control Protocol (TCP) port 2947. Like other UNIX-type software, the source code must be downloaded and the *configure*, *make*, and *make install* commands must be run to install the program. If you are unfamiliar with these procedures, complete information on downloading, compiling, and installing software packages from source code was covered in the last chapter. Documentation for *gpsd* can be downloaded from http://gpsd.berlios.de.

Debian-based Linux distributions such as Ubuntu, install *gpsd* by typing this command at the CLI:

```
sudo apt-get install gpsd
```

Once installed, *gpsd* is started on the CLI by typing the command "*gpsd*" followed by the device designator of the port into which the GPS receiver is plugged. The *gpsd* program normally runs without further configuration, and will self-determine any parameters needed for communicating with the GPS receiver. For example, if the GPS receiver is plugged into the first serial port on the laptop, usually known as device */dev/ttyS0*, then the command would be:

```
gpsd -p /dev/ttyS0
```

If the GPS receiver is plugged into the second Universal Serial Bus (USB) port on the laptop, usually known as *device /dev/ttyUSB1*, then the command would be:

```
gpsd -p /dev/ttyUSB1
```

In order to have Kismet report and record the information coming from *gpsd*, you also have to edit the *kismet.conf* file. Open *kismet.conf* located in the */etc/kismet* directory, in your favorite text editor, just like you did previously with *kismet_ui.conf*. Find the line marked:

```
gps=false
```

and change it to read:

```
gps=true
```

Now save the *kismet.conf* file and close the editor. Now, run Kismet again. If everything is working correctly, you will see GPS data in the form of the current longitude and latitude listed on the bottom boarder of the main Kismet panel. Additionally, you should see a "2D" or "3D" status flag, depending on whether the GPS has locked on to enough satellites to determine a full three-dimensional location or only a two-dimensional location. A full three-dimensional location has the longitude, latitude, and altitude, so if a full three-dimensional location is being tracked by the GPS, all three figures will be displayed. Otherwise, for a two-dimensional location, only the longitude and latitude will be shown.

Typical GPS Problems

There are several potential stumbling blocks to using your GPS receiver with Kismet. If you experience problems getting the GPS data, you need to do a bit of troubleshooting.

The first requirement to getting a GPS unit to work with Kismet is to get the GPS to transmit its data over some manner of communications link. Most GPS receivers will output location data in the National Marine Electronics Association (NMEA) 0183 data protocol, using a serial cable. Technically, the NMEA 0183 output is EIA-422A data, but for all practical purposes it is the same as RS-232 serial data. This means a GPS that sends NMEA 0183 data will talk to the serial communications (COM) ports used on most computers. Some newer GPS units use Bluetooth low-power radio communications to transmit the NMEA data.

However, before you attempt to use the GPS receiver with Kismet, you must go through an initialization procedure. The procedure needs to be done before the GPS will send out the correct location data. Be sure to read the instructions for your GPS, and go through the setup routine.

The Map Datum from the GPS should be set to the World Geodetic System of 1984 (WGS84). This is the default setting for most GPS receivers, but occasionally the data output is set to the North American Datum of 1927 (NAD27). While the two data sets are very similar, there can be a difference in location of over 100 meters (320 feet) in different sections of the United States. Therefore, using the NAD27 setting may result in inaccurate location information, especially if you later try to map the AP site.

A second problem is that some GPS brands and models need to lock on to the satellite signals and establish their location *before* they send any serial data. More than one person has started checking cables and connections and analyzing RS-232 data protocols, only to realize that the receiver had not seen enough satellite signals to establish a location, and had not sent anything out of the serial port.

Conversely, many GPS units will send out data, but it may not be accurate if the receiver has not locked onto the satellite signals. One chipset used in some popular GPS units is known to initialize itself to Tokyo if it cannot see any satellite signals. That's fine if you happen to be in Tokyo when you start collecting data, but probably isn't of much use to people starting outside of Tokyo.

The lesson here is to make sure your GPS receiver has a satellite lock before you head out to use Kismet. GPS satellite signals are relatively weak since the satellites are in high orbit, and the GPS receiver may need several minutes to figure out where it is on the Earth's surface. If you are inside a building, moving outdoors will help speed up this process, as the receiver will have better "line of sight" to the satellites, and therefore have better signal reception. Also, anything that blocks the GPS receiver's clear view of the sky, from heavy tree cover to a city's "concrete canyons," can hinder the ability of the receiver to determine location. When using Kismet with GPS in a vehicle, you should keep the GPS receiver where it can "see" the sky. In most vehicles, this will be an area on the dashboard under the windshield, or near another window. For the sake of safety, make sure the GPS receiver (or any other device) does not obstruct the driver's field of view.

Tools & Traps

Troubleshooting GPS Problems

If Kismet does not seem to be communicating with your GPS receiver, it is sometimes difficult to determine if the fault lays with the Kismet, *gpsd*, the GPS unit itself, or something else such as the cables and connectors.

The first step is to check if the GPS is sending data to *gpsd*. The *gpsd* program uses TCP 2947 to communicate to other programs and applications; therefore, you are able to use the program Telnet to communicate with *gpsd*, to see if it is working. First, start *gpsd* using the appropriate device:

```
gpsd /dev/ttyS0
```

Then, start Telnet, pointing it to the *gpsd* TCP port on the laptop (known as the *localhost*), and type the command r to have *gpsd* respond with the NMEA data.

```
# telnet localhost 2947
# r
```

If the GPS receiver is working properly, you should see NMEA sentences scroll by on the screen. NMEA sentences should look similar to those below, although the data will differ slightly according to your location.

$GPGSV,3,1,10,17,78,216,38,23,63,311,42,26,56,051,41,15,52,303,43*7E
$GPGSV,3,2,10,18,46,295,49,09,36,152,,29,36,053,,03,09,317,*7C

Continued

```
$GPGSV,3,3,10,10,08,097,,06,04,203,,,,,,,,,,*7C
$GPGLL,4422.2935,N,07313.8332,W,005702.969,A*21
$GPGGA,005702.97,4422.2935,N,07313.8332,W,1,05,2.7,00075,M,,,,*3E
$GPRMC,005702.97,A,4422.2935,N,07313.8332,W,00.0,000.0,150303,15.,W*67
$GPGSA,A,2,17,23,26,18,15,,,,,,,,2.7,2.7,*13
```

If you see information similar to this, then the GPS and *gpsd* are working properly, and you may close Telnet by typing the following commands:

```
# ^c
# e
```

If no characters show at all, then this indicates a probable cable issue. In this case, you may need to purchase a null modem, which will swap the connections of several common lines used in serial connections. Null modems for serial cables can be obtained at most Radio Shack stores for under $10.

A third issue is that RS-232 serial data has its own pitfalls. Almost all serial connections on the GPS receivers are proprietary, so most users will need to purchase a cable from the GPS manufacturer. The plugs and sockets for the PC end of the cable are usually DB9 sub-connectors on most laptops, but sometimes those are also proprietary. Encountering a plug (or socket) on both the laptop and the GPS is quite common, requiring the purchase and use of gender-changer plugs or sockets in order to get the equipment to connect to each other. Another common difficulty with the RS-232 standard is finding that a null modem is required to switch the location of the data lines within the connectors. A gender changer and a null modem are shown in Figure 3.6.

Figure 3.6 A "Gender Changer" Plug and a Null Modem Needed to Connect Various GPS Cables

The final common problem with using a GPS is that many laptops produced in the last few years lack RS-232 serial ports. Instead, the serial ports have been replaced with the faster and more flexible USB ports. However, many GPS receivers still only use an RS-232 serial port. This will require the use of a serial-to-USB converter. Several manufactures such as Belkin make serial-to-USB converters.

Putting It All together: The Complete Kismet Setup

At this point you should have collected all of the pieces. Hopefully, you have been able to configure everything, and confirmed it's all working. No doubt, you are about to head out on your first war drive or at least your first use of Kismet. Before you do, look over these set ups and make sure you are ready. You can see a typical Kismet setup in Figure 3.7. Most setups will include the following or very similar items:

- A laptop with PC Card or Personal Computer Memory Card International Association (PCMCIA) slot(s)

- Wireless network interface card

- Antenna pigtail

- Portable omni-directional Antenna in the 3dBi to 8dBi range, with magnetic mount base

- GPS

- Serial or USB communications cable for GPS, or possibly a Bluetooth link.

Figure 3.7 A Complete Kismet War Driving Rig; Laptop, GPS Receiver, Omni Antenna, and Pigtail

A laptop carrying case (shoulder bag or backpack) is not shown in the photo, but is certainly an item that you don't want to overlook. It helps make carrying all the equipment around a lot easier.

Three other accessories that you may find useful are a mobile power supply for the laptop, a multiple socket cigarette lighter adapter, and a DC–AC power inverter. The multiple cigarette lighter socket adapter allows you to have extra 12-volt power sockets in your vehicle without rewiring, and a DC–AC converter allows you to power devices that you might not own an automotive power supply for, such as a laptop. Independently or together, these two accessories allow you to have a flexible electrical power arraigment in your vehicle.

Summary

This concludes the two chapters on getting Kismet set up and running. You now have all the information you need to get Kismet installed, and how to build from the initial setup using an antenna and a GPS receiver.

From this point on, the remaining chapters in this book will build on these basics, so if you haven't installed Kismet, you at least need to have a good understanding of the procedures and particulars needed and how to go about getting the install done.

## Chapter 4

Kismet Menus

Solutions in this chapter:

- **Main display**
- **Popup windows**
- **Customizing the panels interface**
- **Third party front-ends**

☑ **Summary**

☑ **Solutions Fast Track**

Introduction

Kismet is a text-based application that uses an ncurses/panels interface for its default front-end menus. Visually, the front ends are similar, although the ncurses interface is black and white, while the panels interface users color (see Figure 4.1). As we will see through this chapter, the value of color is immeasurable to Kismet's panels interface in terms of the amount and value of the information it provides. In addition, the ncurses interface is a single, non-interactive display; the various secondary and popup menus specified within this chapter do not work.

Figure 4.1 Ncurses/Panels Interface

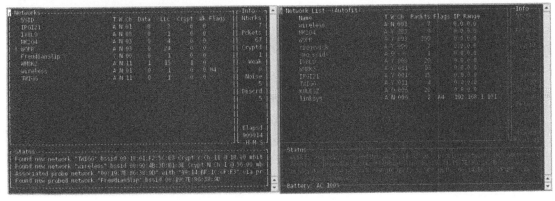

The choice of graphical user interface type to use is specified in the *kismet_ui.conf* file:

```
# Gui type to use
# Valid types: curses, panel
gui=panel
```

This file is typically located in */usr/local/etc*. The panel interface is the default, and is highly recommended. For the remainder of this chapter, all references and figures will use the panels interface.

An important feature of the Kismet panels interface is the integrated help screen. From the primary window, simply press **h** to bring up the help pop-up window (see Figure 4.2).

Figure 4.2 Kismet Panels Interface

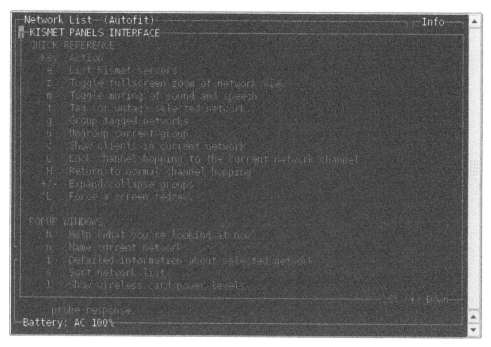

> **TIP**
>
> In any of Kismet's pop-up windows, the bottom right corner of the window
> provides you with data regarding the amount of information being
> displayed. In the case of Figure 4.2, this data tells us that only 26 percent
> of the help pop-up screen is displayed, and that you should scroll down for
> more information.

Main Display

The primary window or main display provides a general overview of Kismet's
operations (see Figure 4.3).

Figure 4.3 Kismet's Main Display

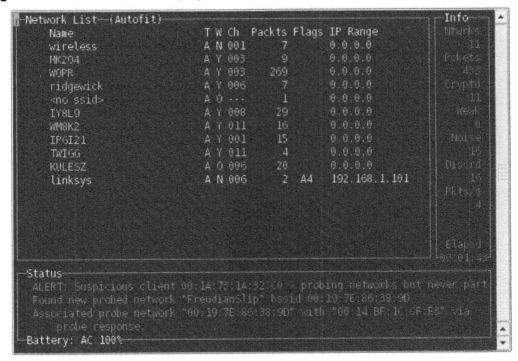

The display is divided into three panels: the network list panel, the information panel, and the status panel.

Network List Panel

The primary source of information on Kismet's main display is the network list panel (see Figure 4.4). This panel consumes a considerable amount of screen space, and desires to strike a balance between displaying as many networks as possible, while still providing valuable information about each of those individual networks. In this section, we'll discuss the various options to sort networks as well as the default columns and colors displayed by Kismet in the network list panel, and how they provide information to users.

Figure 4.4 Network List Panel

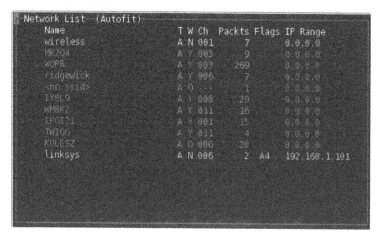

Sorting

As you will note in Figure 4.4, Kismet's default sorting mode is known as *autofit*. The goal of autofit is to display as many currently active networks as possible. While using autofit, network selection, tagging, grouping, scrolling, and so forth is disabled. To use any of these features, simply sort the network list by another method. To bring up the sort options, simply press **s** (see Figure 4.5).

Figure 4.5 Sort Options

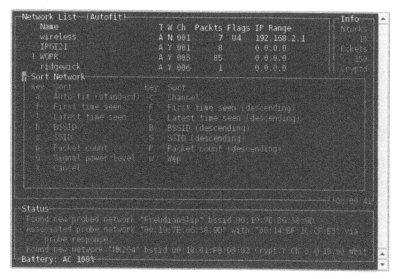

The sort options displayed in Figure 4.5 are self-explanatory; although, as previously explained, you'll need to choose something other than autofit to do anything useful. Service Sent Identifier (SSID) is common, and displayed in Figure 4.6:

Figure 4.6 Networks Sorted by SSID

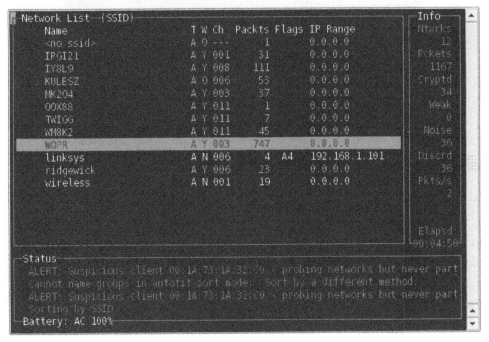

Sorting also gives you a cursor-enabled selection bar that indicates which network is currently highlighted. Note in Figure 4.6, that the sort is ascending by default. In the case of first time seen, latest seen, Basic Service Sent Identifier (BSSID), SSID, and packet count, the capital letter equivalent (S rather than s) is a descending sort.

Columns

Kismet supports in excess of 20 column descriptions, although only the nine listed below are displayed by default (see "Customizing the Panels Interface" below for more information). Kismet will display as many columns as it can within the space provided.

TIP

If the Kismet window isn't big enough to display all of the columns, simply use the left and right arrow keys to scroll in the appropriate direction.

Decay

The first column is *decay*, although it has no header and may not be immediately obvious. Decay is a measure of network activity and the amount of time passed, and is controlled by the decay variable in the *kismet_ui.conf* file. The default setting is three seconds:

- **Active** If the network is active within the decay time, an exclamation point "!" is displayed prior to the network name.

- **Recent** If the network was active within two periods of the decay time (i.e., six seconds), a period "." is displayed prior to the network name. See the "WOPR" network in Figure 4.4 for an example.

- **Inactive** In all other cases (i.e., the network has not been active within six seconds), nothing is displayed.

Name

The network name is the most prominent column in the network list display. Typically, this lists the SSID, although you can change the name of any particular network with the "n" pop-up window. If a network is not broadcasting the SSID, Kismet can still infer its presence and will publish the network as *<no ssid>* until it can determine the name.

Type

The T column specifies the type of network:

- **A (Access Point)** A wireless access point (AP) or wireless router; by far the most common network type

- **D (Data Network)** Data packets have been seen, but Kismet has not captured any beacons or management frames and thus cannot yet tell what kind of network it is

- **G (Group)** Networks that have been manually grouped together by the user (*t* to tag networks, *g* to group tagged networks together)

- **H (Ad-hoc)** Typically a wireless network set up between multiple laptops or clients without using an AP

- **P (Probe Request)** A client probing for an AP that has not yet associated

- **T (Turbocell)** Turbocell/Karlnet/Lucent router (uncommon)

WEP

The W column denotes whether or not encryption is being used on the network. However, it is more relevant to ask the question, "*is WEP being used, or something else?*" to understand the possible responses:

- **Y (Yes)** Wireless Encryption Protocol (WEP) is in use

- **N (No)** The network is not encrypted

- **O(Other)** The network is encrypted with something other than WEP (for example, WPA)

Channel

The channel of the network is displayed in the C column:

- For the more common 802.11b/g networks, the associated channels are 1–11 in the United States and 1–14 outside the United States.

- For 802.11a, the following are allowable channels with the United States: 36, 40, 44, 48, 52, 56, 60,64, 149, 153, 157, 161, and 165. Outside of the United States, particularly in Europe and Japan, more channels are available.

Packets

"Packts" is simply a cumulative total of packets captured for that particular network.

Flags

The Flags column displays brief information about the network:

- **F (Factory Configuration)** The bells should be going off in your head; this user has not changed anything from the original factory configuration

- **W (WEP Decrypted)** This is a WEP-encrypted network that has been decrypted with a user-supplied key

If Kismet can determine the address range and Internet Protocol (IP), it will display in the Flags column the method by which it obtained this information:

- **T (TCP)** The address range was determined via Transmission Control Protocol (TCP) traffic

- **U (UDP)** The address range was determine via User Datagram Protocol (UDP) traffic

- **A (ARP)** The address range was determined via Address Resolution Protocol (ARP) traffic

- **D (DHCP)** The address range was determined via Dynamic Host Configuration Protocol (DHCP) traffic

In addition, the T, U, and A flags may display a number (1–4), which indicates the number of octets discovered. For example, referring again to Figure 4.4, the *linksys* network displays the A4 flags, indicating that the address was discovered using ARP traffic, and all four octets have been discovered.

IP

By monitoring traffic, Kismet attempts to determine the IP address of the network, and this is displayed in the "IP Range" column. Kismet will display 0.0.0.0 until it finds some useful data via one of the methods described in the Flags section above. As you might suspect, more traffic collected from a particular network will provide a greater likelihood of finding the IP range, and more particularly, the exact IP address.

Size

The size column displays the total size of all the packets collected for that particular network.

Colors

While it is not accurately reproduced in a grayscale screenshot, the Kismet interface also displays to the shrewd observer, some valuable information by color-coding the networks:

- **Networks in yellow** are not encrypted, meaning they are not using WEP or WPA. While these networks are coded as unencrypted, they still may be using a Virtual Private Network (VPN) or some other form of authentication after associating with the network. Yellow networks also indicate that at least some settings have been changed from their factory defaults.

- **The red** color code is the signature of a network that is using the factory defaults. You may also see the F flag with this network. If the user hasn't changed the factory configuration, you just might find that they haven't changed the default password either!

- **Networks in green** are using some form of encryption, usually either WEP or WPA. If Kismet cannot determine between the two, the Kismet *.dump* file can be imported into Wireshark, and the exact form of encryption determined there.

- **Blue** networks are using SSID cloaking or are not broadcasting the SSID. An active scanner such as Network Stumbler (for Windows), which relies on the broadcast frame to determine the SSID, would not be able to locate this network.

GPS

When a supported Global Positioning System (GPS) is used together with Kismet, the applicable GPS data will be displayed along the bottom edge of the network list panel (see Figure 4.7).

Figure 4.7 GPS Status Information

Lat 39.143 Lon -76.612 Alt 22.9m Spd 0.016m/s Hed 303.376 Fix 3D

As is typical of coordinates without north/south/east/west labels, positive latitudes indicate north, while negative latitudes indicate south. Likewise, positive longitudes indicate the eastern hemisphere, while negative longitudes indicate the western. In Figure 4.7, our coordinates are north of the equator, and in the western hemisphere (central Maryland to be more precise). Also included is a measure of altitude, speed, heading, and quality of fix.

Information Panel

The information panel labeled as "Info" is a small vertical panel to the right of the network list panel (see Figure 4.8).

- **Ntwrk** Total number of collected networks

- **Pckets** Total number of collected packets

- **Cryptd** Total number of collected packets that were encrypted

- **Weak** Total number of weak packets collected

- **Noise** Worthless garbage packets

- **Discrd** Total number of discarded packets; includes noise and packets discarded from the use of filters

- **Pkts/s** Rate of packet collection (per second)

- **Elapsd** Total time (HH:MM:SS) since the Kismet was started

Figure 4.8 Info Panel

Status Panel

The status panel occupies the bottom section of the Kismet interface (see Figure 4.9). The status panel provides scrolling messages to the user:

- **Updates** Kismet will post a message to the status panel when it finds a new network, and provide additional information about networks when it becomes available

- **Problems** Kismet will alert you to information regarding potential problems with Kismet's connection to other services; for example, if Kismet cannot connect to gpsd

- **Alerts** These are primarily useful when using Kismet as an intrusion detection system (IDS); provides integration with third-party systems (i.e., Snort)

- **Battery Meter** Kismet will indicate if you are plugged into external power (AC), and display the percentage of battery life remaining; when using the battery Kismet will display an estimate of how much life is left. Keep in mind that you'll need an APM-enabled kernel for battery life to report correct estimates.

NOTE

Even though Kismet places your wireless adapter in *rfmon* mode (meaning it does not transmit), simply having your wireless adapter radio on consumes more power from your battery. It is estimated that your battery life will be somewhere between 2–7 percent shorter. While this is not necessarily a hugely significant amount, it makes the battery meter all the more useful.

Figure 4.9 Status Panel

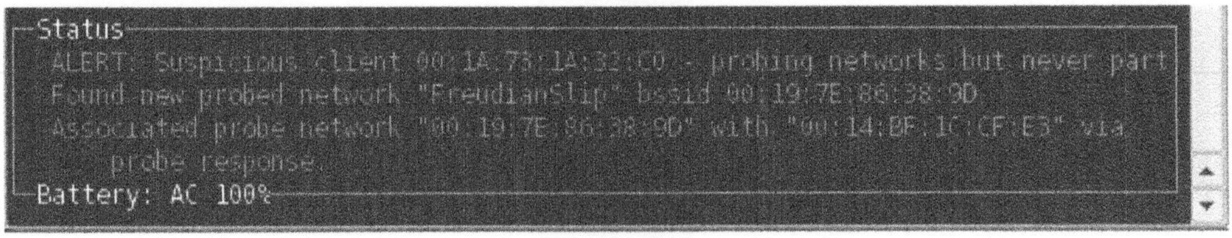

Pop-up Windows

All of Kismet's windows beyond the main display are secondary displays or pop-up windows. These exist primarily as a means of displaying further information on a particular network, group, or client; providing statistics and useful information regarding packet rates and types; and other interesting data.

Network Details

The network details window displays the most comprehensive and detailed information collected about a particular network. When sorting by any mode other than autofit, simply scroll to the network of your choice and press **enter** or **i** (see Figure 4.10).

The network details window is useful if you need more information then is already provided in the network list. For example, the network list may show a particular network with the WEP flag "O," which signifies the network is encrypted, but with something other than WEP. Under some circumstances, Kismet's network details may be able to tell you specifically what type of encryption is being used. Be sure to scroll down as there is likely to be more than one screen of information.

Figure 4.10 Network Details Window

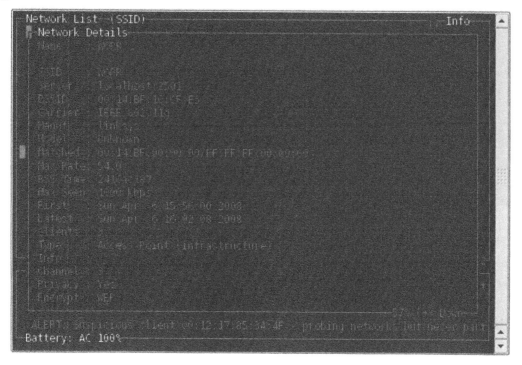

From the network details window, **n** will move you to the next network or group, while **p** will return you to the previous network or group. Alternatively, you can close the pop-up (**q**) and scroll to a different network. The network details window is one means of getting to the client list (**c**); you can also type (**c**) directly from the network list.

Client List

The client list window is very similar in both display and functionality to the network list panel. The default sort mode is also autofit, and the client list can be sorted in a similar manner.

Figure 4.11 Client List Window

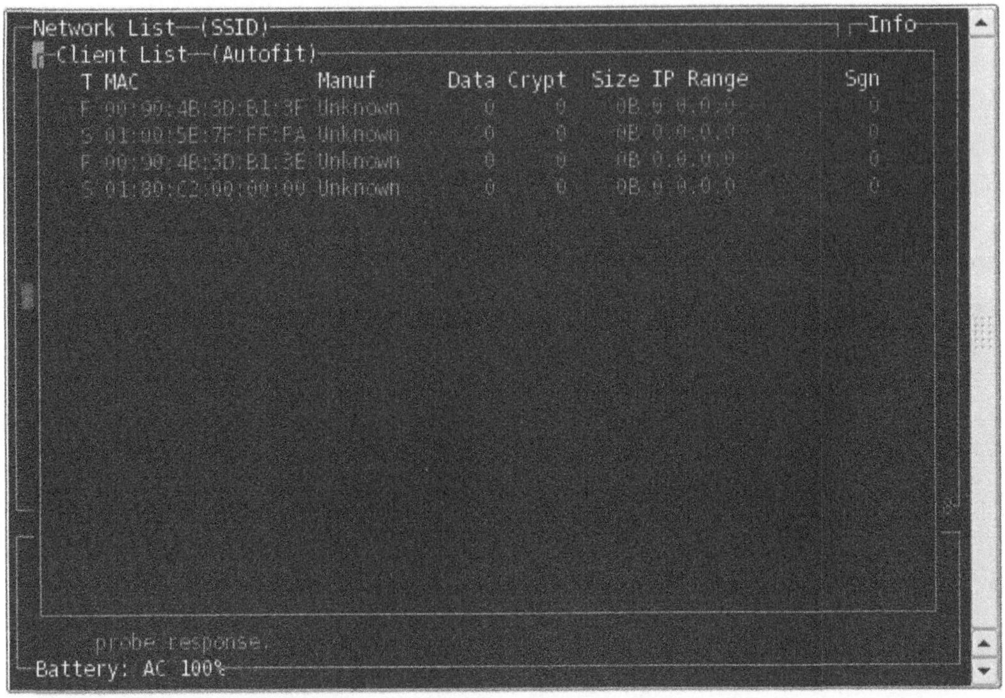

The **n** and **p** keys display the client list of the next and previous network or group, respectively. Once a particular client is highlighted, the **i** key (or pressing **enter**) changes to the client details display.

Columns

The following columns are displayed by default (again, as with the network list panel, see "Customizing the Panels Interface" later on in this chapter for changing the defaults):

Decay

The decay variable for a client is the same as it is for a network. As with the network list panel, the column is unlabeled and unseen unless a client is active or recent.

Type

The T column denotes the type of client. The client types are as follows:

- **F (From DS)** From a wireless distribution system (WDS) or AP to a wireless client; normally this means the client is wired

- **T (To DS)** To a WDS/AP from a wireless client; normally this means the client is wireless

- **I (Intra DS)** A node of the WDS/AP communicating to another node within the system

- **E (Established)** Most often a wireless client entering and leaving the WDS/AP

- **S (Sent To)** A client that has received data but not yet responded

- **(Unknown)** Self-explanatory

Manufacturer

The "Manuf" displays the manufacturer of the client based on the first three octets of the Media Access Control (MAC) address, which is known as the Organizationally Unique Identifier (OUI). As the name suggests, each manufacturer is assigned a specific block of octets that designate their equipment. Kismet attempts to match the client MAC with a list of OUIs in the *client_manuf* file. If a match is made, the manufacturer will be shown; otherwise *unknown* will be displayed.

NOTE

In some cases, Kismet may also be able to fingerprint the fourth octet of the MAC address, which is the first octet of the Network Interface Control (NIC)-specific portion of the MAC address. In this case, potentially more detailed information about a specific wireless adapter may be learned, such as the exact model of the particular device. In other cases, especially newer or rare equipment, Kismet may return *unknown* because it simply doesn't know the MAC address. Likewise, a spoofed MAC address will fool Kismet as to the original manufacturer.

TIP

Kismet's *ap_manuf* and *client_manuf* files are intentionally small to reduce memory use and Central Processing Unit (CPU) consumption. For those users that desire to use the full Institute of Electrical & Electronics Engineers, Inc. (IEEE) OUI list, Kismet provides a script (in the extras directory) called *ieee-manuf-tr.sh*, which will convert the OUI text file into a Kismet readable format. Of course, this will result in increased memory and CPU usage.

Data

This column displays the total number of data packets transferred by the client.

Crypt

The "Crypt" column displays the total number of encrypted packets transferred by the client.

Size

Size displays the total amount of data transferred by the client.

IP Range

"IP Range" displays the last known IP address of the client.

Sgn

The "Sgn" column displays the most recent signal strength of the client. As with all other issues related to signal strength, the accuracy of this data is entirely dependent upon the proper reporting of the data by the driver and/or firmware of the wireless adapter you're using. To reiterate: if your card and/or driver does not support proper signal reporting, this value is useless.

Client Details

In the same way that the network details window shows the comprehensive collection of details about a particular network, the client details provides the same level of data for a particular client. Figure 4.12 provides an example of the level of client detail. Notice the client type is now a little clearer. This particular client is "From DS" or from the AP to a wireless client. As we know, these clients are typically wired. In fact, in this particular case, this client is the AP itself.

Figure 4.12 Client Details Window

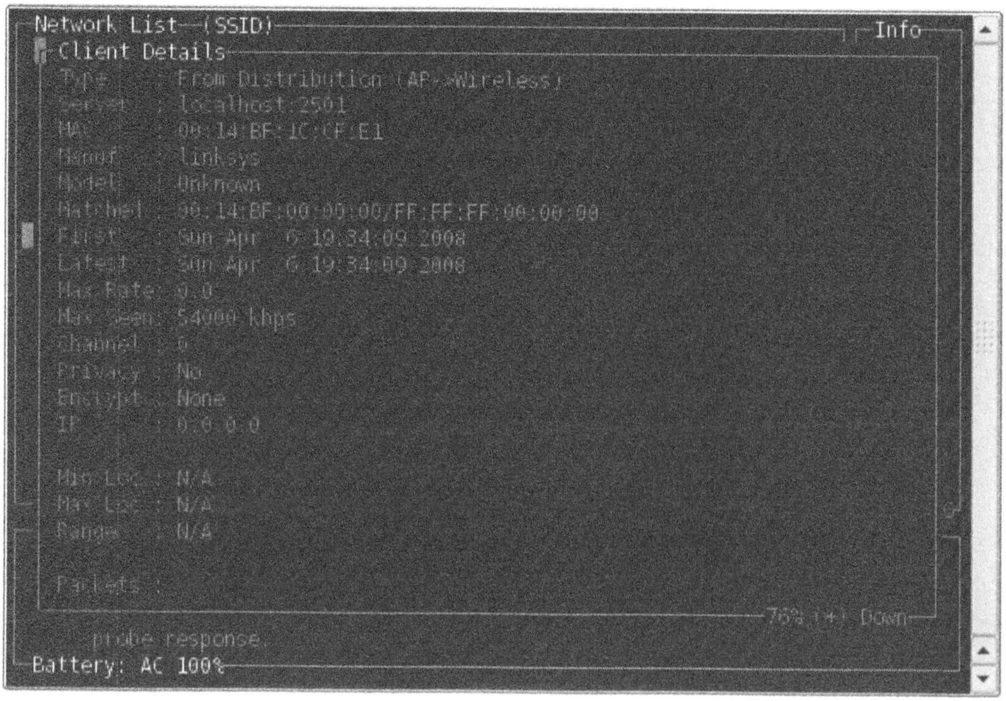

The **n** and **p** keys display the details of the next and previous client, respectively. Similarly to the network details display, scrolling down will provide you with more information.

Packet rate

Kismet's packet rate window will display a 5-minute history of the packet rate per second (see Figure 4.13).

Figure 4.13 Packet Rate Display

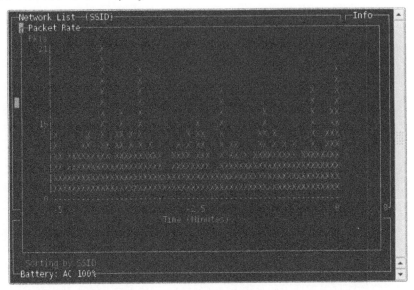

Packet Types

Kismet will also dump the packet type information to the screen (see Figure 4.14).

Figure 4.14 Packet Type Display

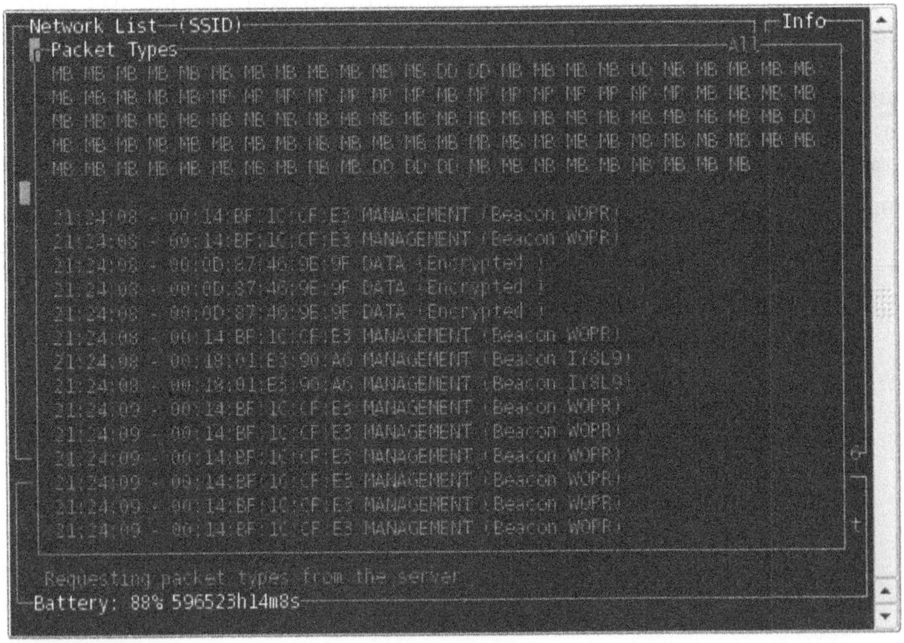

The packet types panel is divided into two sections: the top displays a history of packet types by abbreviation (see the list below), while the bottom displays a scrolling list of the most recent packets with more detailed information. By default, Kismet will display packet types from all networks. However if you have tagged individual networks you can toggle between "all" and "tagged" with the **a** key. The following is a list of the applicable packet types:

```
'N' - Noise
'U' - Unknown
'Mx' - Management frame
        'Ma' - Association request
        'MA' - Association response
        'Mr' - Reassociation request
        'MR' - Reassociation response
        'Mp' - Probe request
        'MP' - Probe response
        'MB' - Beacon
        'MM' - ATIM
        'MD' - Disassociation
        'Mt' - Authentication
        'MT' - Deauthentication
        'M?' - Unknown management frame
'Px' - Physcial frame
        'Pt' - Request to send
        'PT' - Clear to send
        'PA' - Data Ack
        'Pc' - CF End
        'PC' - CF End+Ack
        'P?' - Unknown phy frame
        'Dx' - Data frame
        'DD' - Data frame
        'Dc' - Data+CF+Ack
        'Dp' - Data+CF+Poll
        'DP' - Data+CF+Ack+Poll
        'DN' - Data Null
        'Da' - CF Ack
        'DA' - CF Ack+Poll
        'D?' - Unknown data frame
```

Statistics

Kismet will display overall statistics that include the time you started the program, how many servers are currently running, the number of networks (broken down into *encrypted* and *default*), total number of packets seen, and maximum packet rate. In addition, Kismet provides both a graph and chart, which display channel usage information. See Figure 4.15 for the statistics window.

Figure 4.15 Statistics Display

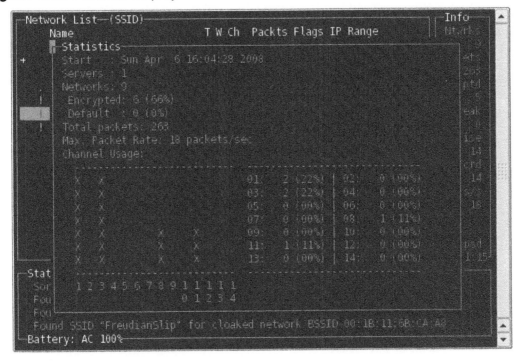

Wireless Card Power

The **1** key will display signal power as well as report noise (see Figure 4.16). The name of this display is a bit of a misnomer, because it is not reporting the power of *your* wireless card; rather it is reporting the signal strength of the particular network or client. Remember that Kismet places your wireless card in *rfmon* mode, therefore your card is precluded from transmitting while Kismet is running.

WARNING

Kismet does not calculate signal power or noise; rather it simply displays information provided by the wireless card driver and/or firmware. Some drivers or firmware may not report this information (especially while in *rfmon* mode), and in this case Kismet will not provide you with anything useful. Furthermore, even when cards do properly report this data, there is no consistency in terms of a scale, so comparing signal and noise levels among different cards is more or less useless.

Figure 4.16 Wireless Card Power Display

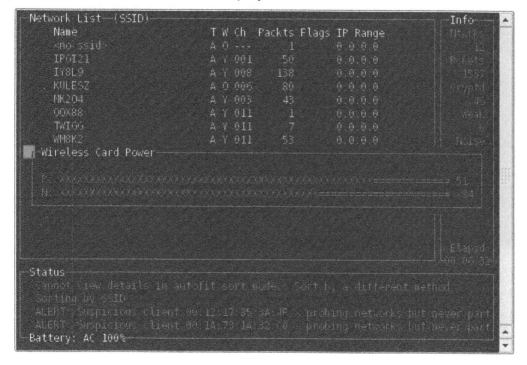

Network Location

Kismet has a nice (and not very well known) feature that will attempt to geo-locate a network. The accuracy of this information is wholly dependent upon GPS location data. Since estimating range based upon non-existent signal and noise standards is virtually impossible, this data is (unfortunately) not very useful in geo-location. Rather Kismet will guess location based upon a sample of GPS-logged locations.

Furthermore, Kismet does this on the fly; therefore it is advantageous to get sample data from a variety of locations to get a better guess. See Figure 4.17 for an example of the network location feature.

Figure 4.17 Network Location Display

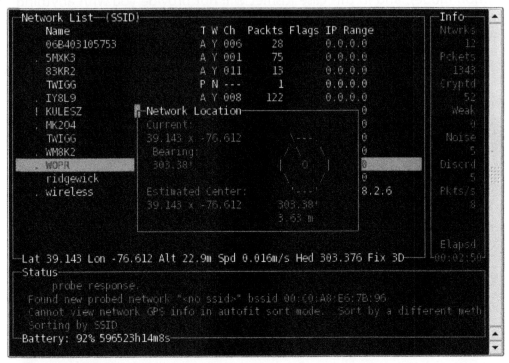

Essentially, network location compares the location of where you were versus where you are now. This also assumes that your laptop is facing the direction of travel.

Customizing the Panels Interface

As has already been noted, Kismet can display a wealth of information about a network or client on the network and client lists (respectively), the only limitation being size. Should you find your work requires additional information to be available to you from one of these two displays, you can easily modify Kismet's user interface configuration file to add or remove columns. Also, Kismet provides the ability to change colors to suit your needs.

Customizing the Network List Window

As we have seen, Kismet's main display contains a significant amount of useful information in the network list section. All of the information for a particular network is available in the network details window. Any or all of this information can be displayed in the main window by modifying the *kismet_ui.conf* file. The recognized columns, and their appropriate descriptions, are as follows (default columns are bold):

bssid   BSSID (MAC address) of the network

channel   Last-advertised channel for network

clients   Number of clients (unique MACs) seen on network

crypt   Number of encrypted packets

data   Number of data packets

decay   Displays '!' or '.' or blank, based on network activity in the
            last 'decay' seconds (controlled by the 'decay' variable in the config file)

dupeiv   Number of packets with duplicate IVs seen

flags   Network status flags (Address size, decrypted, etc)

info   Extra AP info included by some manufacturers

ip   Detected/guessed IP of the network

llc   Number of LLC packets

manuf   Manufacturer, if matched

maxrate   Maximum supported rate as advertised by AP

name   Name of the network or group

noise   Last seen noise level

packets   Total number of packets

shortname   Shortened name of the network or group for small displays

shortssid   Shortened SSID for small displays

signal   Last seen signal level

signalbar   Graphical representation of signal strength

snrbar   Graphical representation of signal-to-noise ratio

size   Amount of data transfered on network

ssid   SSID/ESSID of the network or group

type   Network type (Probe, Adhoc, Infra, etc)

weak   Number of packets which appear to have weak IVs

wep   WEP status (does network indicate it uses WEP)

To modify the default columns in the main window, edit the *kismet_ui.conf* file at the following location:

```
# What columns do we display?  Comma seperated.  Read the documentation for what
# columns are valid.
columns=decay,name,type,wep,channel,packets,flags,ip,size
```

Figure 4.18 shows a modified network list panel showing network name, manufacturer, total number of data packets by network, signal and noise information, and amount of data transferred per network.

Figure 4.18 Modified Network List Window

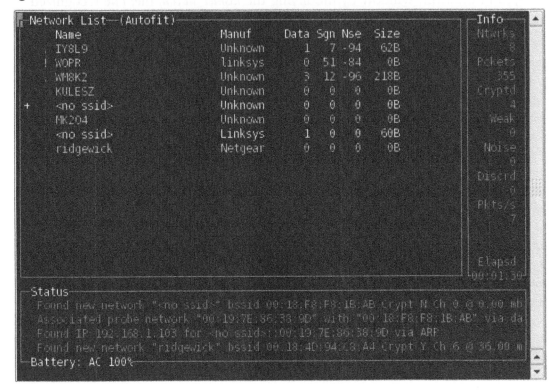

Customizing the Client List Window

Similarly, the columns in the client window can be modified (all are on by default except "maxrate"):

```
crypt        Number of encrypted data packets transfered by client
data         Number of data packets transfered by client
decay        Displays '!', '.', or ' ' based on network activity
ip           Last seen IP used by client
mac          MAC address of client
manuf        Manufacturer of client (if known)
maxrate      Maximum rate client seen transfering
```

```
noise        Last seen noise level of client
signal       Last seen signal level of client
size         Amount of data transfered by client
type         Type of client (Established, To-DS, From-DS, etc)
weak         Number of packets which appear to have weak IVs
```

To modify the default columns in the client window, edit the *kismet_ui.conf* file at the following location:

```
# What columns do we display for clients? Comma seperated.
clientcolumns=decay,type,mac,manuf,data,crypt,size,ip,signal,quality,noise
```

Customizing Colors

Kismet's colors can be turned on or off, the background and border colors can be changed, and the default colors listed above can be changed by modifying the applicable portion of *kismet_ui.conf*:

```
# Colors (front, back) of text in the panel front. Valid colors are:
# black, red, yellow, green, blue, magenta, cyan, white
# optionally prefixed with "hi-" for bold/bright colors, ie
# hi-red, hi-yellow, hi-green, etc.

# Enable colors?
color=true
# Background
backgroundcolor=black
# Default text
textcolor=white
# Window borders
bordercolor=green
# Titles
titlecolor=hi-white
# GPS and APM info
monitorcolor=hi-white
# WEP network color
wepcolor=hi-green
# Factory network color
factorycolor=hi-red
# Open color
opencolor=hi-yellow
# Decloaked network color
cloakcolor=hi-blue
```

Third Party Front-ends

While the large majority of this chapter has focused on Kismet's native panels interface, there are a number of third-party interfaces that have been developed over the years. These third-party front-ends are designed primarily as a way of enhancing the look or changing the interface from an ncurses/panel one to a truly graphical one. This section is not meant to be an exhaustive review of such graphical user interfaces (GUIs), but rather a brief survey of some of the options that are available.

> **NOTE**
>
> It is important to note that these third-party front-ends are simply replacements for the Kismet client (interface), and don't actually do anything by themselves. They still require you to run Kismet in server mode and connect to it with the particular interface of your choice.

gkismet

One example of a popular Linux-based Kismet front end is *gkismet* (see Figure 4.19). The gkismet interface is designed to supplement or replace the native Kismet panels interface for those that prefer something more GUI-based. Many of the same features are available, and development is ongoing to remain compatible with the latest version of Kismet. For more information about gkismet, see http://gkismet. sourceforge.net/.

Figure 4.19 gkismet

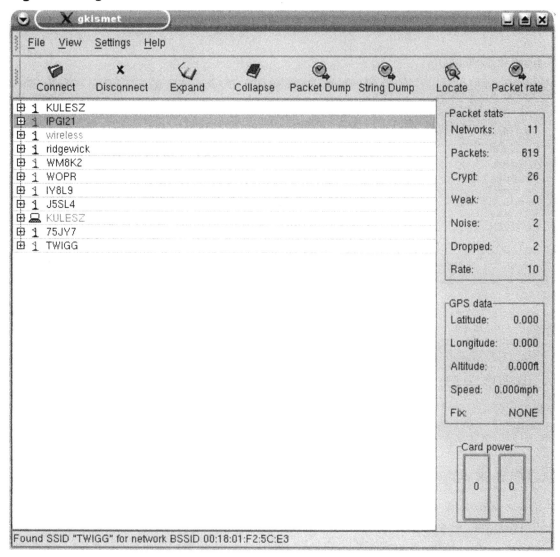

KisWin

KisWin (not to be confused with RenderMan's Kismet for Windows package also known as KisWin, and located at http://www.renderlab.net/projects/wrt54g/) is a Windows-based GUI front-end for Kismet (see Figure 4.20). Whether you are running Kismet on Windows/Cygwin using a remote drone (such as a modified Linksys WRT54G), using CACE Technologies' AirPcap adapter, or simply running Kismet over a network to a Windows PC, *KisWin* provides you with a GUI interface. For more information about *KisWin*, see http://kiswin.taz00.com/

Figure 4.20 KisWin

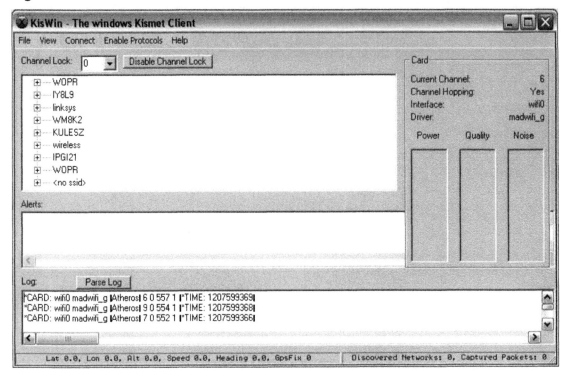

dumb kismet client

The last interface we'll mention is *dumb kismet client* for Win32. This particular client is lightweight, and should be able to run in front of any of the same Windows/ Cygwin configurations as KisWin. While *dkc* is designed for Windows, it also worked fine under Linux using *wine*. For information about *dumb kismet client*, see http://www.d3tr.de/dkc/.

Figure 4.21 dumb kismet client

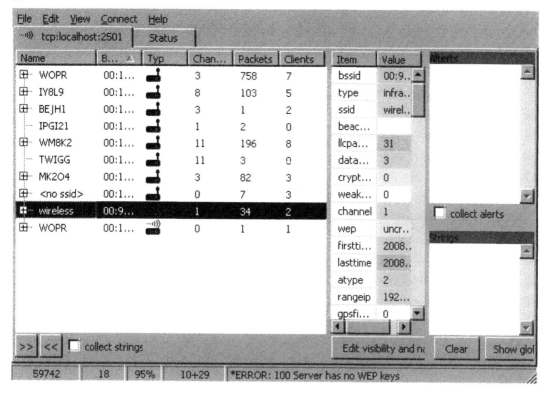

Further information

Once again, this section is not designed to be the end-all solution for third-party front-ends for Kismet, rather a sampling of some of the solutions that are available to users. See http://www.kismetwireless.net/links.shtml for more information on third-party tools for Kismet.

Summary

The Kismet client is the primary interface between the Kismet server and the user. The default display is the panels interface, which is a lightweight, interactive GUI display. The primary display provides the user with a general overview of Kismet's collected data, and can be manipulated and modified to the user's content. The remainder of the windows are secondary displays or pop-up windows that provide additional and amplifying information about selected networks, groups, or clients, as well as statistics and additional interesting information. Some of these displays can also be modified to the user's liking. Lastly, there are a number of third-party front-ends to supplement or replace the default Kismet client.

What happens when you have a question? Your first source of information should be Kismet itself. Most if not all of the displays have integrated help screens (always the **h** key). Your second source should be the online documentation, found at www. kismetwireless.net/documentation.shtml. Of particular interest to this chapter are sections 10 (Ncurses/panel interface), 17 (Troubleshooting, and 18 (Frequently Asked Questions). You would benefit greatly from reading the documentation in its entirety (all the way to the end!). Once you exhaust those sources, move on to the Kismet forums (http://www.kismetwireless.net/forum.php), being sure to search before you post. Finally, consider using your best friend Google who, more often than not, can find something that will guide you in the right direction.

Solutions Fast Track

Main Display

☑ The Kismet panels display is the primary interface between the Kismet client and server and the user.

☑ The main display is divided into the network list panel, status panel, and information panel; and is designed to provide the user with an overview of Kismet's collected information.

☑ Kismet's integrated help feature is the gateway to more detailed information about a particular network.

Popup Windows

☑ All windows beyond the main display are secondary or pop-up windows, and provide additional and amplifying information about selected networks, groups, or clients, as well as statistics and additional interesting information.

☑ The information provided on the wireless card power and network location pop-up windows is wholly dependent upon the wireless card drivers and/or firmware. Kismet does not calculate signal or noise information, rather it simply reports it.

Customizing the Panels Interface

☑ Both the network list and client list can be modified to the user's specifications by editing the *kismet_ui.conf* file.

☑ Kismet's color scheme, including the background, borders, and default color-coding of networks, can be modified as well.

Third-Party Front-ends

☑ Third-party front-ends are GUIs designed to supplement or replace the Kismet client panels interface.

☑ Third-party clients are available to run on both Linux and Windows.

## Chapter 5

Configuring the Kismet Server

Solutions in this chapter:

- The Kismet Config File

- Kismet.conf

☑ Summary

Introduction

The Kismet server is controlled primarily from one big scary configuration file. Usually located in */usr/local/etc*, the *kismet.conf* file is where you'll spend most of your configuration time. Anyone who's spent any time working on config files will find themselves pretty comfortable. It is an untapped resource for both the Kismet beginner and even for experts who have been using Kismet for a while. Not many people go through and check out the extent of the configuration options available to them. There's a great amount of information that can be tracked and recorded by Kismet, as well as filtering and targeting of certain information. Understanding what options are available will help you use Kismet in the best possible way for your needs.

The Kismet Config File

The config file is not as scary as it may seem. It is very large, however, because Dragorn was kind enough to leave a lot of very verbose comments about the various options. Some areas are fairly self-explanatory while others are not. This section will go through, almost line-by-line and examine and explain each of them. The comments are good, however some areas are open to tweaks not specified in the comments, and a lot of power can be revealed once you start digging into the config file.

Kismet Parameters

The *kismet.conf* config file can be edited directly with your favorite UNIX text editor (such as vi, pico, emacs), just be aware of word wrapping and UNIX file format. The config file is parsed at runtime by the server and expects a UNIX text file. DOS and UNIX use different control characters for their text files and as such, using a DOS or windows editor on a UNIX text file will probably change it and make the file unreadable to the server. In general, if you are editing the *kismet.conf* file, use a UNIX editor. This can be either a native Linux application, or an editor through Cygwin if you are running under windows or some other UNIX text format-capable editor.

Comments in the *kismet.conf* file are lines starting with a "#" symbol. These are often comments or example configurations and can usually guide you to what options you need to set. Lines that do not start with a comment are the actual parameter variables acted upon by the server. It's a good idea to comment out the existing line by putting a "#" in front of the line and adding a new line with the adjusted parameter. This way if something goes wrong, you know what the original parameter was.

Kismet.conf

```
# Kismet config file
# Most of the "static" configs have been moved to here -- the command line
# config was getting way too crowded and cryptic. We want functionality,
# not continually reading --help!
```

The Kismet server used to be controlled through command-line parameters (many of which still can be used), but as the program and functionality grew, it became a huge effort to set all the command-line arguments for sources, ports, and so forth. So everything was moved into the *kismet.conf* file. The above lines are the beginning of the *kismet.conf* file, and is a throwback to those early days when people spent forever looking at the –help command line switches.

```
# Version of Kismet config
version=2007.09.R1
```

This line indicates the version of the config file itself, not the version of the server or any other portion of the program. A lot of people confuse this line with the server version and wonder why their server is three versions back. The config file doesn't change as often as the rest of the tool suite, so it has a separate version number listed on this line.

```
# Name of server (Purely for organizational purposes)
servername=Kismet
```

This parameter is one of those often-overlooked sections of the config, and it's right at the top. The *servername* parameter allows you to name the server for your own organizational purposes. This is particularly useful if you are monitoring several remote servers with one client instance. You could have servers named after location (*server_north_east, server_north_west, warehouse*) or channel (*server_ch1, server_ch2*) or however you want to keep things sane. The server name must not contain any spaces, so use underscores or dashes in place of spaces. This allows you to know which server you're connected to and it's location for either troubleshooting purposes or for incident tracking. It has no real affect on performance; it's just useful for keeping you sane, particularly in large installations.

```
# User to setid to (should be your normal user)
suiduser=your_user_here
```

This line is often a misunderstood by people just beginning with Kismet. This is the user that Kismet will run it's processes as once it's started. Kismet requires root access to set monitor mode and other options, then it drops privileges on the Kismet processes to the user specified in this parameter.

```
suiduser=foo
```

The above is an example, where "foo" is a normal user account on the system.

NOTE

As noted in the chapter on basic Kismet install, unless you build Kismet Set User ID (SUID) root, you need to have a normal non-privileged user on the system. This is for security reasons. The user specified here also has to have write permission on the directory where you are storing your captured data and logs. A major problem people trip on is that they run Kismet as root and specify root as the SETUID user. Unless you built it SETUID root, this will halt Kismet from starting. They also make the mistake of logging in as root, running Kismet from /root and the server fails to start as the SETUID user does not have write permission on the /root directory. The simple solution is to login as a normal user and either su to root or use sudo to start Kismet.

Specify the username of a non-privileged (non-root) user on the system and make sure that wherever you store the data it has write permission. The logical place for this is the non-privileged users home directory. The best order to run Kismet to avoid problems is to login as a normal user, change to the directory you want the resulting data saved to, then "su" to root and then run Kismet.

```
# Do we try to put networkmanager to sleep? If you use NM, this is probably
# what you want to do, so that it will leave the interfaces alone while
# Kismet is using them. This requires DBus support!
networkmanagersleep=true
```

This line in the config file tells Kismet to use Dbus to disable Network Manager, the common gnome desktop manager applet, to disable itself for the duration of the Kismet session. After Kismet exits, the network manager will resume control.

> **NOTE**
>
> Many modern Linux distributions use fancy X widgets to control the network cards. It's an attempt at making the system user friendly and avoiding users to have to go to the command line to connect to a wireless network. The problem is, if we want to do anything weird with the card, such as monitor mode, these network monitor programs fight for control of the card and can cause no end of grief for Kismet.
>
> If you have any weird scanning situations such as things randomly stopping scanning or getting stuck on one channel and not hopping, this is a likely candidate. For the most part, you'll want this option enabled.
>
> In some situations, this may cause issues. The most common will be when you are scanning with one interface but using the network manager to control another for communication (such as an intrusion detection system (IDS) setup reporting to a server. Kismet disables network manager for all interfaces, wired and wireless. If you run into problems with the network manager being disabled, you may want to not use the network manager at all and manually configure the other interfaces.

```
# Sources are defined as:
# source=sourcetype,interface,name[,initialchannel]
# Source types and required drivers are listed in the README under the
# CAPTURE SOURCES section.
# The initial channel is optional, if hopping is not enabled it can be used
# to set the channel the interface listens on.
# YOU MUST CHANGE THIS TO BE THE SOURCE YOU WANT TO USE
```

Probably one of the most important areas of the config file; where do we get our data. The source line tells Kismet what it needs to know to get data into the program so we can start scanning. Each source has three parameters: a Kismet source name for the specific type of card, the interface name, and a logical name found in the Kismet client. The Kismet README has a list of compatible sources and their proper interface names.

```
hostap    Prism/2    Linux    HostAP 0.4
            http://hostap.epitest.fi/
            Capture interface: 'wlanX'
            HostAP drivers drive the Prism/2 chipset in access point
```

```
mode, but also can drive the cards in client and monitor
modes. The HostAP drivers seem to change how they go
into monitor mode fairly often, but this source should
manage to get them going.
```

The README has many entries, such as this one for hostap-compatible cards. You'll need to find the one for your card type and follow any special instructions to get it to work (different drivers or patches, and so forth).

For the above card, the source line would be "*source=hostap,wlanx,hostap*" where *hostap* is the name of the type of card (according to the readme), and *wlanx* is the interface name for that card (usually will be wlan0 or wlan1). The last part is a logical name for your information. The client displays the status of each card and what channel it is currently on. It is useful to give a short descriptive name so you know which is which. Identifying on board network cards vs. add-on cards can be especially useful so you know which one is active and on what channel.

You can also specify the initial channel the cards start on when Kismet is started by adding a fourth parameter after a comma. If you want the card to start on channel 11, you simply add a ",11" after the logical name. The source line would now read "*source=hostap,wlanx,onboard,11.*" This is especially useful if you have multiple cards and want to monitor different channels on each; you can have Kismet set the channels instead of manually doing it. This setting does not affect much if channel hopping is enabled and only works for static channel monitoring.

Drones are also specified here in the *source=* line. Drones are like any other source except that we specify a remote address of the drone device instead of a local interface.

If we have a drone running on a computer at 192.168.0.45, the *source=* line would look like:

```
source=kismet_drone,192.168.0.45:3501,Drone
```

Just as with local interfaces, we specify the type of device, in this case *kismet_drone*, the address of the device and the port the drone is running on (default is 3501), and a logical name for the device that is shown in the client.

Drones need to be running before the Kismet server is started or the server will fail to start. If a drone disconnects for any reason, you will need to restart the Kismet server to reconnect to that drone. This limitation is being addressed in the development of Kismet-Newcore.

```
# Per-source special options
# sourceopts=srcname:options
```

```
# srcname * indicates "all sources". Individual source options can be turned
# off with "no", ie "noweakvalidate". Some sources may have special options.
# sourceopts=demo:fuzzycrypt,weakvalidate
# sourceopts=demo2:nofuzzycrypt
```

Sources can have special parameters for what type of data to collect. If we have multiple sources, you can specify some sources to collect all data, and others to ignore some. For the most part, it's not necessary to change any of these as each driver is unique and there is no way to tell what options are available to change.

```
# Comma-separated list of sources to enable. This is only needed if you defined
# multiple sources and only want to enable some of them. By default, all defined
# sources are enabled.
# For example:
# enablesources=prismsource,ciscosource
```

This is a very useful parameter for multi-source installations, or for situations where you use different cards for different types of detection. Define all your potential sources (different cards, or configurations of cards) above in the *source=* lines and depending on the logical names you specify for each source, you can toggle them here by either editing the *enablesource=* line or setting up multiple lines with different combinations of cards and commenting out with a "#" at the start of the lines you don't need. Remember that only one *enablesources=* line should be uncommented at once.

For example, if you had a configuration for wardriving with two cards, you could have a line that says "*enablesources=engenius1,engenius2*" and another one for direction finding as "*enablesources=proxim.*" This becomes particularly useful when dealing with large numbers of drones. You can enable and disable groups very quickly and easily by setting up multiple lines and just commenting and uncommenting different ones.

```
# Automatically destroy VAPs on multi-vap interfaces (like madwifi-ng).
# Madwifi-ng doesn't work in rfmon when non-rfmon VAPs are present, however
# this is a fairly invasive change to the system so it CAN be disabled. Expect
# things not to work in most cases if you do disable it, however.
vapdestroy=true
```

Some WiFi drivers create Virtual interfaces, VAP's, off a parent device for different functions. Madwifi-ng is the most common of these. With Madwifi-ng, the parent device is typically called something like wifi0 and all VAP's are named ath0, ath1, and so forth, depending on the specifics of the card. You can have a single card operating in multiple modes simultaneously, however that doesn't mean they work properly. Madwifi-ng in particular has great problems operating with one VAP in monitor mode and channel hopping when there's another VAP trying to connect and/or stay connected to a network.

Setting vapdestroy=true tells Kismet that if there is a parent/virtual device driver in use, destroy all the VAP's and create an interface for Kismet in monitor mode. If you have some reason for needing those other VAP's, you'll have to create the monitor mode interface manually. Don't be surprised if things like monitor mode and channel hopping don't get along with other VAP's present. If in doubt, enable it and let Kismet sort out the interfaces.

```
# Do we channelhop?
channelhop=true
```

This is fairly obvious. It specifies whether or not to invoke the channel-hopping sections (if channel hopping is possible on the source). Set to *channelhop=false* if you want to lock to a specific channel. This will have the source card scan the channel it is on when Kismet is started, or the channel specified in the optional initial source parameter on the source= line for that source.

```
# How many channels per second do we hop? (1-10)
channelvelocity=5
```

You can tweak the speed at which you hop channels. This is mostly something you have to fine tune yourself. If you hop slow, it takes longer to get through all the channels. If you hop fast, there's the chance you could miss something. Generally, if you're wardriving or traveling fast, you want to hop fast. If you're on foot or can take the time to be thorough, you can hop slow. If you are traveling fast and only in range of an access point (AP) for a split second, you want to scan through as many channels as you can to hopefully be on the correct channel when you're in range. If you're on foot or moving slow as you would be for rogue hunting, you can take your time and make sure to check channels. Default is 5, but might need to be tweaked depending on your situation and preference.

```
# By setting the dwell time for channel hopping we override the channelvelocity
# setting above and dwell on each channel for the given number of seconds.
# channeldwell=10
```

This setting overrides the channel velocity setting and specifies that, rather than a certain number of channels per second, Kismet should spend a certain amount of time on each channel. This is a more useful setting for static installations and drones. This way you can thoroughly inspect each channel. It's up to you to determine which works for you to make the most of your time and coverage. Increments of 1 second can be adjusted.

```
# Do we split channels between cards on the same spectrum? This means if
# multiple 802.11b capture sources are defined, they will be offset to cover
# the most possible spectrum at a given time. This also controls splitting
# fine-tuned sourcechannels lines which cover multiple interfaces (see below)
channelsplit=true
```

Channel splitting enables Kismet to cover more spectrums at any given time when multiple sources are in use. If you have two cards, both hopping, Kismet will make sure that they are both always on different channels at any given time. If card 1 is on channel 5, card 2 is on a channel other than 5, maximizing the covered spectrum. This is especially useful for situations of several cards, where having all of them on one channel makes little or no sense. If you are using several drones or other situations where you need blanket coverage of a channel across several locations, consider disabling this.

```
# Basic channel hopping control:
# These define the channels the cards hop through for various frequency ranges
# supported by Kismet.  More finegrain control is available via the
# "sourcechannels" configuration option.
#
# Don't change the IEEE80211<x> identifiers or channel hopping won't work.
# Users outside the US might want to use this list:
# defaultchannels=IEEE80211b:1,7,13,2,8,3,14,9,4,10,5,11,6,12
defaultchannels=IEEE80211b:1,6,11,2,7,3,8,4,9,5,10

# 802.11g uses the same channels as 802.11b…
defaultchannels=IEEE80211g:1,6,11,2,7,3,8,4,9,5,10

# 802.11a channels are non-overlapping so sequential is fine. You may want to
# adjust the list depending on the channels your card actually supports.
# defaultchannels=IEEE80211a:36,40,44,48,52,56,60,64,100,104,108,112,116,120,124,
128,132,136,140,149,153,157,161,184,188,192,196,200,204,208,212,216
```

Here you can specify what channels, by default, a source should hop through. More fine control is available in the *sourcechannels=* line later on, we are just specifying the channels that are possible here.

> **NOTE**
>
> This setting also allows you to set the channels for your regulatory domain. By default, it is set up for the North American regulator domain, which is for channels 1–11, but not all users are in the North American regulatory domain and can use more or less channels. This is also where you can hack things a bit. If your card supports all 14 channels, or more than your regulatory domain allows, you can specify all the possible channels, even the ones not technically allowed in your regulatory domain. Check your local laws before doing this, however.
>
> Since we are not transmitting in Kismet it shouldn't be a problem (check your local laws) to listen to see if someone has set up a rogue AP on channels not normally used or allowed, to try and avoid detection. Please don't abuse this as the regulations are there for a reason.

```
# Combo cards like Atheros use both 'a' and 'b/g' channels. Of course, you
# can also explicitly override a given source. You can use the script
# extras/listchan.pl to extract all the channels your card supports.
defaultchannels=IEEE80211ab:1,6,11,2,7,3,8,4,9,5,10,36,40,44,48,52,56,60,64
```

You can also specify channels to be covered by a/b/g combo cards if you happen to have one. The *listchan.pl* script in the extras directory of the install package will poll your card(s) to see what channels are supported. A useful thing to see if your card is capable of more than you thought it was.

```
# Fine-tuning channel hopping control:
# The sourcechannels option can be used to set the channel hopping for
# specific interfaces, and to control what interfaces share a list of
# channels for split hopping.  This can also be used to easily lock
# one card on a single channel while hopping with other cards.
# Any card without a sourcechannel definition will use the standard hopping
# list.
# sourcechannels=sourcename[,sourcename]:ch1,ch2,ch3,…chN

# ie, for us channels on the source 'prism2source' (same as normal channel
# hopping behavior):
# sourcechannels=prism2source:1,6,11,2,7,3,8,4,9,5,10
```

This parameter is where you can fine-tune the channel hopping. In the *defaultchannels* parameter, we specified what channels were available, now we can specify which ones we specifically want to listen on and what order to sequence through.

Notes from the Underground

Hack

There is a very cool hack possible here. For b/g networks, channels 1, 6, and 11 are statistically the most popular since they don't overlap. If we have one card, it makes no sense to spend only 8/11th's of our time on channels less likely to have something on them. You can specify channels more than once and the sequence will loop back to the beginning when done. So if you specify channels 1, 6, and 11 more than once, you'll end up spending more time there overall and even out your distribution of time/channels.

```
sourcechannels=prism2source:1,6,11,2,7,1,6,11,3,8,1,6,11,4,9,1,6,11,5,10
```

With the above line we are spending 6/10th's of our time checking the most popular channels. You can tweak this distribution to your liking, but it has been tested and tends to work for high-speed scanning such as highway speed wardriving. You can also specify additional channels such as 12–14 if your card supports it and add those to the mix.

You can do the same for 802.11a channels. Either adding them to the mix of b/g channels if you have an a/b/g card or just the 802.11a channels f you have a single mode card.

```
# Given two capture sources, "prism2a" and "prism2b", we want prism2a to stay
# on channel 6 and prism2b to hop normally. By not setting a sourcechannels
# line for prism2b, it will use the standard hopping.
# sourcechannels=prism2a:6
```

If you don't specify a *sourcechannels* parameter and *channelhop=true*, the system will automatically hop through the default channels. If you have multiple sources, you can have a specific *sourcechannels* for one device and have it monitor a few specific channels, while the other one checks the remainder. This is effective with wardriving. One source spends all it's time checking 1, 6, and 11 where there are most likely going to be signals, and the other can check the remaining channels.

You can also use this to break up the workload across multiple sources. Once card can do the lower channels, the other the higher channels, and be able to sequence through everything much faster than a single card.

```
# To assign the same custom hop channel to multiple sources, or to split the
# same custom hop channel over two sources (if splitchannels is true), list
# them all on the same sourcechannels line:
# sourcechannels=prism2a,prism2b,prism2c:1,6,11
```

You can also nest multiple sources in an assigned *sourcechannel*. If *channelsplit=true*, Kismet will cycle through the channels, and make sure that no two sources are on the same channel at the same time, maximizing the time spent on high–usage channels, and making sure not to overlap scanned channels. In the config file example, three sources would cycle through each of three channels without overlapping.

```
# Port to serve GUI data
tcpport=2501
```

Here you can specify what TCP port the server will serve clients on. There should be no real reason to change this setting. If you feel the need to change this, make sure to make the appropriate change in the *kismet_ui.conf* file.

```
# People allowed to connect, comma seperated IP addresses or network/mask
# blocks. Netmasks can be expressed as dotted quad (/255.255.255.0) or as
# numbers (/24)
allowedhosts=127.0.0.1
```

This is where remote monitoring can be set up. By default, for security reasons, only the host running the server can connect a client (localhost). If you want to use the Kismet client on another system and connect to a remote server, you need to specify the network address of the host that will be connecting to the server. This is accomplished by appending it to the existing line with a comma and no space.

```
allowedhosts=127.0.0.1,192.168.0.34,10.0.50.45
```

You can also specify valid netblocks; *allowedhosts=127.0.0.1,192.168.0.0/24* or *allowedhosts=127.0.0.1,192.168.0.0/255.255.255.0* will allow the entire 192.168.0.x netblock to connect.

It is best to limit what hosts can connect. If you're monitoring your corporate network and you let anyone connect, you could end up giving access to your data dumps to an attacker, since Kismet does not do any authentication beyond this.

```
# Address to bind to. Should be an address already configured already on
# this host, reverts to INADDR_ANY if specified incorrectly.
bindaddress=127.0.0.1
```

The Kismet server can be bound to specific addresses on a multi-homed system. By default, Kismet will bind to all addresses configured and listen on all interfaces. If you want to limit it to only one address, specify it here.

```
# Maximum number of concurrent GUI's
maxclients=5
```

This specifies exactly what it says; the maximum number of clients that can connect to a server. The more clients, the more work the server has to do, so it's best not to allow too many or run too many.

```
# Do we have a GPS?
gps=true
```

This is a pretty self-explanatory parameter. If you want to use a GPS, you need to set this to true in order to use it. If it's set to false, you can save a little memory on really slim systems.

```
# Host:port that GPSD is running on. This can be localhost OR remote!
gpshost=localhost:2947
```

Kismet uses GPSD for getting GPS coordinates into Kismet and in turn into your logs. GPSD interfaces with your serial/Universal Serial Bus (USB) port and takes the incoming NMEA data and puts it out over a TCP port. Kismet connects to that port and puts the data into the server.

Specify where GPSD is running and on what port. Most configurations have GPSD running on the same system as *kismet_server*, so it would be set to "*gpshost=localhost:2947*" or "*gpshost=127.0.0.1:2947*" depending on if name resolution is working or not.

NOTE

If for some reason you have GPSD on another machine on the same network as the *kismet_server* and GPSD is available on it, you can specify that system's address instead. Note: If you get your GPS data from a source other than one attached to the system running *kismet_server*, then all your locations will seem to be from the location at the remote system, skewing your results. This is also true if you are running remote drones. If your GPS location is not at the location of your sensor, then your GPS data will not be correct.

```
# Do we lock the mode? This overrides coordinates of lock "0", which will
# generate some bad information until you get a GPS lock, but it will
# fix problems with GPS units with broken NMEA that report lock 0
gpsmodelock=false
```

This parameter is a workaround for GPS's that don't send proper data until you get a lock on the GPS satellites. Set this to "true" if your GPS is giving you issues on startup. You may also want to check for updated firmwares for your GPS.

```
# Packet filtering options:
# filter_tracker - Packets filtered from the tracker are not processed or
#                   recorded in any way.
# filter_dump   -  Packets filtered at the dump level are tracked, displayed,
#                   and written to the csv/xml/network/etc files, but not
#                   recorded in the packet dump
# filter_export -  Controls what packets influence the exported CSV, network,
#                   xml, gps, etc files.
# All filtering options take arguments containing the type of address and
# addresses to be filtered. Valid address types are 'ANY', 'BSSID',
# 'SOURCE', and 'DEST'. Filtering can be inverted by the use of '!' before
# the address. For example,
# filter_tracker=ANY(!00:00:DE:AD:BE:EF)
# has the same effect as the previous mac_filter config file option.
# filter_tracker=…
# filter_dump=…
# filter_export=…
```

Kismet can filter out specific MAC addresses at various levels of the program. This can be useful if you wish to eliminate known AP's and clients from your logs or display. You can also limit how far the packet gets in the client server chain and if it's recorded or not in the logs.

- **filter_tracker=** If any packets match the specified parameters, they are not added to the display or any of the log files, and are simply dropped on the floor.

- **filter_export=** If any packets match the specified parameters, they are not included in the CSV, network, xml, gps, etc files but are recorded in the dump file.

- **filter_netclient=** If a packet comes from a specific network client, don't record it.

The MAC addresses can be specified as SOURCE, DEST (destination), BSSID, and ANY. Source and destination are useful for eliminating known clients, BSSID is for specifying the MAC of a wireless AP. ANY will filter any packets with that MAC, regardless of where it appears in the frame. Just specifying the MAC will activate the filter on a match to that address, or you can specify the inverse with an exclamation point at the beginning to filter everything but the specified address.

```
filter_tracker=ANY(!"00:00:DE:AD:BE:EF")
```

This will filter any packet out of the logs and packet tracker that does not match the specified MAC of *00:00:DE:AD:BE:EF*

```
filter_dump=BSSID("00:00:DE:AD:BE:EF")
```

This line will filter out packets from the AP with the BSSID of *00:00:DE:AD:BE:EF* from the dump file.

```
filter_tracker=ANY("00:00:DE:AD:BE:EF")
```

This line would drop any packets with the MAC of *00:00:DE:AD:BE:EF* from the display and the logs. This is particularly good if you want to monitor for rogue networks and eliminate known networks and clients from the logs and display.

```
# Alerts to be reported and the throttling rates.
# alert=name,throttle/unit,burst/unit
# The throttle/unit describes the number of alerts of this type that are
# sent per time unit. Valid time units are second, minute, hour, and day.
# Burst rates control the number of packets sent at a time
# For example:
# alert=FOO,10/min,5/sec
# Would allow 5 alerts per second, and 10 alerts total per minute.
# A throttle rate of 0 disables throttling of the alert.
# See the README for a list of alert types.
```

Kismet has some rudimentary IDS capability to detect certain patterns in packets known to be attacks, or the presence of certain pieces of software that could be used maliciously.

These alerts can give a network administrator a great deal of power in determining if their network is under attack, or if problems are from some other source. While a certain amount and types of alerts are normal, excessive amounts can indicate problems or attacks.

These alert patterns are built into the Kismet source and are not easily changed. The threshold for triggering an alert is configurable, however. The "*alert=*" line specifies an alert built in the source and it's threshold before triggering a note in the alert log. If you want to disable the alert, just add a comment "#" in front of it.

Each alert has it's own parameters. *alert=FOO,10/min,5* would enable the FOO alert. When the FOO event happens 5 times in a second. it triggers an alert. After that initial trigger, it would spawn another alert if FOO occurred again in the same time frame, to a maximum of 10 alerts per minute, so as to avoid clogging the alert window with thousands of the same alerts.

These alerts will clue you in to the presence of some active network discovery applications, and some odd patterns that denote attacks. Passive sniffers such as Kismet, cannot be detected, and offline attacks obviously cannot be detected either. It is not an exhaustive IDS system, but it can be useful for quickly identifying common attacks and problems.

```
alert=NETSTUMBLER,10/min,1/sec
```

This alert detects the presence of the Netstumbler network discovery tool through unique packets being broadcast while it is in use.

```
alert=WELLENREITER,10/min,1/sec
```

This alert detects the presence of another network discovery tool, Wellenreiter. Specifically this alert detects Wellenreiter's SSID bruteforcer. If a network is not broadcasting it's SSID, it is possible to reveal the SSID by probing using a dictionary and listening for responses. This alert is triggered by certain behaviors of Wellenreiter when it is doing this, namely between each probe attempt, it resets the card to probe for "*this_is_used_for_wellenreiter.*"

```
alert=LUCENTTEST,10/min,1/sec
```

This alert is for the presence of lucent networks link test. This is a site survey tool that could be used for rudimentary stumbling and reconnaissance.

```
alert=DEAUTHFLOOD,10/min,2/sec
```

This detects deauthentication floods. If an attacker is spoofing deauthentication packets from the MAC of the AP to clients, an alert is generated. An alert is not triggered if the disassociation is normal, but only if excessive deauthentications are occurring.

```
alert=BCASTDISCON,10/min,2/sec
```

This alert is for broadcast floods, which should never occur normally. In a broadcast flood, the attacker floods a network with disassociation or deauthentication packets in an attempt to get clients to disassociate with their current AP and associate to a rogue network.

```
alert=CHANCHANGE,5/min,1/sec
```

This alert notes if a previously detected network suddenly changes channels. This is a good indication of an attempt at spoofing a network, since most networks don't change channels on a regular basis.

```
alert=AIRJACKSSID,5/min,1/sec
```

This alert looks for the probe SSID name of "airjack," the initial SSID of airjack tools. The airjack tools allow for raw mode injection and reception, and are used in a number of possibly malicious tools. This alert only detects the SSID of airjack and not the tools themselves. A skilled attacker could easily change the initial SSID to something more innocuous.

```
alert=PROBENOJOIN,10/min,1/sec
```

If a client probes for an existing network and is accepted but does not join, this is an indication of some firmware-based network discovery tools such as Netstumbler. In some situations, this can generate a great number of false positives and may not be indicative of an attack. This can also be triggered by some network client applications waiting for user input before associating.

```
alert=DISASSOCTRAFFIC,10/min,1/sec
```

If a client appears to disassociate from the AP, it should normally not be attempting to communicate with the AP right afterwards. If this alert is triggered, it is likely the client specified in the alert has been the victim of a disassociation attack where an attacker sends a forged packet to the AP indicating the client is leaving.

```
alert=NULLPROBERESP,10/min,1/sec
```

This is an indication of an attack against some firmware versions by many manufacturers that have a fatal error if they receive a SSID probe of null length (no length). This can be a sign of a Denial of Service (DoS) attack or misbehaving client.

```
alert=BSSTIMESTAMP,10/min,1/sec
```

Each packet from an AP is time-stamped and should be received in something resembling a continuous stream. It is not possible to spoof the time stamp with normal drivers, so a wildly different time stamp received is an indication that someone may be trying to spoof the AP's SSID and/or MAC address. This may trigger some false positives in situations of high loss where not all packets are being received.

```
alert=MSFBCOMSSID,10/min,1/sec
```

Several exploits exist for drivers of several manufacturers of wireless cards. The Metasploit project exploit framework contains an exploit for some broadcom drivers. This exploit uses an overly large SSID to cause a buffer overflow in the driver. This alert will tell you if someone is attempting to exploit this.

```
alert=LONGSSID,10/min,1/sec
```

The IEEE spec allows for a maximum of 32 bytes in the SSID field. If frames are detected with SSID's over 32 bytes, it's a very good indication that someone is doing something bad to your network. This alert will let you know if something is amiss.

```
alert=MSFDLINKRATE,10/min,1/sec
```

Metasploit contains an exploit for a D-link driver. The exploit revolves around how the driver handles an overly long accepted data rate field. This alert detects the usage of this exploit, and likely, someone doing something bad.

```
alert=MSFNETGEARBEACON,10/min,1/sec
```

Just like the D-link and Broadcom cards, some drivers for Netgear are exploitable, this time through oversized beacon frames. This alert indicates as the others do, that someone is using Metasploit to do something possibly bad to your network.

```
alert=DISCONCODEINVALID,10/min,1/sec
alert=DEAUTHCODEINVALID,10/min,1/sec
```

Both the *DISCONCODEINVALID* and *DEAUTHCODEINVALID* are alerts for related issues. In this case, it relates to the way some APs and client adapters handle unknown or invalid reason codes in disassociation or deauthentication packets. This alert is indicative of problems on the network or possibly an attack against exploitable equipment.

```
# Known WEP keys to decrypt, bssid,hexkey. This is only for networks where
# the keys are already known, and it may impact throughput on slower hardware.
# Multiple wepkey lines may be used for multiple BSSIDs.
# wepkey=00:DE:AD:C0:DE:00,FEEDFACEDEADBEEF01020304050607080900
```

If you are monitoring your own network, hopefully it is encrypted. If you use WEP it can be useful to have the packets decrypted for passing to snort or other third-party programs. With the *wepkey=* parameter, you can specify the BSSID of the particular network and the key in hexadecimal format. Multiple keys can be specified with multiple *wepkey=* lines. Keep in mind that if you are decrypting traffic, the server host system has to work harder to decrypt everything on the fly, and that the captured data will be in plaintext in the dump file. You want to keep access to it secure.

Hopefully you are not running WEP and are using something stronger like WPA. WEP can be cracked in less than 60 seconds using freely available tools. At this time, there is no way to decrypt a WPA network on the fly through Kismet.

```
# Is transmission of the keys to the client allowed? This may be a security
# risk for some. If you disable this, you will not be able to query keys from
# a client.
allowkeytransmit=true
```

Depending on your configuration and monitoring needs, you may not want the Kismet server to inform the Kismet client what the keys are. Change to false if you don't want this, particularly if others can read the data from the server or the dump file.

```
# How often (in seconds) do we write all our data files (0 to disable)
writeinterval=300
```

By default, Kismet writes the logs to disk every 5 minutes (300 seconds). You can adjust this if you like, but as the size of the logs grow, the longer it takes to save them. If you specify a time too low, then it might cause your system to thrash its hard disk in a constant save cycle.

```
# How old (and inactive) does a network need to be before we expire it?
# This is really only good for limited ram environments where keeping a
# total log of all networks is problematic. This is in seconds, and should
# be set to a large value like 12 or 24 hours. This is intended for use
# on stationary systems like an IDS
# logexpiry=86400
```

In some situations you may want to have networks expire from the list. If you are running the server for several days and want to limit the amount of resources used, you can set the *logexpiry=* parameter to a reasonable expiry time. This is particularly of interest when used as an IDS and you want to automatically remove networks that haven't been active for quite a while (such as clients passing by or way off nets that you might have gotten a lucky reflection and a single packet).

```
# Do we limit the number of networks we log? This is for low-ram situations
# when tracking everything could lead to the system falling down. This
# should be combined with a sane logexpiry value to flush out very old
# inactive networks. This is mainly for stationary systems like an IDS.
# limitnets=10000
```

Some situations such as limited resource machines or noisy environments, might make you want to limit the number of networks. Most situations usually require that you record everything, so it may not be the best solution. Smart usage of the *logexpiry=* parameter above can hopefully help keep your system logs from growing beyond the capabilities of your system.

```
# Do we track IVs? this can help identify some attacks, but takes a LOT
# of memory to do so on a busy network. If you have the RAM, by all
# means turn it on.
trackivs=false
```

This parameter can be useful for some real time tracking of possible attacks. If you track IV's, you can keep an eye on the rate at which they appear and see if someone is attempting to perform any injection attacks. This can also be useful if you are attempting to collect enough IV's to break WEP, and are using Kismet to do the collection. On most modern systems it's not a bad idea to turn it on.

```
# Do we use sound?
# Not to be confused with GUI sound parameter, this controls whether or not the
# server itself will play sound. Primarily for headless or automated systems.
sound=false
```

The server can be made to play sounds on events (new network, and so forth), which is not to be confused with sound events from the client (controlled from the *kismet_ui.conf* file). This is useful for headless and automated systems. If you have a rig in the back of your car with no monitor, there's not much need to run a client, but you still need to keep an eye (or more correctly, an ear) on the status of the server to make sure it's operating properly. So having it beep or squawk it's status is a useful thing to have.

```
# Path to sound player
soundplay=/usr/bin/play
```

If the server is to play sound, it obviously needs to know what program on your system it should use to play them. By default it's */usr/bin/play*, but adjust to your system's specific sound player.

```
# Optional parameters to pass to the player
# soundopts=--volume=.3
```

If you want to get fancy, you can also pass parameters such as sound volume or any other command-line parameters for your player program. Simple specify them as you would on the command line.

```
# New network found
sound_new=@sharedatadir@/kismet/wav/new_network.wav
# Wepped new network
# sound_new_wep=@sharedstatedir@/kismet/wav/new_wep_network.wav
# Network traffic sound
sound_traffic=@sharedatadir@/kismet/wav/traffic.wav
# Network junk traffic found
sound_junktraffic=@sharedatadir@/kismet/wav/junk_traffic.wav
# GPS lock aquired sound
# sound_gpslock=@sharedatadir@/kismet/wav/foo.wav
# GPS lock lost sound
# sound_gpslost=@sharedatadir@/kismet/wav/bar.wav
# Alert sound
sound_alert=@sharedatadir@/kismet/wav/alert.wav
```

Each event can have it's own sound, and if you want, your own custom sound. Simply load your own WAV files onto your system and point each event at the sound you want to use. You can also only enable specific event sounds such as the new network or GPS lock lost by commenting out un-needed sounds lines.

```
# Does the server have speech? (Again, not to be confused with the GUI's speech)
speech=false
```

The server, just like with sounds on a headless system, can also speak. Using festival, the server can speak out the names of the networks. If your system has festival installed, just change speech to true. This is best used by headless and automated systems, and should not be confused with the client speech configuration in the *kismet_ui.conf* file.

```
# Server's path to Festival
festival=/usr/bin/festival
```

Kismet also needs to know where festival is installed if you want to use it. Depending on your system, just point your config to the festival executable. By default it is */usr/bin/festival*.

```
# Are we using festival lite? If so, set the above "festival" path to also
# point to the "flite" binary
flite=false
```

If you are using festival lite, you can set this option to true and set the path on the above *festival=* line and point it to the *flite* binary.

```
# Are we using Darwin speech?
darwinsay=false
```

If you built Kismet for OSX on a Mac, you can use Darwin's speech functionality in place of festival to speak server events.

```
# What voice do we use? (Currently only valid on Darwin)
speech_voice=default
```

Darwin also has a selection of voices that can be used. Choose the voice in the system preferences, and Kismet will use that voice as the default option in the config file.

```
# How do we speak? Valid options:
# speech       Normal speech
# nato         NATO spellings (alpha, bravo, charlie)
# spell        Spell the letters out (aye, bee, sea)
speech_type=nato
```

If we are using festival and speech, how do we want it to speak? Setting this to "speech" has festival speak (or approximately speak) the names of the networks that are detected. Setting *speech_type* to *nato* will use the nato alphabet to "speak" each letter (linksys is read out as "LIMA, INDIA, NOVEMBER, KILO, SIERRA, YANKEE, SIERRA"). If you set it to "spell", festival will read out each letter as a normal "L,I,N,K,S,Y,S."

```
# speech_encrypted and speech_unencrypted - Speech templates
# Similar to the logtemplate option, this lets you customize the speech output.
# speech_encrypted is used for an encrypted network spoken string
# speech_unencrypted is used for an unencrypted network spoken string
#
# %b is replaced by the BSSID (MAC) of the network
# %s is replaced by the SSID (name) of the network
# %c is replaced by the CHANNEL of the network
# %r is replaced by the MAX RATE of the network
speech_encrypted=New network detected, s.s.i.d. %s, channel %c, network encrypted.
speech_unencrypted=New network detected, s.s.i.d. %s, channel %c, network open.
```

You can customize the output of festival and construct the sentences that it speaks. There are separate lines for encrypted and unencrypted networks. Festival will speak whatever words you put after the equals sign in the *speech_encrypted=* or *speech_unencrypted=* lines, with specific symbols replaced by the settings for the network being read out.

```
speech_encrypted=New network detected, s.s.i.d. %s, channel %c, network encrypted.
```

The default lines would read out the above-detected linksys network as "New network detected SSID LINKSYS Channel 6 network encrypted" if it was encrypted. You can easily shrink this to "Detected SSID LINKSYS" if you change the line to "*speech_encrypted=Detected, s.s.i.d. %s*" for both the *speech_encrypted* and *speech_unencrypted* parameters.

```
# Where do we get our manufacturer fingerprints from? Assumed to be in the
# default config directory if an absolute path is not given.
ap_manuf=ap_manuf
client_manuf=client_manuf
```

All manufacturers register the MAC addresses of their devices with the IEEE OUI database. From this we can tell what manufacturer made the devices we are detecting. Kismet comes with a database for APs and client devices, but sometimes this gets out of date or you may want to adjust or update it. You can adjust or replace the files or just set the *ap_manuf=* line to the path of the file you want Kismet to use. If it is not in the default config directory (*usually /usr/local/etc/*) then you should specify an absolute path.

```
# Use metric measurements in the output?
metric=false
```

Kismet can automatically change measurements from imperial (feet, miles) to metric (meters, kilometers). False uses imperial (default) and true uses metric measurements.

```
# Do we write waypoints for gpsdrive to load? Note: This is NOT related to
# recent versions of GPSDrive's native support of Kismet.
waypoints=false
```

If we are using *gpsdrive*, we can, in semi-realtime, plot discovered networks on the GPSDrive map. The file is purged when *Kismet_server* starts and is read by GPSDrive periodically, and used to generate waypoints on the map. This is good for a low spec laptop that might not be able to run other mapping utilities. It also gives you access at the same time to GPSDrives' other functions (track log, and so forth). It is not able to determine closed or open networks or use special symbols, but it is a quick and dirty way of mapping your networks. There is approximately a 15-second delay between a network being detected and GPSDrive picking up the change to the file.

Provided you have not restarted the *kismet_server*, you can copy the Kismet waypoints file specified in the following parameter to another file name and open it in GPSDrive for a basic map of your route and results.

```
# GPSDrive waypoint file. This WILL be truncated.
waypointdata=%h/.gpsdrive/way_kismet.txt
```

This parameter specifies the file write network information and location for GPSDrive to load as waypoints. By default, it looks in the home directory *.gpsdrive/* directory.

```
# Do we want ESSID or BSSID as the waypoint name ?
waypoint_essid=false
```

When Kismet parses the waypoint file, do you want to use the ESSID or the BSSID as the network name? Extended Service Set Identifier (ESSID) is false, BSSID is true.

```
# How many alerts do we backlog for new clients? Only change this if you have
# a -very- low memory system and need those extra bytes, or if you have a high
# memory system and a huge number of alert conditions.
alertbacklog=50
```

If a new client connects to the server, we want to fill it in on any alerts that have occurred. This parameter sets how many alerts we buffer for newly connecting clients. If you have a low memory system, you can save a bit of memory here by turning this down or even to 0. Conversely, if you have the memory and are running a logging system without a client running all the time (such as a network logging/monitoring system on your network), you can catch up to the alerts when you connect a client by setting this high.

```
# File types to log, comma seperated
# dump     -    raw packet dump
# network  -    plaintext detected networks
# csv      -    plaintext detected networks in CSV format
# xml      -    XML formatted network and cisco log
# weak     -    weak packets (in airsnort format)
# cisco    -    cisco equipment CDP broadcasts
# gps      -    gps coordinates
logtypes=dump,network,csv,xml,weak,cisco,gps
```

What type of log files do we want to save:

- **pcapdump** The raw packet dump file; everything recorded is derived from here.

- **gpsxml** XML log of the network's locations.

- **netxml** XML list of the networks detected, network settings, and so forth.

- **nettxt** TXT file output list of all the networks detected.

```
# Do we track probe responses and merge probe networks into their owners?
# This isn't always desireable, depending on the type of monitoring you're
# trying to do.
trackprobenets=true
```

Sometimes we detect the clients looking for networks before we detect the network itself, so this setting controls whether we merge these detected client probes in when we detect the network in the probes. Sometimes you may want to keep client broadcasts separate, in which case, you should change this to false.

```
# Do we log "noise" packets that we can't decipher? I tend to not, since
# they don't have anything interesting at all in them.
noiselog=false
```

Some packets are just garbage, but if you are trying to diagnose problems, it might be useful to capture them to dissect later. Set this to true if you want to capture them, normally though, it's best to keep it on false and save the disk space since they are usually truly garbage.

```
# Do we log corrupt packets? Corrupt packets have enough header information
# to see what they are, but someting is wrong with them that prevents us from
# completely dissecting them. Logging these is usually not a bad idea.
corruptlog=true
```

Corrupt packets can be very useful in troubleshooting network problems, and should probably be recorded. Setting *corruptlog* to false will save you disk space, but overall, not very much.

```
# Do we log beacon packets or do we filter them out of the dumpfile
beaconlog=true
```

This parameter specifies if we want to record SSID beacon frames. Most networks by default, spew these out at a fairly high rate, so it might save some disk space if you don't want them. Setting *beaconlog* to false would be a good idea on a headless monitoring system or an automated system with limited storage space.

```
# Do we log PHY layer packets or do we filter them out of the dumpfile
phylog=true
```

Logging PHY layer packets is usually a good idea for troubleshooting purposes. Set to false if you don't want to.

```
# Do we mangle packets if we can decrypt them or if they're fuzzy-detected
mangledatalog=true
```

If we receive a damaged packet and we can mangle it into being correct, should we decrypt it? Normally this is a good idea, but packets decoded this way may not be 100 percent correct, but can be useful for troubleshooting.

```
# Do we do "fuzzy" crypt detection? (byte-based detection instead of 802.11
# frame headers)
# valid option: Comma seperated list of card types to perform fuzzy detection
# on, or 'all'
fuzzycrypt=wtapfile,wlanng,wlanng_legacy,wlanng_avs,hostap,wlanng_wext,
ipw2200,ipw2915
```

Sometimes it may be necessary to detect packets for encryption based on their size, rather than what the packet flags say. This depends a lot on the card type, as some drivers add extra information. Comment out the *fuzzycrypt=* line if you need or want to trust the frames to report their encryption status, rather than actually checking the bytes in the packet.

```
# Do we do forgiving fuzzy packet decoding? This lets us handle borked drivers
# which don't indicate they're including FCS, and then do.
fuzzydecode=wtapfile,radiotap_bsd_a,radiotap_bsd_g,radiotap_bsd_bg,radiotap_bsd_b,
pcapfile
```

Some drivers are better than others for claiming one set of capabilities and reporting another. As above, if you want to double check packets and make sure all is as is being reported, enable this option.

```
# Do we use network-classifier fuzzy-crypt detection? This means we expect
# packets that are associated with an encrypted network to be encrypted too,
# and we process them by the same fuzzy compare.
# This essentially replaces the fuzzycrypt per-source option.
netfuzzycrypt=true
```

This parameter overrides the *fuzzycrypt*= parameter and basically assumes that if a network is encrypted, any associated clients must be encrypted too.

```
# What type of dump do we generate?
# valid option: "wiretap"
dumptype=wiretap
```

At this point, Kismet will only generate wiretap dump files. In the future, more options may be available, but for now, just leave it at wiretap.

```
# Do we limit the size of dump logs? Sometimes ethereal can't handle big ones.
# 0 = No limit
# Anything else = Max number of packets to log to a single file before closing
# and opening a new one.
dumplimit=0
```

Sometimes you may want to limit the size of your dump files. Maybe you have limited storage or want to make things more manageable for storage. A setting of 0 is the default and has no size limit. Anything else is the number of packets to record before closing the file and starting a new one.

```
# Do we write data packets to a FIFO for an external data-IDS (such as Snort)?
# See the docs before enabling this.
#fifo=/tmp/kismet_dump
```

This setting allows you to pipe the data out a First In, First Out (FIFO) pipe to share real time information with other programs that can read from a file. This requires that the program connect to the FIFO pipe before Kismet will start. The *fifo*= setting specifies the location of the FIFO pipe. The third-party program needs to have access to where the FIFO pipe is, so make sure that if your program is running as a normal user and that you don't have the FIFO pipe in a root-only directory.

```
# Default log title
logdefault=Kismet
```

The log file output filename can be tweaked to your hearts content. Kismet by default has a name structure of "Kismet" - "Month – Date –Year" and the number of file in the sequence (i.e., Kismet-Sep-26-2006-1.gps). The *logdefault* parameter starts the file name specifying "Kismet" by default. If you want a different start to the filename, just change it here (no spaces).

```
# logtemplate - Filename logging template.
# This is, at first glance, really nasty and ugly, but you'll hardly ever
# have to touch it so don't complain too much.
```

```
#
# %n is replaced by the logging instance name
# %d is replaced by the current date as Mon-DD-YYYY
# %D is replaced by the current date as YYYYMMDD
# %t is replaced by the starting log time
# %i is replaced by the increment log in the case of multiple logs
# %l is replaced by the log type (dump, status, crypt, etc)
# %h is replaced by the home directory
# ie, "netlogs/%n-%d-%i.dump" called with a logging name of "Pok" could expand
# to something like "netlogs/Pok-Dec-20-01-1.dump" for the first instance and
# "netlogs/Pok-Dec-20-01-2.%l" for the second logfile generated.
# %h/netlots/%n-%d-%i.dump could expand to
# /home/foo/netlogs/Pok-Dec-20-01-2.dump
#
# Other possibilities: Sorting by directory
# logtemplate=%l/%n-%d-%i
# Would expand to, for example,
# dump/Pok-Dec-20-01-1
# crypt/Pok-Dec-20-01-1
# and so on. The "dump", "crypt", etc, dirs must exist before kismet is run
# in this case.
logtemplate=%n-%d-%i.%l
```

As the comments for the log template say, it looks scary, but it isn't. Using the listed % variables, you can change the order and even the whole filename of the log files. Specifying the *%l/* variable at the beginning will split the log files into separate log files, based on the type of file (*dump/ crypt/* and so forth).

The possibilities are endless, so adjust to your needs. The default of *logtemplate=%n-%d-%i.%l* is replaced with Kismet, *%d* is replaced with the date, *%i* is replaced with the log increment, and *%l* is the file type, in this case it is also used as an extension.

```
# Where do we store the pid file of the server?
piddir=/var/run/
```

The *pid* file of the server when it's running. There should be no reason to change this unless you are running an odd UNIX variant and need to specify something else.

```
# Where state info, etc, is stored. You shouldnt ever need to change this.
# This is a directory.
configdir=%h/.kismet/
```

This setting is where Kismet stores it's state info. This directory is usually in the home directory of your SUID user. There shouldn't be a need to change this at all.

```
# cloaked SSID file. You shouldn't ever need to change this.
ssidmap=ssid_map
```

The *ssidmap=* parameter specifies the file that Kismet should use to keep a tab on what BSSID matches each SSID. This is usually stored within the directory specified in the *configdir* parameter. If you discover the BSSID from a cloaked network and you have previously determined the SSID, this will fill in the blank automatically from this file. You shouldn't need to change this parameter unless you are running on a weird distribution without home directories.

```
# Group map file. You shouldn't ever need to change this.
groupmap=group_map
```

The *groupmap=* parameter specifies the file that Kismet should use to keep a running list of network groups as specified by the user. This is usually stored within the directory specified in the *configdir* parameter. You shouldn't need to change this parameter.

```
# IP range map file.  You shouldn't ever need to change this.
ipmap=ip_map
```

The *ipmap=* parameter specifies the file that Kismet should use to keep a tab on what networks are using what IP range. This is usually stored within the directory specified in the *configdir* parameter. This file holds the previously detected mappings of networks and their IP spaces to help fill in the blanks. You shouldn't need to change this parameter.

Kismet Server Command Line

The Kismet server, in addition to the config file, can be controlled at start by command-line switches. Previously this was how all parameters were set on early versions of Kismet, but the config file became necessary when so many options were added. There are times, however, that you want to change a parameter for that one run of the server, and many are still available as command-line switches.

These options override the settings in the config file, and require that the server be launched separate from the client. You can't use the Kismet command/script to start the server and client, you will need to start the *kismet_server* and *kismet_client* separately:

```
Usage: kismet_server [OPTION]
```

Like most command-line programs, just list the switch after the *kismet_server* command, usually with a dash "-," just as the following list shows.

```
-I, --initial-channel <n:c> Initial channel to monitor on (default: 6) Format
capname:channel
```

You can specify the initial channel to monitor for each source you are monitoring. If you have channel hopping enabled, then this is not that useful since the server will immediately start hopping. However, using the *–force-no-channel-hop* switch, you can turn off hopping and the *–initial channel* switch will lock to the channel number you specify.

```
-x, --force-channel-hop    Forcibly enable the channel hopper
```

If you have channel hopping disabled, you can enable it with this:

```
-X, --force-no-channel-hop  Forcibly disable the channel hopper
```

Disabling channel hopping is the more likely option you might use. *–force-no-channel-hop* if best used with *–initial-channel* or else the card will monitor a random channel, or at least whatever channel it was last set to.

```
-t, --log-title <title>   Custom log file title
```

This will specify a customized log file title. This overrides the *logdefault=* parameter in the config file. Use this if you want to change the log file name for this run temporarily. This can be particularly useful if you are rogue hunting and want to separate your logs when you get close to each target for later processing.

```
-n, --no-logging    No logging (only process packets)
```

Most of the time, Kismet is being used because it logs, but sometimes, particularly when testing something, you can disable logging easily.

```
-f, --config-file <file>   Use alternate config file
```

Alternate config files are the most common reason to use command switches. Typically on a single system, there is one install of Kismet and one Kismet server config file. If you find yourself altering configurations often, you can have multiple config files on your system, one for each configuration. Just specify the config you want when you start the server, rather than having to go and edit the config each time.

One config could be with just the onboard wireless chipset, and another could be for directional rogue hunting with an external antenna and another wireless card. Just copy the default config file somewhere and make your *changes.* When you start the server, you can specify *kismet_server -f /<path to config>/kismet-alterrnate.conf* and the server will use the alternate config file. This is particularly powerful in combination with scripting.

You can also use this to launch several Kismet servers at the same time on the same system. Just be careful of using the same sources between them, as the servers may fight for control of things like channel hopping and channel locking.

```
-c, --capture-source <src>  Packet capture source line (type,interface,name)
```

If you want to add a source at runtime that is not set up and enabled in the config file, you can specify it at the command line. Just like in the config file, specify the type, interface name, and a logical name for the device, just like in the *source=* parameter of the config file.

```
-C, --enable-capture-sources Comma separated list of named packet sources to use.
```

If you have specified all yours sources in the config file but don't need all of them enabled, you can specify which ones to enable with the *-C* option. This overrides the *enablesources=* parameter of the config file.

```
-l, --log-types <types>   Comma separated list of types to log,
                          (ie, dump,cisco,weak,network,gps)
```

You can specify which log types you want to record. Just list the various types of logs you want (e.g., dump, network, csv, xml, weak, cisco, gps)

```
-d, --dump-type <type>  Dumpfile type (wiretap)
```

For the moment, Kismet only supports wiretap dump files, so there should be no reason to change this.

```
-m, --max-packets <num>  Maximum number of packets before starting new dump
```

Some systems may have issues with single large files, or for organizational purposes you may want to split your log files evenly. The *—max-packets* switch will tell the server when a certain number of packets is reached, at which point, Kismet will start a new file.

```
-q, --quiet    Don't play sounds
```

If you want, you can temporarily quiet the server and disable all sounds with the *—quiet* switch. This is useful if you're rogue hunting and want to sneak up on the target.

```
-g, --gps <host:port>   GPS server (host:port or off)
```

To change the location of the GPSD source used by Kismet, specify the host and port running the server.

```
-p, --port <port>    TCPIP server port for GUI connections
```

On occasion, sometimes with third- party scripts or clients you will need to adjust which port the client should connect to. Just remember not to specify one in use by another program.

```
-a, --allowed-hosts <hosts> Comma separated list of hosts allowed to connect
```

Allowing remote hosts to connect clients should be done carefully, as you are giving full access to the sniffed data. If you want to temporarily add a remote network to the allowed list, specify it here at runtime. Just as in the config file, you can specify single addresses or whole netblocks.

```
-b, --bind-address <address>  Bind to this address. Default INADDR_ANY
```

By default Kismet will bind to any address on the system and clients can connect through any of them. If you want to limit which interface, or to temporarily relax a restriction, you can do so at runtime here with the *–bind-address.*

```
-r, --retain-monitor    Leave card in monitor mode on exit
```

If your plans include using a tool needing monitor mode after leaving Kismet, you can leave it in monitor mode with the *–retain-monitor* switch.

```
-s, --silent    Don't send any output to console.
```

Sometimes the server output can be too verbose and you just want it to go away. *--silent* will suppress this output.

```
-N, --server-name    Server name
```

If you want to change the server name (as seen in the client) at runtime, you can do that here.

```
--daemonize    Background server in daemon mode
```

This switch is very useful if you are going to run the client immediately afterwards on the same system. Once the server starts, it goes into the background and returns you to the shell prompt, the perfect place to start the client from.

```
-v, --version    Kismet version
```

If you're like me and upgrade often, sometimes you need to know what version of the server you are running. *kismet_server –version* will output the current version of the installed *kismet_server* binary.

```
-h, --help    What do you think you're reading?
```

This will output the list of command-line switches we just went through. A very useful thing in case you don't have this book handy.

Summary

The Kismet server configuration file, *kismet.conf*, has a great deal of untapped power. From setting up sources, to limiting log sizes, to filtering out known SSID's, you can do a lot. In combination with the command-line switches, the server can perform many neat tricks.

Exploring all the available options in the server configuration file can greatly expand your ability to monitor your wireless network.

## Chapter 6

Kismet Client Configuration File

Solutions in this chapter:

- **The Kismet Client Config File**
- **Command-Line Switches**

☑ **Summary**

Introduction

Like the Kismet server, the Kismet client is controlled from a single configuration file. On the surface, this file seems as scary as the server configuration; however, it's just as well commented and fairly easy to understand when you dig in. The client configuration file is usually in */usr/local/etc* and is named *kismet_ui.conf*. For the most part, after you come up with a client configuration that suits your needs you will not need to change it much. That being said, there is a very large and often untapped amount of configuration of the client available. Most people don't seem to change much beyond the standard configuration.

The Kismet Client Config File

The config file is not as large as the server configuration file, but offers the same amount of flexibility and options. There are lots of very verbose comments about the various options listed. Some areas are fairly self-explanatory while others are not. This section will go through, almost line-by-line, and examine and explain each of them. The comments are good, however some areas are open to tweaks not specified in the comments and a lot of power can be revealed once you start digging into the config file.

Kismet Parameters

The *kismet.conf* config file can be edited directly with your favorite UNIX text editor (such as vi, pico, emacs), just be aware of word wrapping and UNIX file format. The config file is parsed at runtime by the server and expects a UNIX text file. DOS and UNIX use different control characters for their text files and as such, using a DOS or windows editor on a UNIX text file will probably change it and make the file unreadable to the server. In general, if you are editing the *kismet_ui.conf* file, use a UNIX editor. This can be either a native Linux application, or an editor through Cygwin if you are running under windows or some other UNIX text format-capable editor.

Comments in the *kismet_ui.conf* file are lines starting with a "#" symbol. These are often comments or example configurations and can usually guide you to what options you need to set. Lines that do not start with a comment are the actual parameter variables acted upon by the server. It's a good idea to comment out the existing line by putting a "#" in front of the line and adding a new line with the adjusted parameter. This way if something goes wrong, you know what the original parameter was.

```
# Kismet GUI config file

# Version of Kismet config
version=2004.10.R1
```

The Kismet client configuration has its own version number, separate from the package release number and other config files. The config file doesn't change as often as the rest of the tool suite, so it has a separate version number listed on this line.

```
# Do we show the intro window?
showintro=true
```

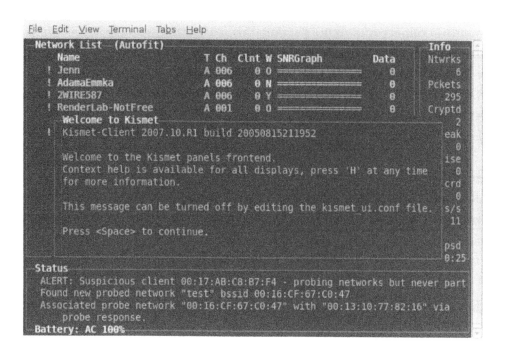

By default, Kismet shows an intro screen with some instructions on accessing help menus and other information. This is often a very annoying thing for early users of Kismet. Changing the *showintro=* line to false will prevent this intro message from showing up every time you start the client. This is probably the first thing that you should adjust.

```
# Gui type to use
# Valid types: curses, panel
gui=panel
```

Depending on your system's capabilities, your options for the type of Graphical User Interface (GUI) to use may need to change. By default, Kismet uses panels for its display. For most modern Linux-based systems, this is not a problem. For some systems like handheld devices, or low power or embedded systems, your options for shell GUI's may be limited, in which case, you may need to use the curses libraries, and change the *gui=* parameter to curses if needed. This is a more advanced feature, and if you are working on a system with limited resources you may need it.

```
# Server to connect to (host:port)
host=localhost:2501
```

This parameter is where the client is told where the server is to connect to. The default is to connect to a server running on the local computer, port 2501. If you want to connect to a remote server, this is where to specify it. To connect to a remote computer over the Local Area Network (LAN) or Internet, just specify the Internet Protocol (IP) address in the *host=* line. To connect to a server running on 192.168.0.45, just change the line to "*host=192.168.0.45:2501*." However, if you do this, you need to make sure to add the address of the client your connecting to the *allowedhosts=* parameter in the server configuration, or the server will not allow the remote client to connect.

Several servers can be specified and monitored at once with separate host lines, but all detected data will be mashed together in the client. If you want to keep the data separate, it is better to run separate instances of the client for each server.

```
# Network traffic decay (active/recent/inactive) and packet click rate - increase
# this if you are doing prism2 channel hopping.
Decay=3
```

Traffic decay is the exclamation point and period that appear to the left of the SSID in the default client layout. They indicate the presence of activity for that network within the recent amount of time. When the data for that network is seen, an exclamation point shows beside the Set User ID (SUID). If no data is seen, in the next update (typically 1 second) the symbol changes to a period. If nothing is seen on the next update, no symbol is shown. In this case, the *decay=* parameter allows you to configure how many updates (seconds) this transition takes. Some cards, like prism2 (hostap drivers) may take a few updates to properly report seeing data. Adjust this higher if things don't seem to be updating right.

```
# What columns do we display? Comma separated. Read the documentation for what
# columns are valid.
columns=decay,name,type,wep,channel,packets,flags,ip,size
```

This is where the rubber meets the road and some good configuration can make Kismet more useful to you. Columns are the various types of info listed in the client window. Things like the SSID, channel, number of packets seen, and so forth, are all configurable in terms of which are shown and in what order. By default, Kismet shows for a typical network, from left to right.

- Recently seen decay (see above parameter)

- The BSSID of the network

- Type of network (ad-hoc, infrastructure)

- Security protocol in use (if any)

- Channel of the network

- Number of packets seen

- Any special flags set on the packets from the network

- IP range in use on the network (if it can be determined)

- Total size of the packets collected for the network

For most people this is enough information for basic scanning, however there are a great many other options available to use in the client beyond the default ones listed above. These can allow you to customize the display on the client to whatever information you need. Not everyone needs to know what flags are coming from the server or the IP range of the network. If you specify more columns than the display can handle, the display can be scrolled to the right with the arrow keys.

To customize the columns displayed, put them in a comma separated list (no spaces) on the *columns=* line. The available options are:

- **BSSID** The BSSID (MAC address) of the network. The BSSID is the advertised name of the network.

- **Channel** The last channel advertised by the network. If the network changes channels, the display is updated to reflect this change.

- **Clients** The number of unique client MAC addresses seen on the network. This includes wireless stations and wired stations sending packets (broadcast and direct) to wireless stations. The client's menu will show you which stations are which and further info.

- **Crypt** This is the number of encrypted packets. This is usually the same as the data column, unless the network is switching from encrypted to un-encrypted, which it should generally not be unless something is going very wrong.

- **Data** The number of data packets. The total number of data packets is just the total Transmission Control Protocol (TCP)/IP packets, not the 802.11 management frames. This is actual data being passed around the network, not just management overhead. Typically if the network is encrypted, the data and crypt counters will be the same.

- **Decay** Displays "!" or "." or blank, based on network activity in the last "decay" seconds (controlled by the "decay" variable in the config file). Decay is the column mentioned earlier that indicated to the user if there has been data seen in the last few updates. Typically if data is seen on the latest update, an exclamation point will be shown (!), if the next update doesn't have any new data (as typically happens with channel hopping), a period will be shown (.), and if no data is seen recently, this column is blank. The rate at which this updates can be controlled by the *decay=* parameter mentioned earlier.

- **dupeiv** The number of packets with duplicate IVs seen. It is sometimes useful to know if networks you're monitoring are generating a lot of duplicate IV's, particularly in stationary Intrusion Detection System (IDS) situations. This only applies to Wireless Encryption Protocol (WEP) networks. If you are seeing excessive duplicate IV's on a WEP network, either the access point (AP) is misbehaving (old firmware problems, and so forth) or if you are seeing large numbers of duplicate IV's with excessively high data packet rates, you may be under an active injection attack on your network. Not a useful thing for wardriving, but for security monitoring of a legacy WEP network, it can be very useful.

- **Flags** Network status flags (address size, decrypted, and so forth). The Kismet server sets various flags on each network to indicate some status information. This information is a very brief overview of what has been discovered about a network.

The various flags (from the client help menu) are:

- **F** Vulnerable factory configuration. Many people don't bother to ever change the configuration on their WAP. This is bad.

- **T#** Address range of # octets found via TCP traffic

- **U#** Address range of # octets found via User Datagram Protocol (UDP) traffic

- **A#** Address range of # octets found via Address Resolution Protocol (ARP) traffic

- **D** Address range found via observed Dynamic Host Configuration Protocol (DHCP) traffic

- **W** WEP'd network decrypted with user-supplied key

These flags can be useful to quickly note to other apps that something is amiss or should be noted (such as a default-configured network).

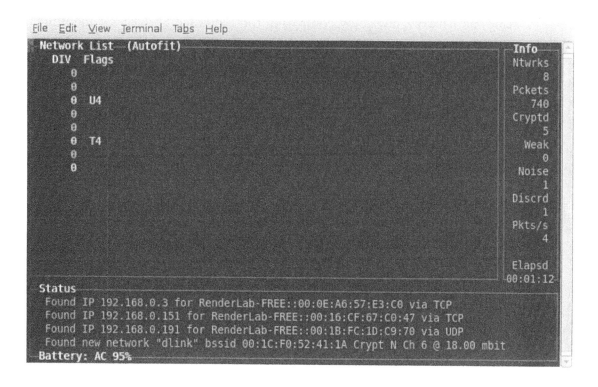

- **Info** The extra AP info included by some manufacturers. Some manufacturers include extra information in their traffic about the APs, which may or may not be of use to your scans. If you do want it, add "info" to the list of columns displayed.

- **IP** The detected/guessed IP of the network. Kismet can make a guesstimate of what IP addresses are in use on a network through dissection of the packets it sees. Kismet will display any IP addresses it sees in the traffic. This only applies to open networks. Encrypted networks typically do not divulge their addresses since they are encrypted. If there are more than one network address spaces in use over a wireless link, Kismet may switch between address spaces on the client display.

- **LLC** The number of LLC packets. The LLC column is a counter for beacons and other management frames. These are the logical link layer packets that manage the wireless link. This counter is separate from the data and crypt columns.

- **Manuf** The manufacturer, if matched. Kismet can guess what manufacturer made the network device by comparing the Extended Service Set Identifier (ESSID) (MAC address) with the Organizational Unique Identifier (OUI) database. Network device manufacturers register the address spaces they make their devices in with the Institute of Electrical & Electronics Engineers, Inc. Using this list, Kismet can look at the addresses seen and compare to this list to make an educated guess about who made the device. This obviously does not work if the network address for the device has been changed for whatever reason.

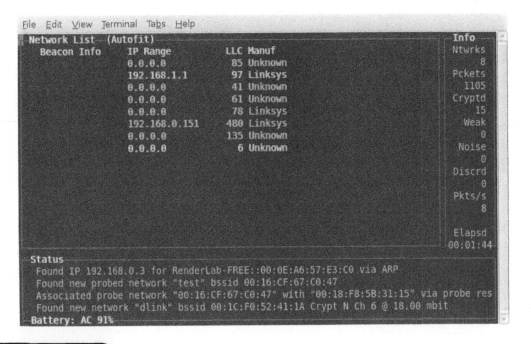

- **Maxrate** The maximum supported rate as advertised by the AP. Networks advertise the maximum data rate available so that incoming clients know what the maximum rate they should try when connecting.

- **Name** The name of the network or group. Typically this is the ESSID of the network Service Set Identifier (SSID), but some manufacturers add additional fields for things like location or other organizational data.

- **Noise** The last seen noise level. The noise column shows the noise level reported by the wireless driver. The problem with the signal and noise readings from wireless cards is that there is no standard unit of measurement across all the different chip sets and drivers. This means that any values reported by various drivers are pretty much useless. The reason that commercial products can do this is that they have access to documentation that open source developers do not, to decode some of this information. They typically also have a limited number of cards they work with that they have had access to the documentation for.

- **Packets** The total number of packets. The packet counter column is the cumulative total of all the packets seen, data, crypt, and LLC.

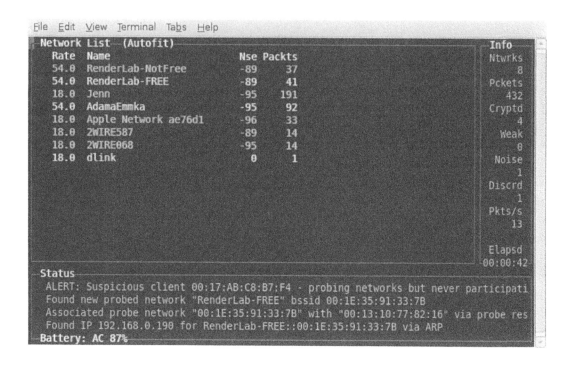

- **Shortname** The shortened name of the network or group for small displays. Use this column for systems with smaller displays. This column is not as wide as the "name" column and can fit in skinnier displays without as much whitespace on the right. If the name is too long for the column, it is truncated.

- **Shortssid** The shortened SSID for small displays. Much like the shortname column, this column is useful for smaller display systems. However, the SSID shown is often the same as the name column, so you may be duplicating some information.

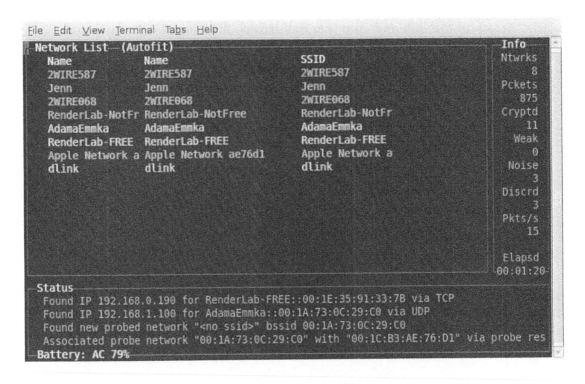

- **Signal** The last seen signal level. Like the noise column, this reports the signal level reported by the driver of the card you're using. Also, like the noise column, there is no standard units for reporting this information and it is a hit or miss venture to use. However, it can be useful in giving you an idea of the relative strength of one network to another.

- **Signalbar** The graphical representation of signal strength. The signalbar column just gives a graphical representation of the signal strength. This, however, is just as reliable as the numeric values from the signal column for the same reasons.

- **Snrbar** The graphical representation of signal-to-noise ratio (SNR). The SNR bar column attempts to show graphically, the signal as compared to the noise levels. As before however, this graph is hit or miss depending on what driver and chipset you are using. It can be useful for comparing the relative strength of the various networks detected.

- **Size** The amount of data transferred on network. The size column is the total (in Bytes, Kilobytes, etc) of the captured data packets, giving a relative comparison of which networks are transmitting the most data.

- **SSID** The SSID/ESSID of the network or group. The SSID column shows the ESSID of the network. This is also pretty much the same as the name column.

- **Type** The network type (Probe, Adhoc, Infra, and so forth). The type column indicates what type of network this is (probing client, AP, and so forth). From the Kismet help menu:

  - **P** Probe request No associated connection yet.

  - **A** Access point Standard wireless network.

  - **H** Ad-hoc point-to-point wireless network.

  - **T** Turbocell Turbocell (aka Karlnet or Lucent outdoor router) network.

  - **G** Group of wireless networks.

  - **D** Data Data only network with no control packets

This column is only a single character wide and only shows a title of "T."

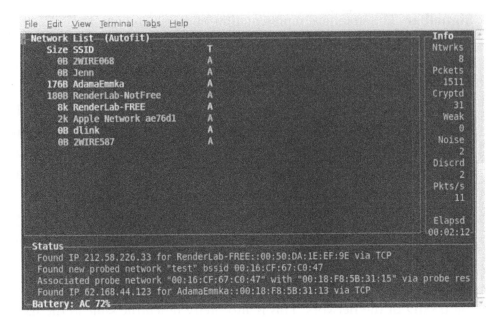

- **Weak** The number of packets that appear to have weak IV's. Weak IV's used to be an issue with early WEP cracking tools. Most modern AP firmware doesn't leak weak packets as much as they used to. It may be useful to use this column to monitor for excessive amounts of weak IV's, which could indicate attack or something else going wrong.

- **WEP** The WEP status (does network indicate it uses WEP). This column is one of the most useful but sadly mislabeled, because Kismet grew organically with changes and updates being made as they were introduced and integrated into the program.

The WEP column is actually the encryption status. Early on, WEP was the only option available, so it was a simple Y/N status indication. Since those days, WPA and WPA2 (802.11i) have been added. From the client help:

- **N** No encryption detected
- **Y** Standard WEP encryption
- **O** Other encryption methods detected

The "O" indicator shows if WPA/WPA2 is present, as well as if other proprietary methods are available. The network information screen shows more specific information of what encryption is available. However, this does not necessarily mean that the strongest encryption available is in use.

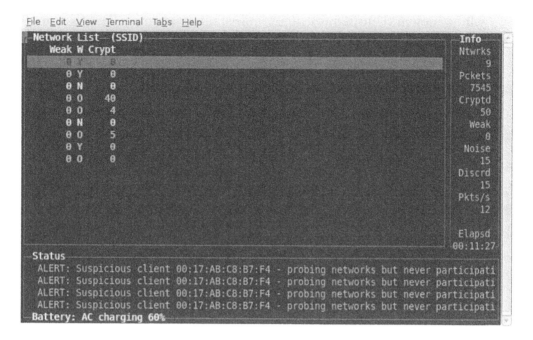

What columns do we display for clients? Comma seperated.

```
clientcolumns=decay,type,mac,manuf,data,crypt,size,ip,signal,quality,noise
```

Like the main network display, we can specify the columns to be shown when we are in the client information screen that gives us information about the clients associated with that network.

The options, just as with the main screen, are added, comma separated with no spaces, to the *clientcolumns=* line.

The available columns are:

- **Crypt** The number of encrypted data packets transferred by client. The crypt counter, like the main network screen, shows the total number of encrypted packets transferred to and from the client. If the network is open, this counter does not count anything.

- **Data** The number of data packets transferred by client. The data counter counts all data packets to and from the client, both unencrypted and encrypted packets.

- **Decay** Displays "!," ".," or '' based on network activity. Once again, the client's recent activity can be tracked through the decay column. This column shows the user if there has been data seen from or too a client in the last few updates. Typically if data is seen on the latest update, an exclamation point will be shown (!), if the next update doesn't have any new data (as typically happens with channel hopping), a period will be shown (.), and if no data is seen recently, this column is blank.

- **IP** The last seen IP used by client. Kismet can dissect packets to determine the IP a client is using. This only works on unencrypted networks.

- **Mac** The MAC address of client. The MAC address of the client's are on every packet sent to or from the client and is listed here for your tracking enjoyment.

- **Manuf** The manufacturer of the client (if known). As with the APs, we can use the OUI database to make a best guess about the manufacturer of the client adapters. The manufacturer's guess is to be taken with a grain of salt, as it's trivial to change the MAC address of client adapters to anything else in the allowable range of addresses.

- **Maxrate** The maximum rate client seen transferring. Kismet can track the maximum rate the client has seen transferring. This can be useful in diagnosing client's complaining of low transfer speeds.

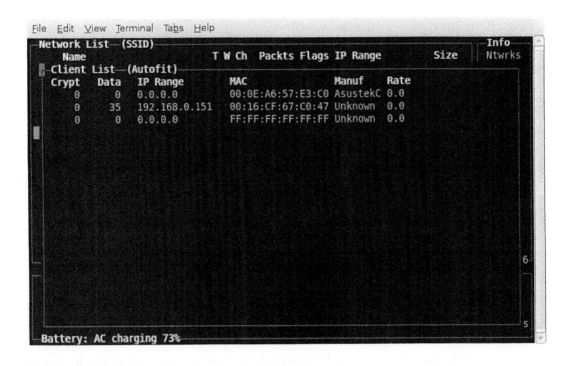

- **Noise** The last seen noise level of client. The noise level column refers to the Kismet server's level of noise between it and the client, not the client to it's associated AP. The server could be seeing a lot of noise that is not being experienced between the client and the AP. All readings should be taken with a grain of salt. Once again, with differences in drivers and a lack of standard reporting of signal levels, this value is not an absolute and only useful for relative comparison.

- **Signal** The last seen signal level of client. Same as the noise, this is the value of the signal strength between the client and the Kismet server, not the client and the AP. All values should be taken with a grain of salt due to the lack of standards in the drivers and chipsets.

- **Size** The amount of data transferred by the client. The size column counts the size of the packets (in bytes, kilobytes, and so forth) collected from and to the client.

- **Type** The type of client (Established, To-DS, From-DS, and so forth). Clients can be wired or wireless. Kismet can tell this depending on the direction of traffic and if telltale wireless traffic is seen.

The clients list shows the following (from the client help menu):

- **F From DS** The client broadcast from wireless distribution system. These clients are typically wired systems.

- **T To DS** The client transmitted over the wireless to the distribution system. These clients are typically wireless nodes.

- **I Intra DS** The client is a node of the distribution system talking to another node in the distribution system.

- **E Established** The client has been seen entering and leaving the DS. These are typically wireless nodes.

- **S Sent-to** The data has been sent to this client, but no data has been seen FROM this client, possibly a hidden node.

- **U Unknown** The client is in an unknown state. Depending on what flag is set, you can make a reasonable guess as to what clients are wireless and which are wired.

- **Weak** The number of packets which appear to have weak IV's. This column counts the number of packets with weak IV's. Not a problem commonly seen nowadays, but excessive weak packets could be an indication of problems or an attack.

```
# Does the GUI use sound?
# NOT to be confused with "sound" option later, which is for the SERVER to make
# noise on whatever host it's running on.
sound=true
```

The sound option enables the client (as opposed to the server) sound options. The client can make noises and play sounds on various events (new network, and so forth). This can be very useful for systems where you can't keep your eye on the system (like in a moving car).

It's best to use either the server sound or the client sound, but not both at the same time or it will be awfully confusing and noisy.

```
# Path to sound player
soundplay=/usr/bin/play
```

If the client is to play sound, it obviously needs to know what program on your system it should use to play them. By default it's */usr/bin/play*, but adjust to your system's specific sound player.

```
# Optional parameters to pass to the player
# soundopts=--volume=.3
```

If you want to get fancy, you can also pass parameters such as sound volume or any other command-line parameters for your player program. Simple specify them as you would on the command line.

```
# New network found
sound_new=@sharedatadir@/kismet/wav/new_network.wav
# Wepped new network
# sound_new_wep=@sharedstatedir@/kismet/wav/new_wep_network.wav
# Network traffic sound
sound_traffic=@sharedatadir@/kismet/wav/traffic.wav
# Network junk traffic found
sound_junktraffic=@sharedatadir@/kismet/wav/junk_traffic.wav
# GPS lock aquired sound
# sound_gpslock=@sharedatadir@/kismet/wav/foo.wav
```

```
# GPS lock lost sound
# sound_gpslost=@sharedatadir@/kismet/wav/bar.wav
# Alert sound
sound_alert=@sharedatadir@/kismet/wav/alert.wav
```

Each event can have its own sound, and if you want, your own custom sound. Simply load your own WAV files onto your system and point each event at the sound you want to use. You can also enable only specific event sounds such as the new network or Global Positioning System (GPS) lock, lost by commenting out un-needed sounds lines.

```
# Do we automatically make a group for probed networks or do we show them
# amidst other networks?
autogroup_probe=true
```

The client can take and group all the probe networks (clients looking for networks) together. They will be listed under the *<probe networks>* group, and can be expanded by selecting the group and pressing **Enter** to show information about all the probe networks. If a probe is seen and then associated with a network, it will be moved to the client list for that network.

```
# Do we autogroup data-only networks?
autogroup_data=true
```

Like probe networks, the client can group *data-only networks* together in the same manner. Select the data networks group and press **Enter** to see the data networks.

```
# Do we autogroup adhoc networks?
autogroup_adhoc=true
```

Once again, we can group ad-hoc networks together just like probe and data networks. It is sometimes a good idea to set this as false, to see if anyone may be setting up ad-hoc networks that circumvent your security policies.

```
# Display battery status?
apm=true
```

If your system has APM enabled, Kismet can report your battery status at the bottom left of the client. Useful if your running around on battery power and want to keep an eye on your time left before you have to plug in and charge up.

```
# Does the GUI talk to us with Festival?
speech=false
```

Using *festival*, the client can speak out the names of the networks. If your system has festival installed, change the speech to true. This should not be confused with the server usage of festival.

```
# Where is festival located for the GUI?
festival=/usr/bin/festival
```

Kismet also needs to know where festival is installed if you want to use it. Depending on your system, point your config to the festival executable. By default it is */usr/bin/festival*.

```
# Are we using festival light? If so, point the above "festival" path to the
# "flite" binary.
flite=false
```

If you are using festival lite you can set this option to true and set the path on the above *festival=* line and point it to the *flite* binary.

```
# Are we using speech on Darwin?
darwinsay=false
```

If you built Kismet for OSX on a Mac, you can use Darwin's speech functionality in place of festival, to speak server events. Set this to true if you want to use Darwin's speech.

```
# What voice do we use? (currently only supported on darwin)
speech_voice=default
```

Darwin also has a selection of voices that can be used. Choose the voice in the system preferences and Kismet will use that voice as the default option in the config file.

```
# How do we speak? Valid options:
# speech      Normal speech
# nato        NATO spellings (alpha, bravo, charlie)
# spell       Spell the letters out (aye, bee, sea)
speech_type=nato
```

If we are using festival and speech, how do we want it to speak? Setting this to "speech" has festival speak (or approximately speak) the names of the networks that are detected. Setting *speech_type* to *nato* will use the nato alphabet to "speak" each letter (linksys is read out as "LIMA, INDIA, NOVEMBER, KILO, SIERRA, YANKEE, SIERRA"). If you set it to "spell," festival will read out each letter as a normal "L,I,N,K,S,Y,S."

```
# speech_encrypted and speech_unencrypted - Speech templates
# Similar to the logtemplate option, this lets you customize the speech output.
# speech_encrypted is used for an encrypted network spoken string
# speech_unencrypted is used for an unencrypted network spoken string
#
# %b is replaced by the BSSID (MAC) of the network
# %s is replaced by the SSID (name) of the network
# %c is replaced by the CHANNEL of the network
# %r is replaced by the MAX RATE of the network
speech_encrypted=New network detected, s.s.i.d. %s, channel %c, network encrypted.
speech_unencrypted=New network detected, s.s.i.d. %s, channel %c, network open.
```

You can customize the output of festival and construct the sentences that it speaks. There are separate lines for encrypted and unencrypted networks. Festival will speak whatever words you put after the equals sign in the *speech_encrypted=* or *speech_unencrypted=* lines with specific symbols replaced by the settings for the network being read out.

```
speech_encrypted=New network detected, s.s.i.d. %s, channel %c, network encrypted.
```

The default lines would read out the above detected linksys network as "New network detected SSID LINKSYS Channel 6 network encrypted" if it was encrypted. You can easily shrink this to "Detected SSID LINKSYS" if you change the line to "*speech_encrypted=Detected, s.s.i.d. %s*" for both the *speech_encrypted* and *speech_unencrypted* parameters.

```
# Simple borders (use - and | instead of smooth vertical and horizontal
# lines. This is required on Zaurus, and might be needed elsewhere if your
# terminal doesn't display the border characters correctly.
simpleborders=false
```

Depending on your terminal, you may need to change from straight lines to terminal characters. Usually this in not an issue unless you're running Kismet on some exotic hardware and not a standard laptop.

```
# Colors (front, back) of text in the panel front. Valid colors are:
# black, red, yellow, green, blue, magenta, cyan, white
# optionally prefixed with "hi-" for bold/bright colors, ie
# hi-red, hi-yellow, hi-green, etc.

# Enable colors?
color=true
# Background
backgroundcolor=black
```

```
# Default text
textcolor=white
# Window borders
bordercolor=green
# Titles
titlecolor=hi-white
# GPS and APM info
monitorcolor=hi-white
# WEP network color
wepcolor=hi-green
# Factory network color
factorycolor=hi-red
# Open color
opencolor=hi-yellow
# Decloaked network color
cloakcolor=hi-blue
```

If the default black, green, and yellow color scheme for the client is not to your liking, you can change any of the elements colors you want. Just change any of the elements config lines to black, red, yellow, green, blue, magenta, cyan, white, or add "hi-" in front of the color name to make it bold.

Command-Line Switches

Just as the server, you can specify command-line switches for the Kismet client. This does require you to start the Kismet server separately using *kismet_sever*. You can't use the Kismet script that launches both the server and client together. The command-line switches override any settings in the *kismet_ui.conf* file.

```
-f, --config-file <file>   Use alternate config file
```

Some of the options for the client come from the server config file, so if you specify an alternate server config file, the client needs to know about it.

```
-u, --ui-config-file <file>  Use alternate UI config file
```

Some users like to have one config file with the columns a certain way, and another with different columns listed. Using the *−u* switch, you can easily change from one to another.

```
-q, --quiet    Don't play sounds
```

Sometimes sound is useful, other times it's not. This option will disable it for you for this run of the client.

```
-s, --server <host:port>    Connect to Kismet host and port
```

Probably the most common use of command-line switches for the client, is specifying an alternate server. If you're running multiple servers, maybe in an IDS setup, you can specify the IP and port at runtime with the *–s* switch.

```
-g, --gui <type>    GUI type to create (curses, panel)
```

If you need to switch between a panel and curses interface for a session (there shouldn't be many) you can specify it here. There are only two choices: panel and curses.

```
-c, --columns <list>    Columns to display initially (comma seperated)
```

Instead of multiple config files, you can manually specify what columns you want, in the order you want from the command line. Valid options are the same as in the config file, listed earlier in the chapter or in the Kismet README file.

```
-r, --reconnect    Try to reconnect after the client/server connection fails.
```

If you are on a flakey or a high latency connection to a remote server, the client might disconnect occasionally. The *–r* switch will automatically have the client try and reconnect the client to the server if it is disconnected.

```
-C, --client-columns <list>  Columns to display for client info
```

As with the network columns, you can specify as comma-separated names, which columns and the order you want them for client devices that are detected. Valid options are the same as in the config file, listed earlier in the chapter or in the Kismet README

```
-v, --version    Kismet version
```

The *–v* option will print the version number of the client to the command line.

```
-h, --help    What do you think you're reading?
```

Finally, the *–h* option will pull up the list of command-line switches in case you don't have this book handy.

Summary

The Kismet client has a great deal of configuration available to it. Proper configuration can give you the information you want, where and when you need it. Adjusting the columns puts the information at your fingertips and can make your life easier and hopefully more productive.

## Chapter 7

Server.conf File Advanced Configuration

Solutions in this chapter:

- **Asus EEEPC installation**
- **Kismet On Windows**
- **Wardriving in a Box**
- **Monitor Installation**

☑ **Summary**

Introduction

Kismet is capable of some amazing feats. It's highly useful in a mobile, rogue-hunting role as it is in a stationary IDS setup. This chapter will show you the various ways that Kismet can be used. Kismet is used all over, from mobile rogue-hunting systems, to site surveys, to full IDS setups for monitoring the airwaves around your wireless installations.

Asus eeePC Installation

In 2007, Asus released the eeePC, a diminutive sub-notebook running Linux. These laptops use a solid state drive, which means fast boot times and they can put up with a lot of movement. The eeePC comes with xandros Linux installed and with an atheros wireless chipset, making it a nice light and portable Kismet rig.

The eeePC's are all fairly identical except for disk space and random access memory (RAM), but the chipsets are consistent. Installation on the default Linux install is fairly easy. A few downloads and packages and you're good to go. You may choose to put another Linux distro or even Windows onto an eeePC, however, those instructions are in other chapters. In this case, we are going to use the eeePC as a quick and light mobile search and sniff rig for your office.

Installation and Updating

Once you've opened your eeePC, the first thing you want to do is update it. This isn't necessary for the Kismet install, but is a good idea since the eeePC originally shipped with a vulnerable version of samba, which could lead to bad things.

To update you can use the update features of the add/remove software under the settings menu on the eeePC, but we'll be using the command line since it's more thorough.

First connect your eeePC to the Internet and open a command shell with:

```
ctl-alt-t
```

You'll need to change to the super user, which is easiest with:

```
sudo su
```

Be careful from now on, you are now super user and if you aren't careful, you can cause major damage to your operating system installation.

Now we need to update the *apt* cache:

```
apt-get update
```

This tells the system to see what packages are available from asus, and if any are newer than what are installed. Upgrade your system to the latest versions available with:

```
apt-get upgrade
```

Apt will probably give you a large list of packages to install and ask for confirmation. This can take a few minutes.

Install Development Tools

By default, the eeePC does not ship with a compiler and most of the basic development tools, however, we can add them, but not from the asus source.

The eeePC is based on Xandros Linux, which is debian-based. This basically means that we can use debian packages fairly safely with the default operating system (OS). This is fairly easy and just requires us to add the debian stable packages to our repository list and load away.

To start, if you haven't already got one open, open a terminal window with:

```
ctl-alt-t
```

Also, make sure you are root with:

```
sudo su
```

Now, you'll need to select a mirror site to download your packages from. Go to http://www.debian.org/mirror/mirrors_full and select a mirror from the list. For the examples, we'll be using the generic ftp.debian.org. You'll need to add the mirror and path you choose to the */etc/apt/sources* list.

```
deb http://ftp.debian.org/debian/ stable main contrib non-free
```

Once again, we need to update our sources to include the new repository:

```
apt-get update
```

Once *apt* knows about the new packages available, we can install the build tools we need to build Kismet:

```
apt-get install build-essential
```

If all goes well, *apt* will load the necessary build tools. We can now load the dependencies we need to install to build Kismet. The required ones are:

- libncurses5-dev
- libpcap0.8-dev
- zlib1g-dev

This is necessary to get Kismet running. If you want to include gpsmap, you'll need to include the following:

- imagemagick
- libexpat1-dev
- libgmp3-dev

You can add all of these in one *apt-get* install command, just list them all on one line with spaces between packages.

```
Apt-get install libncurses5-dev libpcap0.8-dev zlib1g-dev imagemagick libexpat1-dev
libgmp3-dev
```

This should take a few minutes.

Once everything is installed, you can download the latest Kismet stable package from http://www.kismetwireless.net. Check the downloads section for the latest release version. If you want to track any changes to the source since the last release, you'll need to install subversion to get the bleeding-edge development source. Fortunately, this is easy since we have *apt* set up:

```
Apt-get install subversion
```

followed by:

```
svn co http://svn.kismetwireless.net/code/trunk kismet-devel
```

This will download the latest source into the *kismet-devel* directory you are working in, so make sure it's where you want it. If you want to update this source in the future, go to the directory and type **svn update** and any new source changes will be merged into the existing source. Once you have the source, if you need to unpack it, do so now. Switch to the Kismet source directory and just like any other install, run:

```
./configure
make
make install
```

Check the output from configure and make sure all dependencies that you want/ need are satisfied, and hopefully all will work fine when you run *make*. Once Kismet is built and installed, you still need to configure the server. This part is easy once you know what needs to happen. The *Kismet.conf* file needs the following lines changed:

```
suiduser=user
source=madwifi_g,wifi0,<descriptive name here>
```

Once you do this, Kismet still will not run. For some reason, Kismet cannot properly set up the wireless card for monitor mode without manual help. You have to manually destroy the virtual *ath0* interface to leave the parent wifi0 interface:

```
Wlanconfig ath0 destroy
```

This command will allow Kismet to control monitor mode and let Kismet run. If everything is set up right, you can run Kismet and be looking at your very own Kismet installation on your eeePC.

Kismet on Windows

Kismet is primarily developed on and for Linux systems, due to the abundance of open source wireless drivers that allow for monitor mode. Kismet can run on Windows, but with some restrictions. Most if not all consumer wireless drivers do not support monitor mode and given their closed source and proprietary nature, are unlikely to. Kismet on Windows will run with drones as a source, and also one particular Universal Serial Bus (USB) adapter.

The exception is the Airpcap from Cacetech. Available as a USB adapter, these adapters come with a driver capable of monitor mode as well as a full development kit. Compared to others, if you need monitor mode on Windows, this is the cheapest and easiest way.

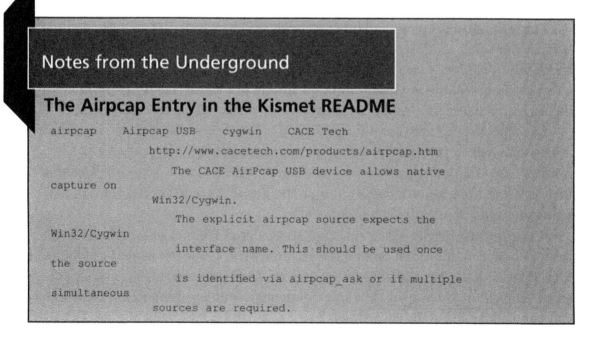

Notes from the Underground

The Airpcap Entry in the Kismet README

```
airpcap    Airpcap USB    cygwin    CACE Tech
                http://www.cacetech.com/products/airpcap.htm
                    The CACE AirPcap USB device allows native
capture on
                Win32/Cygwin.
                    The explicit airpcap source expects the
Win32/Cygwin
                    interface name. This should be used once
the source
                    is identified via airpcap_ask or if multiple
simultaneous
                sources are required.
```

The Airpcap is the only Windows adapter supported by Kismet. Cacetech has worked with the open source security tool community, including Kismet, to include support and ongoing improvements. As part of this, they have made a Windows build of Kismet available for free on their Web site. Kismet on Windows can be a useful thing if you have an existing monitoring station on your network running Windows, and do not want to run an additional station or a VM to monitor your drones.

Kismet on Windows uses Cygwin to run. Cygwin is a library that emulates Linux application program interfaces (APIs) and allows for some portability of applications from UNIX to Windows. It is not perfect, but for the purposes of Kismet, it's been pretty reliable. Building your own install of Kismet in Cygwin for Windows is possible; however, Cacetech has been kind enough to provide an installable build of Kismet for Windows on their Web site: http://www.cacetech.com/support/downloads.htm.

This installable Windows package also provides a very nice interface for setting up your sources, including drones, which means that you don't even need to have an Airpcap to use this package for monitoring drones.

Installation

The first step is to install the Airpcap software. This installs Winpcap and other needed libraries. The Airpcap driver installer is located on the same download page as the Kismet installer on the Cacetech. Double-click the downloaded file and follow the instructions.

This will install Winpcap and other libraries that are needed. If you already have Winpcap installed, the Airpcap installer may ask you to upgrade to its version. Double check which version is newer and if the Airpcap version is newer, let it overwrite the older. If you have a newer version installed already, just cancel the Winpcap part of the Airpcap installer (this won't cancel the whole thing, just the Winpcap part).

After the Airpcap software is loaded, run the Kismet installer. Follow the installer's instructions, which consist of pressing the **next** button three times. After it is installed, you will find a Kismet entry in your Start menu list of programs. Listed in there is a link for a command-line prompt, the Kismet executable, the Kismet configuration, and a shortcut to the logs folder.

If you run the Kismet executable right away, things will fail since you need to configure sources. Instead of editing the *kismet.conf* file, Cacetech made a configuration utility to pass all the options for sources to the Kismet executable, making life easier. Launch the Kismet for Windows configuration utility through the Start menu and you will see the available options.

The upper left corner is for setting up local sources (or specifying that you have none). At this point, the Airpcap is the only supported local adapter. If you have one installed, you can select it from the drop-down box. The adapter name will be in the format \\.\airpcapXX where XX is the number of the adapter (00, 01, 02, and so forth). If you have more than one adapter, the Airpcap utilities can flash the LED's on different adapters to select the right one, or just select "Enable all sources" and use everything

The upper right area is for drones. This is as simple as adding the Internet Protocol (IP) address and port the drone is on (usually port 3501). You can add multiple drones in this area and use them in conjunction with an Airpcap adapter, or set the airpcap section to "No local sources" and just use drones as a source.

In the lower left corner you can choose to enable disk logging. The log files are the same as Kismet on Linux. They are stored in the logs folder in the installed directory. You can find a shortcut to it in the Start menu. The lower right corner has three buttons for launching a manual edit of the various config files. The editor that launches takes care of making sure the config file is UNIX text file formatted so Kismet can still read them when you save them.

Select the options and configure your sources then click the "Apply and run Kismet" button in the lower left corner to do exactly that; apply the settings and launch the Kismet server. Once Kismet starts, if your sources are set up correctly, everything operates just as it does in Linux.

Troubleshooting

One note about Kismet on Windows with an Airpcap. If you do not get data, get slow data, or get random weird stuff coming up on the Kismet client display, start the Airpcap control panel and make sure that the capture type drop down is set to "802.11 + Radio." Also, if you don't have the Airpcap set to capture radio headers, Kismet doesn't get all the information it expects to see and generally does not work.

Wardriving in a Box

Kismet's ability to operate on different hardware and its client/server model, means that you can operate a Kismet server in a very small package.

If you're into war driving, you know that it's a pain to haul all your gear to the car and back. One of the most useful things you can do with Kismet is build a war driving appliance to sit on the dash or back shelf of your vehicle.

There are an infinite number of ways that you can build such a device, but for the purposes of this section, we'll focus on ease of build and use. There are different ways to accomplish the same thing, but fundamentally you just need:

- A central processing unit (CPU) that runs a version of Linux

- A compatible wireless network card

- Storage media

NOTE

This guide is meant as an inspiration. If you want more ideas, check out "Linksys WRT54G Hacking" by Paul Asadoorian and Larry Pesce. They explore a lot of the potential of the WRT54G as an embedded platform.

For the purposes of this guide, only the following parts are needed and the most complex hardware hack is the removal of fur screws:

- Asus WL-500g Premium router

- BU-353 USB Global Positioning System (GPS)

- Atheros mini PCI card

- USB memory stick (any size)

- OpenWRT Kamikaze

The Asus WL-500g is a better platform for this project than a WRT54G because it has more flash space and more RAM. Since this device will be running a server, the more the better. The inclusion by Asus of two USB ports makes this project easy and mod free. The logs will be written to the USB memory stick and the only cable needed is the power cable.

The Asus router comes from the factory with a Broadcom 43xx mini PCI card, which works with Kismet, but due to the lack of an open driver features like channel hopping, are not as well supported as other chipsets. However, since this is a mini PCI card, it is very easy to replace with a different card that has full support. Some judicious use of Ebay can get you one for cheap.

Start off by obtaining a WL-500G Premium router. Make sure it has two USB ports. Other similar models don't have the USB ports. You need both, one for the USB stick and one for the GPS.

As for OpenWRT, the Kamikaze version works well, but the broadcom chipset doesn't channel hop without some effort. As well, the versions of Kismet available currently as Ipkg's don't play nice with the broadcom chipset, so unless you want to cross compile your own server (instructions are part of the Kismet Drone chapter), just replace the mini PCI card with one more compatible; in this case, an Atheros card.

Installation of OpenWRT is a bit trickier than on a WRT54G. The OpenWRT Wiki has more information on that at http://wiki.openwrt.org/OpenWrtDocs/Hardware/Asus/WL500GP.

Notes from the Underground

From the OpenWRT Wiki

To install OpenWrt using Trivial File Transfer Protocol (TFTP) or the Asus firmware restoration tool, you have to put the router in diag mode. To put the router in the diag mode, do this:

1. Unplug the router's power cord.
2. Confirm your PC is configured to request an address via Dynamic Host Configuration Protocol (DHCP).
3. Connect the router's LAN1 port directly to your PC.
4. Push the black **RESTORE** button using a pen or such, and keep the button pushed down.
5. Plug the power on while keeping the RESTORE button pushed for few seconds.
6. When you see a slowly blinking power light, you are in diag mode.
7. Now the router should accept an image via TFTP or via the Asus firmware restoration tool.
8. In diag mode, the router takes address 192.168.1.1. It responds to ping, so you can confirm that it is in diag mode and ready for the TFTP by using "ping 192.168.1.1."

Once the router is in diagnostic mode, upload the firmware by TFTP as usual:

```
tftp 192.168.1.1
tftp> binary
tftp> rexmt 1
tftp> trace
tftp> put openwrt-wrt54g-squashfs.bin
```

Once you have flashed the router, wait 6 minutes. The way the router flashes is that it copies the uploaded flash to RAM, then flashes the flash memory. Interrupting this process can brick the router. Be patient and wait for 6 minutes after flashing to power cycle the router and try to connect to it. Telnet to the router at 192.168.1.1 and change the password so Secure Shell (SSH) is enabled:

```
passwd root
```

Once you have confirmed that the router flash went well, you can swap out the WiFi mini PCI card. The router is held together by four screws underneath the rubber feet on the bottom. Just pop them off and undo the screws to lift the top off the router.

Inside is the mini PCI card. You can see the external antenna connection to the mini PCI card u.fl connector (http://en.wikipedia.org/wiki/U.FL). This is the first thing that needs to be removed. The u.fl connector connects flat to the card, just get the thin edge of a knife or screwdriver to *very gently* pop the u.fl connector off the card.

Once you have the antenna cable disconnected, slide the tabs on the sides out and the card should pop up. Once the card has been released, pull it out and reverse the process to insert the new one. If the card has two u.fl connectors (most do) make sure you reconnect the external antenna to the primary connector, not the auxiliary or secondary one. Look for tiny printing to that affect on the card by the connectors. That's it for the internal tinkering, the rest is just software and plug-and-play.

To set up the router to talk to the Internet to get some necessary files, edit the */etc/config/network* file. The config files are well documented on the openwrt wiki. http://wiki.openwrt.org/OpenWrtDocs/KamikazeConfiguration. It contains all the options, but the few you will probably want to edit are under the "config interface LAN" section:

```
option ipaddr  192.168.1.1
```

If you want to change the IP address of the router:

```
option netmask  255.255.255.0
```

If you need to change the netmask, here is the place to do it:

```
option gateway    192.168.0.1
```

Set your default gateway so that the router can talk to the rest of the Internet:

```
option dns    64.59.184.13
```

You should also set up the router with a domain name system (DNS) server so it can resolve the *openwrt.org* domain to get software.

For example, here is a working LAN config:

```
#### LAN configuration
config interface lan

        option type          bridge

        option ifname        "eth0.0"

        option proto         static

        option ipaddr        192.168.0.75

        option netmask       255.255.255.0

        option gateway       192.168.0.1

        option dns           64.59.184.13
```

After a reboot, you should be able to SSH into the router and ping outside addresses and resolve domains. The easiest way to install the Kismet server is through *ipkg*:

```
ipkg update
ipkg install kismet-server
```

This will download and install the server onto the router. You'll need to make some edits to the */etc/kismet/kismet.conf* file to use the different card and the GPS, as well as a few tweaks for embedded systems.

Change the following lines:

```
source=madwifi_g,wifi0,foo
```

Change the source to use the madwifi driver:

```
channelhop=true
```

Since the madwifi driver works well with Kismet channel hopping, enable it. No special scripts are necessary for channel hopping.

```
allowedhosts=127.0.0.1,<IP other than localhost>
```

It is useful to use another system as a client to the router's server for diagnostic purposes. Set an IP address range that you can use clients on:

```
gps=true
```

Enable the GPS since you have one on the router:

```
writeinterval=XX
```

Since this system can't shut down gracefully, the server won't be able to clean up and write out any remaining data. Adjusting the write interval down to a shorter time means that when you pull the plug, you won't lose as much data. Thirty seconds is reasonable if the system is not in use for a long period of time. Longer usage of the router means larger files and longer write times. If it takes longer than the time interval set in the config, you can end up in a nasty loop and probably lose a lot of data.

You can adjust other options as you like. Since this is a full server, all the options are available to be edited. You will also need to install some other software through *ipkg*:

```
ipkg install kmod-fs-ext3
ipkg install kmod-usb2
ipkg install kmod-usb-uhci-iv
ipkg install kmod-usb-serial-pl2303
ipkg install kmod-usb-storage
ipkg install gpsd
ipkg install hotplug2
ipkg install usbutils
```

These packages are for the GPS and the USB memory stick. Support is not built into the default images, but is easily added.

NOTE

These instructions are assuming an EXT3 formatted memory stick. If you want to use another file system, make sure you load the kernel module for that file system, otherwise the system won't know how to read it. The EXT3 file system is probably the best choice. It tends to deal well with having the power yanked during writes.

Once these packages are installed, it's time to set up some scripting to start GPSD, the Kismet server, and the automount system for the memory stick. Enter these scripts as named into the */etc/init.d* folder.

/etc/init.d/usb

```
#!/bin/sh /etc/rc.common
# Copyright (C) 2006 OpenWrt.org

START=39
```

```
start() {

        [ -d /proc/bus/usb ] && {

                /bin/mount -t usbfs none /proc/bus/usb

        }

}
```

/etc/init.d/gps

```
#!/bin/sh /etc/rc.common
# Copyright (C) 2006 OpenWrt.org

START=10
STOP=10

boot() {
        sleep 10
        start
        }
start() {

        /usr/sbin/gpsd -n /dev/ttyUSB0
        }

stop() {

        kill `ps -ef | grep 'gpsd' | awk '{ print $1 }'`
        }
```

/etc/init.d/kismet

```
#!/bin/sh /etc/rc.common
# Copyright (C) 2006 OpenWrt.org

START=50
STOP=10

boot() {
}
start() {

        echo start
        # commands to launch application
        sleep 3
        cd /mnt/usbdrive
        kismet_server -f /etc/kismet/kismet.conf
```

```
}

boot() {

        echo boot
        # commands to run at boot
        # continue with the start() section
        start

}
```

What happens here is that on startup, the USB script runs and mounts the USB memory stick in */mnt./usbdrive.* The GPS script comes next and starts GPSD on the other USB port. After that, the Kismet server starts up, waits 3 seconds for the other scripts to settle, then switches to the newly mounted */mnt/usbdrive* and then launches the server, saving the data to the memory stick.

Once all this is done and saved, you can restart the router. Log back in and verify that GPSD, the Kismet server, and the hotplug daemon are all running with the *ps* command.

Monitor Installation

This assumes that you are using something like a stripped down PC or a WRT54GL as drones, since they are the cheapest and easiest way to get data into a monitor system.

Planning out your monitoring system is essential. If you are covering one access point, that's as easy as putting the sensor right beside the access point, but multiple access points need a bit more planning as to coverage. As well, you probably want to answer some essential questions about what you want to monitor.

In a typical network, threats come from all around. Monitoring your network is a good idea, but if you don't plan, you'll find yourself buried in data and missing a great deal of information.

Summary

In today's world of everyone using wireless networks, there will almost always be other networks in the area of yours. This means that you probably only want to monitor threats directed at your network. In this case, you probably only want to monitor the channel you are operating your access points on, so as to avoid unnecessary data collection and possibly violating any number of laws regarding privacy and data interception. As well, if you decide to channel hop, it's likely you'll miss a lot of data, which can be a problem if you are looking to monitor usage by users or by an intruder. If you want to monitor for performance reasons, channel hopping may be a good idea, so you can get a view of the wireless landscape of other networks in the area.

Filters will be your friend as well. If you're monitoring your network and all the traffic going over it, filters can be used to limit the amount of data collected to just the minimum necessary and the unusual, otherwise things will become very big, very quickly.

The level of complexity is up to your imagination, but for the purposes of this book, we focus on Kismet's strength as a cheap and effective way to monitor your small network in an office.

## Chapter 8

Kismet Drones

Solutions in this chapter:

- Drone Installation
- PC Drone Setup

☑ **Summary**

Introduction

This chapter hopes to show you the various ways that Kismet drones can be used and integrated into your network monitoring. Kismet has a neat trick in terms of sources. The server doesn't need to be on the same system as the source feeding it. Kismet just receives packets and parses them into a human readable view, it doesn't care where that data comes from. Kismet supports an installation of remote, dumb sensors called *drones*. Drones sniff data from the air and send it down to the server. Kismet can handle several of these and they don't need to be powerful systems. This part of the book will focus on building drones and integrating them with Kismet server.

Drone Installation

A drone is a fairly dumb device. It needs nothing more than a compatible network device that can support monitor mode. In addition, it needs something resembling a CPU that can run a very basic Linux and the drone software. Finally, it needs a backhaul method to get the captured data to the server.

You can run a Kismet drone on any type of system you like, from full, modern PC to small embedded computers and everything in between. Kismet is built with x86 systems in mind, but ARM, MIPS and other processors are possible to use as well.

In this chapter we will show you both ends of the spectrum in terms of difficulty and cost.

Linksys WRT54G

The WRT54GL is the latest version of the WRT54G family of routers that have been a great deal of fun for hardware hackers over the last few years. They contain a MIPS processor, a wireless chipset, and wired Ethernet connections; everything we need.

As hackable and available as they are, WRT54G's are limited. The main problems with them is that they have a small memory footprint, and a proprietary broadcom chip set that limits what we can do to what the manufacturer's driver let's us do, and an open source software development cycle that isn't always up to date.

That being said, their redeeming value of being dirt cheap and well documented means that we can squeeze a lot of capabilities out of these units if you don't want to spend money to get extra features of other hardware, or if those other features are not necessary.

Notes from the Underground…

A Word About Cross Compiling

In some cases it's not possible to compile software on the device it's going to run on. Small embedded systems often have no space for a full compiler, libraries, sources, and so forth, which are needed to build software. The 2 megabytes of memory and 200Mhz processor makes it so we can't compile Kismet directly (natively) on the WRT54GL. Cross-compiling is often necessary to build the software in these cases. Cross-compiling is basically building software on one architecture for another. In the case of the WRT54GL, you can build software on your x86 desktop for the MIPS processor.

Cross-compiling can be more a case of voodoo than an art. Setting up toolchains for other architectures is not something for the timid, or even some of the experienced users out there. A great deal of time and research was spent to try and document building your own cross-compiler to build drones for the WRT54GL, however, it was nearly impossible to document all the variables required. In addition, the ever-changing sources for OpenWRT, Kismet, and all the other software needed means it would require an entire book on it's own to talk about cross-compiling. For the most part though, with drones, you can easily be back several revisions of Kismet and not break anything, since the fields coming across the wire have not changed across versions.

It is highly recommended that if you are using Kismet on architectures other than x86, let the developers of whatever Linux distribution you will be using on the device cross-compile it and package it for you. It will save you from dealing with the same headaches and stress the authors went through.

The OpenWRT Buildroot system is an exception. If everything lines up, the build root takes care of setting up the toolchains necessary, and all the source files for building your own firmware and packages.

In short, if you can compile on the system you are going to be running a Kismet drone on, it's best that you do. If you can't, the developers for your target platform may have a packaged solution that's easier to set up than manually trying to build your own cross-compiler.

Installation

Installation and configuration of a Kismet drone on a WRT seems to be a lot of steps, but it's very easy once you get through your first one. These instructions are adapted from instructions available online from the authors, which have proven very reliable.

NOTE

A whole book could be written about the linksys WRT54GL and its many versions. In fact, there is one from Syngress, "Linksys WRT54G Ultimate Hacking" by Paul Asadoorian and Larry Pesce. A great read if you want to know more about the hardware underlying these systems.

The first step should be to get your hands on a compatible WRT54. The best bet is the WRT54GL. The L designates that this version runs Linux and is compatible for our needs. The OpenWRT wiki has a huge amount of information on specific models and compatibility and should be your first stop.

NOTE

Early WRT versions all ran Linux. When linksys released version 5 of the ubiquitous router, they changed from a Linux-based firmware to a vxworks proprietary firmware and also changed the amount of memory and a few other specifications. The backlash was significant enough that linksys released the wrt54gl models with the original amount of memory and running Linux in order to keep feeding the tinkerer market. (See http://wiki.openwrt.org/OpenWrtDocs/Hardware.)

OpenWRT has two versions available: Whiterussian and Kamikaze. Whiterussian is the older, stable version, while Kamikaze is the new development version. In the first part of the chapter, we will use Whiterussian as an example even though it is no longer being developed. The second part will be about Kamikaze. The reason Whiterussian is included is first, because it's stable. Kamikaze is a moving target and tricky to write about, because they haven't sorted out all the issues that may affect a drone. In the process of writing, several bugs and problems were found and corrected in the development version, so Kamikaze will work but needs the additional step of building your own OpenWRT package with a cross- compiler.

First, we need to get the router set up so we can talk to it. This usually starts with plugging it into your network or to your computer through a crossover cable. A crossover cable is best since you probably don't want to introduce a new Dynamic Host Configuration Protocol (DHCP) server onto your network until you have a chance to turn that off.

Configure the router's address, Domain Name System (DNS), and gateway, so that the router can talk to the rest of the world and we can load packages later. This can be done after OpenWRT is loaded, but we will use the GUI Linksys here to make life easier.

Whiterussian

Download the "OpenWRT Whiterussian" release from http://downloads.openwrt. org/whiterussian/newest/default/.

OpenWRT uses the *jffs* or the *squashfs* file system. Both are writable, so added files and changes are retained through power cycles, meaning that your drone files are not erased on reboot. You can also store scripts for running all the commands, to start up the drone on the router or just have it start up the drone on boot. The *squashfs* system makes it easier to keep from messing up the system, since the base files are read-only. So unless you have a pressing need for the *jffs* file system, you probably want to get the *squashfs* image from the download site.

Select the right firmware for your router type according to the Whiterussian README on the openwrt site (http://downloads.openwrt.org/whiterussian/ newest/00-README) If you select the wrong one, you might turn your router into a useless electronic brick, so make sure to get the right one.

Connect to the Web control panel on the router (presuming you have not removed the Linksys firmware yet or are using another with a Web utility). Using the Upgrade firmware button under Administration | Upgrade Firmware, violate your warranty by loading the *.bin* file you downloaded from the openwrt.org Web site.

NOTE

It is advisable to set the BOOT_WAIT parameter on your router *before* you flash. In case you turn your router into a brick, this gives you a few seconds to try and upload a fresh firmware on powerup. If not, it gets ugly. The OpenWRT Usersguide has instructions for doing this on the default

Linksys firmware, or you can make sure it's the first thing you do after you load a firmware that has the BOOT_WAIT parameter as an option on the Web control panel or command line. At any rate, make sure you turn this on; it will save you many headaches!

It's recommended that you use Trivial File Transfer Protocol (TFTP) to load firmware once you have loaded your first instance of openwrt. This is so you can be sure you can do it should your router become a brick. If you have access to a *nix system on the same network as the router, run the following:

```
tftp <ip of the router>
tftp> binary
tftp> rexmt 1
tftp> tracetftp> put openwrt-wrt54g-squashfs.bin
```

Then power cycle the router while the TFTP program tries to send the firmware. The TFTP program should upload the new firmware, provided the BOOT_WAIT parameter was set and your timing was right on the power cycle.

Once you have loaded the openwrt firmware and left it for a few minutes to boot and sort itself out, Telnet to 192.168.1.1 (or whatever Internet Protocol (IP) you manually set it to) and you should get a prompt and the banner for the OpenWRT firmware. Once you've connected via Telnet, you should immediately set up a root password and Secure Shell (SSH). This is easily accomplished with:

```
passwd root
```

Alternatively, you can connect to the Whiterussian Web interface on the router, by popping the IP of the newly flashed router into a Web browser and clicking on any of the links to change settings. The Web interface will ask you to set a root password before you can change any settings. If you need to adjust anything, here is the time and place to do so.

Provided the router has all the settings for talking to the outside world set (from the earlier steps), you should just be able to run *ipkg* from the command line via SSH:

```
ipkg update
ipkg list
```

If the router complains about not finding hosts, double check your set up DNS and gateway. You may need to set a default gateway with the Web interface or from the command line using:

```
route add default gw <IP Address>
```

and your name server with:

```
echo 'nameserver XX.XX.XX.XX >/etc/resolv.conf
```

where XX is the IP of your DNS server.

> **NOTE**
>
> Because Kismet drones are just shuttling data to the server, they do not need to be the same release version to work. You'll probably find the Kismet drone package listed in *ipkg* is from 2006. This is not an issue, as the drone changes very little with each release, and as long as the version you use supports the wireless device you are trying to use, it's not a problem.

You can download and install the *kismet-drone* package through *ipkg* with:

```
ipkg install kismet-drone
```

This will download and install the kismet-drone binaries to */usr/bin* on the router and the config files to */etc/kismet*.

If you run the Kismet binary now, it will fail in two ways. The *kismet_drone.conf* file is using the wrong device and it cannot find the *wl* command (Broadcom Binary Driver for the Wireless chipset) to enter monitor mode. The *wl* command is easy to install with *ipkg*. Just type:

```
ipkg update
ipkg install wl
```

Now we need to edit some files to get the Kismet drone to use the correct interface. The WRT54G line has several models and the wireless interface changed slightly across revisions. We need to edit the */etc/kismet/kismet_drone.conf* file *source=* line, depending on what model we are using.

If you are using a v1.0 or v1.1 router:

```
source=wrt54g,eth2,wrt54g
```

If your using a v2.0, make sure it's *eth1*.

```
source=wrt54g,eth1,wrt54g
```

If you are using a v3.0 router, change it to:

```
source=wrt54g,eth1:prism0,wrt54g
```

Most users using a v4.0 router, however, WRT54GL or others will use *prism0*

```
source=wrt54g,prism0,wrt54g
```

If you run into problems with the drone not capturing data or not starting due to incorrect interfaces, try another interface name. Revisions to the driver and OpenWRT mean that it's possible for things to change between hardware revisions.

You also need to change your *allowedhosts* line in the *kismet_drone.conf* file to something like:

```
allowedhosts=127.0.0.1,192.168.0.0/24
```

By default, the drone only allows connections from the local system. You will need to add your network segment that you will connect your server from to the list with no spaces. It can be a single IP address, or a whole network using decimal notation and no spaces. If you don't change this, it is still possible to connect to the server, however, no data will come through.

At this point we should set up our server to talk to the drone.

Server Configuration

Set up the *Kismet.conf* file on your laptop/workstation to use *source=kismet_drone, <IP Address>:3501,drone*. You can run other sources at the same time (e.g., wi-fi cards, other drones) on separate source= lines.

The source line breaks down like this:

- **Kismet_drone** indicates this is a remote drone source, as opposed to a local card source.

- **<IP Address>:3501** is the Transmission Control Protocol (TCP)/IP address and port that the drone is running on. You can change the IP address to whatever you set your router to. You shouldn't need to change the port.

- **drone** is just an arbitrary description that is shown in the bottom right corner of the Kismet window in the sources list. You can change this to whatever you want for organizational purposes, be it where the drone is or perhaps what channels it's monitoring.

To run the drone manually, just SSH into the router in another window or terminal and run the following commands:

- **wl ap 0** Put the router in Client mode, just to be sure. We don't want anyone associating while we drive by.

- **wl disassoc** To make sure it's not associated with anything that could screw up our detection.

- **wl passive 1** This throws the router scan engine into passive mode, and prevents any transmissions.

- **wl promisc 1** Why not put it in promisc mode too?

Run the drone, specifying where the config file is:

```
/usr/bin/./kismet_drone -f /etc/kismet/kismet_drone.conf
```

You should then see something like :

```
Suid priv-dropping disabled. This may not be secure.
No specific sources given to be enabled, all will be enabled.
Enabling channel hopping.
Disabling channel splitting.
Source 0 (wrt54g): Enabling monitor mode for wrt54g source interface eth2
channel 6...
Source 0 (wrt54g): Opening wrt54g source interface eth2...
Kismet Drone 2006-04-R1 (Kismet)
Listening on port 3501 (protocol 8).
Allowing connections from 192.168.0.0/255.255.0.0
```

If not, double check your steps.

The last line is the most important. It means that the drone will now accept connections from servers on the 192.168.0.0/24 network, where our server is hopefully set up.

You should then be able to fire up Kismet on your workstation and if everything lines up, you'll see "accepted streamer connection from" in the router SSH session, and Kismet will show a drone with channel "--" in the bottom right corner as a source (This doesn't mean it's not scanning channels, it's just a limitation of the server to know which channel the drone is on). If it's also your only source and you detect networks, you'll know it is working.

Kismet cannot control the channel of the WRT54G; this is a known limitation with the Kismet drone and server. If you want to monitor just one channel, you'll want to disable channel hopping in the *kismet_drone.conf* file by changing the *channelhop=* line to false (purely for organizational purposes, since it doesn't work anyways):

```
channelhop=false
```

Then set which channel you want to monitor in the Web interface, or through the command line with:

```
nvram set channel X
nvram commit
```

where X is the channel you want to monitor. This will set the WRT54G to a single channel that will remain persistent through reboots.

In a lot of cases, you'll want to monitor more than one channel. You can either set up one drone per channel (that's a lot of drones) or have them hop channels. As noted before, Kismet cannot control the channels on the WRT54G hardware, however the *wl* utility can.

Joshua Wright of willhackforsushi.com came up with a channel hopping script that allows for fine control of what channels are monitored.

Using the command line, enter the following in a file called */etc/init.d/S70Wl_scan*:

```
#!/bin/sh
while : ; do
wl channel 1 ; sleep 1
wl channel 6 ; sleep 1
wl channel 11 ; sleep 1
wl channel 2 ; sleep 1
wl channel 7 ; sleep 1
wl channel 3 ; sleep 1
wl channel 8 ; sleep 1
wl channel 4 ; sleep 1
wl channel 9 ; sleep 1
wl channel 5 ; sleep 1
wl channel 10 ; sleep 1
done
```

Now make it executable with:

```
chmod 777 /etc/init.d/S70Wl_scan
```

This will start the channel hopping on startup of the router.

Once you have it there, you can tweak it to your hearts content. Add more sleep to spend longer on a channel, change the order, or copy more lines in to check certain channels more often. (See the Kismet server.conf chapter for more information on tweaking your channel hopping for maximum performance.)

You probably don't want to SSH into the router every time you want to start the drone. You probably want it as an appliance that starts the drone automatically.

To do this, use your favorite text editor to create the file */etc/init.d/S60kismet_ drone* on the router with the following in it:

```
#! /bin/sh
echo "Setting radio for kismet_drone"
mkdir /var/log
/sbin/ifconfig eth1 up
/usr/sbin/wl ap 0
/usr/sbin/wl disassoc
/usr/sbin/wl passive 1
/usr/sbin/wl promisc 1
/usr/sbin/wl monitor 1
echo "Running kismet_drone"
/usr/bin/./kismet_drone -f /etc/kismet/kismet_drone.conf > /dev/null 2>&1 &
sleep 3
echo "kismet_drone now running"
```

Now just make it executable with:

```
chmod 777 /etc/init.d/S60kismet_drone
```

This will start the drone on startup first, followed by the channel hopping script if you chose to use it.

If everything is working fine, you should see data coming in when you start your server and hopefully across all channels. If you don't see anything, check the following:

Troubleshooting

If the server is failing to start:

- Is the source line for your drone correct and do you have source entries for all sources present?

- Can you ping the drone's IP address? Is the Kismet drone shown as running using the *ps* command?

If the server starts, but no data is coming in:

■ Is your server's network on the allowed hosts line in the *kismet_drone.conf?* Is the *source=* line in the *kismet_drone.conf* correct? Is the channel-hopping script listed as running using the *ps* command?

Kamikaze

Kamikaze is the latest version of OpenWRT and is still in development. This means that things that work today, may change and not work tomorrow. This is why if you are building drones for a production environment, you probably want to use Whiterussian, since it's stable and unlikely to change.

Just like Whiterussian, obtain a compatible WRT54G unit and configure it to connect to the Internet.

Select the appropriate firmware from the openwrt Web site for your hardware. Check the release notes for the latest version, to select the right one for your unit (http://downloads.openwrt.org/kamikaze/release.txt).

If you are starting from a fresh router with the default firmware on it, installing opwnwrt Kamikaze, connect to the Web control panel on the router. Using the Upgrade firmware button under Administration | Upgrade Firmware, violate your warranty by loading the *.bin* file.

It's recommended that you use TFTP to load firmware once you have loaded your first instance of openwrt. This is so you can be sure you can do it should your router become a brick. If you have access to a *nix system on the same network as the router, run the following:

```
tftp <ip of the router>
tftp> binary
tftp> rexmt 1
tftp> trace
tftp> put openwrt-wrt54g-squashfs.bin
```

Once you have loaded the openwrt firmware and left it for a few minutes to boot and sort itself out, Telnet to 192.168.1.1 (or whatever IP you manually set it to) and you should get a prompt and the banner for the OpenWRT firmware. If you don't, try a crossover cable between your station and the router. If that still doesn't work, set up your workstation as 192.168.1.2 and try again. If none of those work, try resetting the router, which should hopefully put it back to 192.168.1.1 and you can try again.

Once you've connected via Telnet, you should immediately set up a root password and SSH. This is easily accomplished with:

```
passwd root
```

Configuring the router is a bit different than on Whiterussian. The system no longer uses nvram, but instead uses configuration files to set up all the parameters.

There are a lot of options available for configuring your router, and they are outside of the scope of this book, however there are a few specific ones worth mentioning.

/etc/config contains most of the base system configuration files. Before we can load Kismet, we need to make a few changes.

To set up the router to talk to the Internet to get some necessary files, edit the */etc/config/network* file.

The config files are well documented on the openwrt wiki. http://wiki.openwrt.org/OpenWrtDocs/KamikazeConfiguration contains all the options, but the few you will probably want to edit are under the "config interface lan" section:

```
option ipaddr    192.168.0.75
```

The IP address of the router, if you wanted to change it for some reason:

```
option netmask   255.255.255.0
```

If you need to change the netmask, here is the place to do it:

```
option gateway   192.168.0.1
```

Set your default gateway so that the router can talk to the rest of the Internet:

```
option dns        64.59.184.13
```

You should also set up the router with a DNS server so it can resolve the open-wrt.org domain to get software.

For example, here is my working LAN config:

```
#### LAN configuration

config interface lan

        option type        bridge

        option ifname      "eth0.0"

        option proto       static

        option ipaddr      192.168.0.75
```

```
option netmask    255.255.255.0

option gateway    192.168.0.1

option dns        64.59.184.13
```

After a reboot, you should be able to SSH into the router and ping outside addresses and resolve domains. To install Kismet, it gets a little weirder than Whiterussian.

> **NOTE**
>
> At the time or writing, the Kismet binaries available through the ipkg repository are almost 18 months old and don't work properly on the broadcom chips in WRT54GL. By printing time, a new version will hopefully be available through ipkg, and things will be easy as ipkg installs kismet-drone. If not, there is always building it yourself, which will be covered further.

The easiest way to install the Kismet-drone is through ipkg:

```
ipkg update
ipkg install kismet-drone
```

Any version after 2007-10-R1 should work fine. If that is not available or not working, it is possible to build your own, as you will see later in this chapter.

Once you have the binaries installed, you need to make some adjustments to the config file for it to work properly.

Edit the */etc/kismet/kismet_drone.conf* file. You can edit it to your liking, but the *source=* and *allowedhosts=* parameters are the most important.

For the *source=* line on a *wrt54g*, specify:

```
source=wrt54g,wl0,foo
```

wrt54g is the source type, *wl0* is the interface name, and *foo* is the designation that shows up in the Kismet client in the lower right corner.

If you want to connect to the drone from a remote server, you need to add the server's IP address or network to the *allowedhosts* parameter.

```
allowedhosts=127.0.0.1,192.168.0.0/24
```

Where you specify the IP or the server or the network should be comma separated with no spaces. To make sure everything is working, launch the drone from the command line:

```
kismet_drone -f /etc/kismet/kismet_drone.conf
```

Just like with Whiterussian, you probably want to run the drone as an appliance running on startup of the WRT54G. The scripting is very different than Whiterussian. Kamikaze uses a custom startup scripting system that is fairly easy to use. It really boils down to inserting the commands you want to into one script template, then that template is used to automatically generate other scripts that are needed. All the startup scripts that you need to edit exist in */etc/init.d*. Create a file named Kismet in that directory. Insert the following example script framework:

```
#!/bin/sh /etc/rc.common
# Example script
# Copyright (C) 2007 OpenWrt.org

START=65
STOP=70

boot() {
        echo boot
        # commands to run at boot
        # continue with the start() section
        start
}

start() {
        echo start
        # commands to launch application

}

stop() {
        echo stop
        # commands to kill application

}
```

As you can see in the example script, there are three main sections: *boot, start* and *stop*. Each section contains the command needed to start, stop, or do whatever for the program we want to control.

```
START=65
STOP=70
```

The start and stop lines contain numbers, which control in what order the scripts generated from here start or stop. The higher the number, the later it starts. If you have one program that needs to start before another (i.e. gpsd starting before Kismet), make sure that the first program has a smaller number than the other.

```
boot() {
        echo boot
        # commands to run at boot
        #continue with the start() section
        start
}
```

The boot section runs commands inside it on startup. These commands are run on startup and then the start section runs. This is a good place to put preparation commands if you need them.

```
start() {

        echo start
        # commands to launch application

}
```

The start section is for commands to be run to start the program, but not necessarily on boot. If the boot section does not call the start section, these commands can be run by manually running the script with the *start* command (i.e. scriptname start)

```
stop() {

        echo stop
        # commands to kill application

}
```

The stop section runs commands to end a program. This section is called when the system shuts down. When you have all the commands in the script, make the script executable with:

```
chmod 777 <scriptname>
```

then run the script with the *enable* parameter:

```
./<scriptname> enable
```

This will link the script properly into the rc.d startup folder and take care of things for you.

A lot more information is available from the OpenWRT site:
http://downloads.openwrt.org/kamikaze/docs/openwrt.html-x1-270001.3.2

For your drone appliance, the following script will prep the WRT54G and run the drone on startup:

```
#!/bin/sh /etc/rc.common
# Example script
# Copyright (C) 2007 OpenWrt.org

START=65
STOP=70

boot() {
        echo boot
        # commands to run at boot
        # continue with the start() section
        start
}

start() {
        echo start
        # commands to launch application
        wl ap 0
        wl disassoc
        wl promisc 1
        sleep 3
        kismet_drone -f /etc/kismet/kismet_drone.conf

}
```

The boot section simply calls the start section, which covers the preparation of the router and launching the drone. Here's what it does:

```
wl ap 0
```

Put the router in client mode, otherwise you will see beacons from the router in your data.

```
wl disassoc
```

If the router is changed to client mode, it may associate with a nearby access point, which would be bad for scanning as well as for legal reasons.

```
wl promisc 1
```

This puts the router in promiscuous mode, mostly for the sake of making sure we can get all the data we want.

NOTE

In the Whiterussian setup, the script uses the *"wl passive 1"* command. This is supposed to prevent the router from transmitting anything, however this command doesn't play nice with Kamikaze. It has a nasty habit of changing the *wl0* interface from wireless to a wired interface (as far as the system is concerned), and causes Kismet to fail to start since it's not seeing the interface as wireless. It's not a problem for it not to be there in this script. Its a problem if it is there, so don't get confused between OpenWRT versions.

```
sleep 3
```

To make sure the *wl* commands have completed, wait for 3 seconds before moving along to the next command.

```
kismet_drone -f /etc/kismet/kismet_drone.conf
```

Run the drone command with the *-f* parameter to specify the config file. To enable the script for startup, run the Kismet script with the enable option:

```
/kismet enable
```

The stop section is not needed since there is no way to gracefully shutdown the WRT54G. When you pull the plug, the program and everything else stops.

Server Configuration

Setup the *Kismet.conf* file on your laptop/workstation to use *source=kismet_drone, <IP Address>:3501,drone*. You can run other sources at the same time (e.g., wi-fi cards, other drones) on separate *source=* lines.

The source line breaks down like this:

- **Kismet_drone** indicates this is a remote drone source, as opposed to a local card source.

- **<IP Address>:3501** is the TCP/IP address and port that the drone is running on. You can change the IP address to whatever you set your router to. You shouldn't need to change the port.

- **drone** is just an arbitrary description that is shown in the bottom right corner of the Kismet window in the sources list. You can change this to whatever you want for organizational purposes, be it where the drone is or perhaps what channels it's monitoring.

Cross Compiling with OpenWRT-Buildroot

OpenWRT development has a very cool tool called a buildroot, which is basically a suite of all the compilers and tools you need to build OpenWRT and it's packages. It really takes the sweat out of compiling software for OpenWRT, and we can use it to build a bleeding edge version of Kismet for Kamikaze.

Building your own packages is not the easiest way. Keep in mind that this can introduce unknown and unanticipated problems. Your mileage may vary.

> **NOTE**
>
> This section is meant as a guide only. Both Kismet and OpenWRT are constantly developing, and it's best to use existing, proven releases to build drone devices. If you have a need to experiment or update outside of normal releases, here's how you can do so.

Buildroot Installation

First, you'll need to obtain the buildroot. This is easily done through the subversion system on the openwrt Web site. Goto https://dev.openwrt.org/ and you should see the available options for the buildroots. There should be a current release version and a development version. The development version is bleeding edge and likely to cause problems. If you have loaded a release version, it's best to use the release version.

You'll also want to make sure you have enough free space. The buildroot can grow to several gigabytes (the author's testing grew to over 4.5 Gb's).

To obtain a buildroot, use the *svn* commands listed on the openwrt development site (this is for the stable buildroot):

```
svn cohttps://svn.openwrt.org/openwrt/tags/kamikaze_7.09 openwrt_buildroot
```

This takes a while, but will download all the software needed to build OpenWRT and it's package software. Kismet is in the extended set of packages, and must be added manually by running the following from the command line:

```
make package/symlinks
```

This will install the extra package sources to the buildroot, including the out-of-date Kismet. Once it's downloaded, you can run "make menuconfig" to start up the configuration. There are a huge amount of options here to configure, way more than we need to worry about. All that matters is the target system. This is where you can specify the architecture you are building for. The target system setting for the WRT54GL is "Broadcom BCM947xx/953xx," and the most stable is the 2.4 kernel. For the purposes of this section, we are not going to change anything else except to build Kismet through the buildroot.

The existing Kismet in the buildroot can be enabled in the menuconfig under network | wireless. Select the Kismet modules you want to build (you can build the server, client, and drone) and make sure they are selected as modules (it should say *<M>* beside the name). This builds them as packages rather than into the base openwrt image.

Go back to the main screen and exit, then save the config and you are returned to the command line. If you type "make" at this point, you will download the sources for everything selected, build the base system, base libraries, and any libraries needed by Kismet, as well as the Kismet binaries. Now, if you want to upgrade the version of Kismet that the buildroot builds, you need to edit the Makefile the buildroot uses, and change where it gets it's sources from and adjust a few build options.

Within the buildroot, the packages are built according to a Makefile that contains the location of the source code, the build options, and a list of dependencies. We need to edit this file to use the newer source, as well as make some adjustments to version numbers.

The Kismet package Makefile is located in the buildroot directory under *packages/feeds/packages/kismet*. The existing Makefile should look something like this:

```
#
# Copyright (C) 2006 OpenWrt.org
#
# This is free software, licensed under the GNU General Public License v2.
# See /LICENSE for more information.
#
# $Id$

include $(TOPDIR)/rules.mk

PKG_NAME:=kismet
PKG_VERSION:=2007-10-R1
PKG_RELEASE:=1

PKG_SOURCE:=$(PKG_NAME)-$(PKG_VERSION).tar.gz
PKG_SOURCE_URL:=http://www.kismetwireless.net/code
PKG_MD5SUM:=2100c667e69db0cde35fa2d06c8516e2
```

```
PKG_BUILD_DEPENDS:=libnotimpl libpcap libncurses uclibcxx

include $(INCLUDE_DIR)/package.mk

define Package/kismet/Default
  SECTION:=net
  CATEGORY:=Network
  TITLE:=Kismet
  DEPENDS:= +uclibcxx
  URL:=http://www.kismetwireless.net/
  SUBMENU:=wireless
endef

define Package/kismet/Default/description
  An 802.11 layer2 wireless network detector, sniffer, and intrusion
  detection system.
endef

define Package/kismet-client
$(call Package/kismet/Default)
  TITLE+= client
  DEPENDS+= +libncurses
endef

define Package/kismet-client/conffiles
/etc/kismet/ap_manuf
/etc/kismet/client_manuf
/etc/kismet/kismet.conf
/etc/kismet/kismet_ui.conf
endef

define Package/kismet-client/description
$(call Package/kismet/Default/description)
  This package contains the kismet text interface client.
endef

define Package/kismet-drone
$(call Package/kismet/Default)
  DEPENDS+= +libpcap
  TITLE+= drone
endef

define Package/kismet-drone/conffiles
/etc/kismet/kismet_drone.conf
endef
```

```
define Package/kismet-drone/description
$(call Package/kismet/Default/description)
  This package contains the kismet remote sniffing.and monitoring drone.
endef

define Package/kismet-server
$(call Package/kismet/Default)
  DEPENDS+= +libpcap +dbus
  TITLE+= server
endef

define Package/kismet-server/conffiles
/etc/kismet/ap_manuf
/etc/kismet/client_manuf
/etc/kismet/kismet.conf
endef

define Package/kismet-server/description
$(call Package/kismet/Default/description)
  This package contains the kismet server.
endef

CONFIGURE_ARGS += \
     --enable-syspcap=yes \
     --disable-setuid \
     --disable-wsp100 \
     --disable-gpsmap \

CONFIGURE_VARS += \
     CXXFLAGS="$$$$CXXFLAGS -fno-builtin -fno-rtti -nostdinc++" \
     CPPFLAGS="$$$$CPPFLAGS -I$(STAGING_DIR)/usr/include/uClibc++
     -I$(LINUX_DIR)/include" \
     LDFLAGS="$$$$LDFLAGS" \
     LIBS="-nodefaultlibs -luClibc++ -lm -lnotimpl" \

define Build/Compile
     $(MAKE) -C $(PKG_BUILD_DIR) \
             LD="\$$$$(CC)" \
             all
endef
```

```
#FIXME: remove this package?
define Package/kismet/install
      $(INSTALL_DIR)  $(1)/usr/bin/
      $(INSTALL_BIN)  $(PKG_BUILD_DIR)/scripts/kismet $(1)/usr/bin/kismet
endef

define Package/kismet-client/install
      $(INSTALL_DIR)  $(1)/etc/kismet/
      $(INSTALL_DATA)  ./files/ap_manuf $(1)/etc/kismet/
      $(INSTALL_DATA)  ./files/client_manuf $(1)/etc/kismet/
      $(INSTALL_DATA)  ./files/kismet.conf $(1)/etc/kismet/
      $(INSTALL_DATA)  ./files/kismet_ui.conf $(1)/etc/kismet/
      $(INSTALL_DIR)  $(1)/usr/bin
      $(INSTALL_BIN)  $(PKG_BUILD_DIR)/kismet_client $(1)/usr/bin/
endef

define Package/kismet-drone/install
      $(INSTALL_DIR)  $(1)/etc/kismet/
      $(INSTALL_DATA)  ./files/kismet_drone.conf $(1)/etc/kismet/
      $(INSTALL_DIR)  $(1)/usr/bin
      $(INSTALL_BIN)  $(PKG_BUILD_DIR)/kismet_drone $(1)/usr/bin/
endef

define Package/kismet-server/install
      $(INSTALL_DIR)  $(1)/etc/kismet/
      $(INSTALL_DATA)  ./files/ap_manuf $(1)/etc/kismet/
      $(INSTALL_DATA)  ./files/client_manuf $(1)/etc/kismet/
      $(INSTALL_DATA)  ./files/kismet.conf $(1)/etc/kismet/
      $(INSTALL_DIR)  $(1)/usr/bin
      $(INSTALL_BIN)  $(PKG_BUILD_DIR)/kismet_server $(1)/usr/bin/
endef

$(eval $(call BuildPackage,kismet-client))
$(eval $(call BuildPackage,kismet-drone))
$(eval $(call BuildPackage,kismet-server))
```

There are really only a few lines that we need to worry about updating. Most of the heavy lifting has been done already.

The first six lines that start with *PKG* are what interest us at the moment:

```
PKG_NAME:=kismet
```

Obviously this is the name given to the package:

```
PKG_VERSION:=2007-10-R1
```

This is the version number of the Kismet build we are doing:

```
PKG_RELEASE:=1
```

For organizational purposes, we can tag this as a version 1, 2, 3, and so forth, of the package for the same Kismet version.

```
PKG_SOURCE:=$(PKG_NAME)-$(PKG_VERSION).tar.gz
```

This tells the buildroot the filename of the source code to download. In this case, it is using the previous lines as variables to spell out the name of the package *kismet-2007-10-R1.tar.gz*. You can just enter the exact filename, but sometimes it's easier just to update the PKG_VERSION line.

```
PKG_SOURCE_URL:=http://www.kismetwireless.net/code
```

The buildroot needs to know where to download the above file from. In this case, it's the Kismet Web site. It can also be from a directory on the local filesystem.

```
PKG_MD5SUM:=2100c667e69db0cde35fa2d06c8516e2
```

As an integrity check, you can specify the Message Digest 5 (MD5) checksum of the download package. You can remove this line if you don't want to integrity check the download. We can now edit this file to use a newer source. You can specify a specific release version by changing the PKG_VERSION and the MD5 of the package from the Kismet Web site, or if you're really brave, you can use the development source. On your workstation, download a fresh snapshot of the Kismet stable development branch:

```
svn cohttp://svn.kismetwireless.net/code/trunk kismet-devel
```

This will check out the latest development source into the *kismet-devel* directory. Next, *tar* and *gzip* the source:

```
tar -czvf kismet-devel.tar.gz kismet-devel
```

This leaves you with a tarball named *kismet-devel.tar.gz*. Copy this into your buildroot */dl* directory. This is where the buildroot downloads source code before building it. You should remove any previously downloaded source for Kismet from the directory while you're there.

You may want the MD5 of the tarball so that you can verify integrity later in the build process, just in case something gets downloaded in it's place. Your Linux distribution may or may not come with the MD5 or MD5SUM command. It should be trivial to add it through whatever package management tools are available or through a quick google search.

```
md5 kismet-devel.tar.gz
```

This will spit out a long line of letters and numbers. This is the signature of this particular file. Save this for later. Now you need to edit the Makefile in the *buildroot packages/feeds/packages* directory, specifically the following lines:

```
PKG_VERSION:=devel
```

Since this in not a release, tag it as devel. As mentioned before, this becomes part of the filename. The *PKG_NAME* parameter is Kismet, now the version is devel, so the Makefile fills in the blanks of the *PKG_SOURCE* parameter and looks for *kismet-devel.tar.gz*, which is what you named the tarball you made.

```
PKG_SOURCE_URL:=<PATH TO BUILDROOT>/dl
```

Specify the local directory where you put the development source tarball earlier.

```
PKG_MD5SUM:=<MD5 checksum>
```

If you are using it, change the MD5 sum of the development tarball. Now if you go back to the top level of the buildroot, and run "make," the buildroot will churn through and hopefully build the openwrt system and the Kismet binaries you selected in the menuconfig as packages.

Troubleshooting

A great deal can go wrong when dealing with bleeding edge software. Incorrect versions of libraries, missing files, and so forth. Here are a few tips and tricks.

If you are just trying to build the Kismet binaries, go with the defaults for the rest of the system configuration and just select to build Kismet. This way, only Kismet and it's dependent libraries are built and it limits the scope of the problems. Avoid 2.6 kernels if you can. The 2.4 branches are much more stable.

If the build fails on a dependency of Kismet, see if it's needed. The above Makefile includes Dbus as a dependency. While it is true the kismet-server can use Dbus, since the WRT54G is not running X and in particular, network manager, you don't need Dbus support to be built to disable it.

Go through the Makefile and find instances of Dbus:

```
define Package/kismet-server
$(call Package/kismet/Default)
  DEPENDS+= +libpcap +dbus
```

Remove the +dbus from the *DEPENDS* line for the server, then find the *./configure* options being used and disable dbus support.

The original file shows the following as configure switches:

```
CONFIGURE_ARGS += \
    --enable-syspcap=yes \
    --disable-setuid \
    --disable-wsp100 \
    --disable-gpsmap \
```

To disable dbus support, add "*--disable-dbus* \" (the space at the end and the slash are important), so that it reads:

```
CONFIGURE_ARGS += \
    --enable-syspcap=yes \
    --disable-setuid \
    --disable-wsp100 \
    --disable-gpsmap \
    --disable-dbus \
```

Save these edits and re-run the top level "make" and hopefully everything will compile successfully.

PC Drone Setup

To set up a drone on a full PC-type system is just as easy as installing Kismet normally, and in fact can be easier. As part of the normal Kismet build process, in addition to the server and client being built, a Kismet drone binary is built and installed along with the server and client.

The requirements for a Kismet drone on a PC is the same as installation for Kismet normally; it can even be done on an older, slower computer (old laptops work great here), as long as it meets the normal drone criteria of having a CPU, a compatible wireless device, and a backhaul method to get the data to the server. Install a compatible Linux distro on the PC and follow the normal installation procedure of:

```
./configure
make
make install
```

Once you have the drone binaries built and installed, you can configure the *kismet_drone.conf* file with your source just as with the server configuration.

You may need to build and install setuid root, depending on how your PC drone is configured. If you don't install setuid root, make sure to add a normal user to the system that Kismet can drop privileges to. The added advantage to using a PC is that most compatible cards and driver don't need external scripts to channel hop. Using compatible cards also means that the Kismet server can control channel hopping (locking and re-enabling hopping) and properly report what channel is currently in use. You also need to change your *allowed hosts* line in the *kismet_drone.conf* file to something like:

```
allowedhosts=127.0.0.1,192.168.0.0/24
```

By default, the drone only allows connection from the local system. You will need to add your network segment that you will connect your server from to the list with no spaces. It can be a single IP address, or a whole network using decimal notation and no spaces. If you don't change this, it is still possible to connect the server, however, no data will come through.

Set up the *Kismet.conf* file on your laptop/workstation to use *source=kismet_drone,* *<IP Address>:3501,drone.* You can run other sources at the same time (e.g., wi-fi cards, other drones) on separate *source=* lines.

The source line breaks down like this:

- **Kismet_drone** indicates this is a remote drone source, as opposed to a local card source.

- **<IP Address>:3501** is the TCP/IP address and port that the drone is running on. You can change the IP address to whatever you set up your router to. You shouldn't need to change the port.

- **drone** is just an arbitrary description that is shown in the bottom right corner of the Kismet window in the sources list. You can change this to whatever you want for organizational purposes, be it where the drone is or perhaps what channels it's monitoring.

As for running the drone on startup, it all depends on your distribution's method of starting programs at startup. There are too many to go over in detail, so just check with the documentation for your particular distribution.

Kismet Drone Configuration File

For both embedded (WRT54G and the like) and full PC, there are a few options in the *kismet_drone.conf* file you can tweak. Here are all the available options:

```
# Kismet drone config file
version=Feb.04.01a
```

As with the server and client, the drone configuration version number is separate from the package version number. As of writing, the *kismet_rone.conf* hasn't changed in over four years

```
# Name of server (Purely for organiational purposes)

servername=Kismet
```

You shouldn't need to change this, but if you have a lot of drones, you may want to adjust this to your taste.

```
# User to setid to (should be your normal user)

suiduser=your_user_here
```

Just like the server, Kismet prefers to start as root and then drop privileges. If you want to run as root, just make installsetuid as per the installation chapters.

```
# Port to serve packet data... This probably shouldn't be the same as the port

# you configured kismet_server for, or else you'll have problems running them

# on the same system.

tcpport=3501
```

The *kismet_drone* normally runs on port 2501. If you need to change it for whatever reason, do so here. It's probably best not to use the same port as the server's graphical user interface (GUI) data on (port 2501).

```
# People allowed to connect, comma seperated IP addresses or network/mask

# blocks. Netmasks can be expressed as dotted quad (/255.255.255.0) or as

# numbers (/24)

allowedhosts=127.0.0.1
```

Probably the second most important line in the configuration. The Kismet drone needs to know what address the server will be connecting from. If you allow just anyone to connect, an attacker could connect and sniff all the data on your network.

The address can be a specific address or a whole network segment. The values are comma separated with no spaces.

```
# Address to bind to. Should be an address already configured already on

# this host, reverts to INADDR_ANY if specified incorrectly.

bindaddress=127.0.0.1
```

If the drone has multiple addresses and you want to only connect on one of the interfaces/addresses, specify that address here. Otherwise, the drone will accept connections on any and all interface addresses.

```
# Maximum number of concurrent stream attachments

maxclients=5
```

How many clients of the drone (meaning servers) do we allow to connect? Too many can overwhelm a drone, but then again, you shouldn't need to connect to many servers.

```
# Sources are defined as:

# source=sourcetype,interface,name[,initialchannel]

# Source types and required drivers are listed in the README.

# The initial channel is optional, if hopping is not enabled it can be used

# to set the channel the interface listens on.

# YOU MUST CHANGE THIS TO BE THE SOURCE YOU WANT TO USE

source=none,none,addme
```

This is the most important line in the drone configuration file. The source line tells Kismet what it needs to know to get data into the program so we can start scanning. Each source has three parameters: a kismet source name for the specific type of card, the interface name, and a logical name found in the Kismet client. The Kismet README has a list of compatible sources and their proper interface names.

```
hostap     Prism/2     Linux     HostAP 0.4
                http://hostap.epitest.fi/
                Capture interface: 'wlanX'
                HostAP drivers drive the Prism/2 chipset in access point
                mode, but also can drive the cards in client andmonitor
                modes. The HostAP drivers seem to change how they go
                into monitor mode fairly often, but this source should
                manage to get them going.
```

The README has many entries, such as this one for *hostap*-compatible cards. You'll need to find the one for your card type and follow any special instructions to get it to work (different drivers or patches, etc).

For the above card, the source line would be "*source=hostap,wlanx,hostap,*" where hostap is the name of the type of card (according to the readme), and wlanx is the interface name for that card (usually will be *wlan0* or *wlan1*). The last part is a logical name for your information. The client displays the status of each card and what channel it is currently on. It is useful to give a short descriptive name so you know which is which. Identifying on-board network cards vs. add-on cards can be especially useful so you know which one is active and on what channel.

You can also specify the initial channel the cards start on when Kismet is started, by adding a fourth parameter after a comma. If you want the card to start on channel 11, you simply add a "*,11*" after the logical name. The source line would now read "*source=hostap,wlanx,onboard,11.*" This is especially useful if you have multiple cards and want to monitor different channels on each, you can have Kismet set the channels instead of manually doing it. This setting does not affect much if channel hopping is enabled, and only works for static channel monitoring.

```
# Comma-separated list of sources to enable. This is only needed if you wish

# to selectively enable multiple sources.

# enablesources=prism,cisco
```

If you have multiple source lines, you can specify which ones to enable. This is easier than removing or commenting out *source=* lines. These lines are comma separated, with no spaces.

```
channelhop?

channelhop=true
```

The drones can channel hop, just like the server. To enable channel hopping, set it to true, to disable, and to false. Some platforms require manual channel hopping scripts, as the drone binary can't control the channel.

```
# How many channels per second do we hop? (1-10)

channelvelocity=5
```

You can tweak the speed at which you hop channels. This is mostly something you have to fine tune yourself. If you hop slow, it takes longer to get through all the channels. If you hop fast, there's the chance you could miss something. Most times you can take your time, since drones are typically stationary and we don't have to worry about velocity making detection a problem.

```
# By setting the dwell time for channel hopping we override the channelvelocity

# setting above and dwell on each channel for the given number of seconds.

#channeldwell=10
```

This setting overrides the channel velocity setting and specifies that, rather than a certain number of channels per second, Kismet should spend a certain amount of time on each channel. This is a more useful setting for static installations and drones. This way you can thoroughly inspect each channel. It's up to you to determine which works for you to make the most of your time and coverage. Increments of 1 second can be adjusted.

```
# Do we split channels between cards on the same spectrum? This means if

# multiple 802.11b capture sources are defined, they will be offset to cover

# the most possible spectrum at a given time. This also controls splitting

# fine-tuned sourcechannels lines which cover multiple interfaces (see below)

splitchannels=true
```

Channel splitting enables Kismet to cover more spectrum at any given time when multiple sources are in use. If you have two cards, both hopping, Kismet will make sure that they are both always on different channels at any given time. If card 1 is on channel 5, card 2 is on a channel other than 5, maximizing the covered spectrum. This is especially useful for situations of several cards where having all of them on one channel makes little or no sense. If you are using several drones or other situations where you need blanket coverage of a channel across several locations, consider disabling this.

```
# Basic channel hopping control:

# These define the channels the cards hop through for various frequency ranges

# supported by Kismet.  More finegrain control is available via the

# "sourcechannels" configuration option.

# Don't change the IEEE80211<x> identifiers or channel hopping won't work.

# Users outside the US might want to use this list:

# defaultchannels=IEEE80211b:1,7,13,2,8,3,14,9,4,10,5,11,6,12
```

```
defaultchannels=IEEE80211b:1,6,11,2,7,3,8,4,9,5,10

# 802.11g uses the same channels as 802.11b...

defaultchannels=IEEE80211g:1,6,11,2,7,3,8,4,9,5,10

# 802.11a channels are non-overlapping so sequential is fine. You may want to

# adjust the list depending on the channels your card actually supports.

# defaultchannels=IEEE80211a:36,40,44,48,52,56,60,64,100,104,108,112,116,120,124,
128,132,136,140,149,153,157,161,184,188,192,196,200,204,208,212,216

defaultchannels=IEEE80211a:36,40,44,48,52,56,60,64
```

Here you can specify what channels, by default, the drone should hop through. More fine control is available in the *sourcechannels=* line later on, we are just specifying the channels that are possible here.

This setting also allows you to set the channels for your regulatory domain. By default, it is set up for the North American regulator domain, which is for channels 1–11, but not all users are in the North American regulatory domain and can use more or less channels. This is also where you can hack things a bit. If your card supports all 14 channels, or more than your regulatory domain allows, you can specify all the possible channels, even the ones not technically allowed in your regulatory domain. Check your local laws before doing this, however.

Since we are not transmitting in Kismet, it shouldn't be a problem (check your local laws) to listen to see if someone has set up a rogue access point on channels not normally used or allowed, to try and avoid detection. Please don't abuse this as the regulations are there for a reason.

```
# Combo cards like Atheros use both 'a' and 'b/g' channels. Of course, you

# can also explicitly override a given source. You can use the script

# extras/listchan.pl to extract all the channels your card supports.

defaultchannels=IEEE80211ab:1,6,11,2,7,3,8,4,9,5,10,36,40,44,48,52,56,60,64
```

You can also specify channels to be covered by a/b/g combo cards if you happen to have one. The *listchan.pl* script in the extras directory of the install package will poll your card(s) to see what channels are supported. A useful thing to see if your card is capable of more than you thought it was.

```
# Fine-tuning channel hopping control:

# The sourcechannels option can be used to set the channel hopping for

# specific interfaces, and to control what interfaces share a list of

# channels for split hopping. This can also be used to easily lock

# one card on a single channel while hopping with other cards.

# Any card without a sourcechannel definition will use the standard hopping

# list.

# sourcechannels=sourcename[,sourcename]:ch1,ch2,ch3,...chN

# ie, for us channels on the source 'prism2source' (same as normal channel

# hopping behavior):

# sourcechannels=prism2source:1,6,11,2,7,3,8,4,9,5,10
```

This parameter is where you can fine-tune the channel hopping. In the *default-channels* parameter, we specified what channels were available. Now we can specify which ones we specifically want to listen on and what order to sequence through.

NOTE

There is a very cool hack possible here. For b/g networks, channels 1, 6, and 11 are statistically the most popular since they don't overlap. If we have one card, it makes no sense to spend only 8/11th's of our time on channels less likely to have something on them. You can specify channels more than once and the sequence will loop back to the beginning when done. So if you specify 1, 6, and 11 more than once, you'll end up spending more time there overall and even out your distribution of time/channels.

sourcechannels=prism2source:1,6,11,2,7,1,6,11,3,8,1,6,11,4,9,1,6,11,5,10

With the above line we are spending 6/10th's of our time checking the most popular channels. You can tweak this distribution to your liking, but it has been tested and tends to work for high speed scanning such as highway speed wardriving. You can also specify additional channels such as 12–14 if your card supports it and add those to the mix.

You can do the same for 802.11a channels. Either adding them to the mix of b/g channels if you have an a/b/g card or just the 802.11a channels if you have a single mode card.

```
# Given two capture sources, "prism2a" and "prism2b", we want prism2a to stay

# on channel 6 and prism2b to hop normally. By not setting a sourcechannels

# line for prism2b, it will use the standard hopping.

# sourcechannels=prism2a:6
```

If you don't specify a *sourcechannels* parameter and *channelhop=true*, the system will automatically hop through the default channels. If you have multiple sources, you can have a specific *sourcechannels* for one device and have it monitor a few specific channels while the other one checks the remainder. This is effective with wardriving. One source spends all it's time checking 1, 6, and 11 where there are most likely going to be signals, and the other can check the remaining channels.

You can also use this to break up the workload across multiple sources. One card can do the lower channels, the other the higher channels, and be able to sequence through everything much faster than a single card.

```
# To assign the same custom hop channel to multiple sources, or to split the

# same custom hop channel over two sources (if splitchannels is true), list

# them all on the same sourcechannels line:

# sourcechannels=prism2a,prism2b,prism2c:1,6,11
```

You can also nest multiple sources in an assigned *sourcechannel*. If *channelsplit=true*, Kismet will cycle through the channels, and make sure that no two sources are on the same channel at the same time, maximizing the time spent on high-usage channels, and making sure not to overlap scanned channels. In the config file example, three sources would cycle through each of three channels without overlapping.

Like the server and client, you can specify command-line switches for the drone that override the options in the *kismet_drone.conf* file.

```
-I, --initial-channel <n:c>      Initial channel to monitor on (default: 6)
```

Format capname:channel
This switch sets what channel the enabled sources should start on. If channel hopping is disabled, this will be the channel that is monitored.

```
-x, --force-channel-hop          Forcibly enable the channel hopper
```

If channel hopping is disabled in the config file, -x (lower case x) will force it to be enabled.

```
-X, --force-no-channel-hop       Forcibly disable the channel hopper
```

The capital X switch will disable the channel hopper, if it is not already disabled.

```
-f, --config-file <file>          Use alternate config file
```

If you need to specify an alternate location or an alternate filename for your config file, the *-f* switch will do that for you.

```
-c, --capture-source <src>        Packet capture source line (type,interface,name)
```

Sometimes you need to specify another capture source. Much like in the config file, it consists of the type (see the README for allowed types), the interface name, and a description with no spaces and all comma separated.

```
-C, --enable-capture-sources Comma separated list of named packet sources to use.
```

If you have multiple sources in your config file, you can fine tune which ones are enabled with the –C switch and listing the descriptions you included in the config file.

```
-p, --port <port>                 TCPIP server port for stream connections
```

Due to firewalls or other restrictions, you may need to specify an alternate port to serve up connections from on the drone. If you do so, you'll have to adjust the *source=* line on your server system to connect to the new port.

```
-a, --allowed-hosts <hosts> Comma separated list of hosts allowed to connect
```

To add a host to allow connections from temporarily, use the *-a* switch and the IP address.

```
-b, --bind-address <address>      Bind to this address. Default INADDR_ANY.
```

On multi-homed systems the drone defaults to accepting connections from any configured address. If you want to restrict connections to one address, use the –b switch.

```
-s, --silent                      Don't send any output to console.
```

Particularly useful in testing is to suppress output from the drone when it runs.

```
-N, --server-name                 Server name
```

For organizational purposes, you can change the server's name. This doesn't show up anywhere major with drones, so no need to worry about it.

```
-v, --version                     Kismet version
-v outputs the version of the kismet_drone
-h, --help                        What do you think you're reading?
```

If you find yourself without this book handy, the *-h* switch will show you the options available.

Summary

Drones have limitations and some quirks. You want to be careful how you set up the backhaul to make sure you don't interfere with normal operations. In most situations, you want to backhaul from your drone to the server over a wired network. Some people try to send the data from the sniffer back over a wireless, which can get you into a great deal of trouble. If you are monitoring the data you are backhauling, you're then capturing it again and broadcasting it back to be sniffed again and getting into a very ugly loop that will likely saturate things very quickly. Also, if you are monitoring a heavily used wireless network and sending the captured data back over the same network, you are effectively doubling the amount of data going down the wire. This can be an issue if you are already near capacity.

For the headaches it saves and the extra data you have to deal with, it's best to run the drones over a separate network from what you are monitoring. Be it through separate wires or Virtual Local Area Networks (VLANS), this will save you a great deal of time and effort.

Currently, drones are a pull-type connection. When the server starts, it connects to all the drones listed as *source=* lines and requests data to be sent, and if the drone is functional, it does so. The current architecture of Kismet does not support dynamically adding sources beyond the startup of the server. This means that if a drone goes down, you have to restart the whole server to bring it back up. This is being addressed in kismet-newcore but for now, if something downs a drone, it takes a server restart to bring it back online.

Drones can be a very cheap and efficient way of extending your view of the network into the RF layer and to see beyond just TCP/IP packets and see what is going on in the lower layers of the stack at remote locations. Drones can be nearly any type of system that runs Linux, has a backhaul method, and a compatible wireless device. Some devices have their own quirks and issues. A bit of research and development will save you some headaches and hopefully some money.

## Chapter 9

Kismet and Mapping

Solutions in this Chapter:

- GPSMap/KisMap
- WiGLE
- WiGLE Google Map
- IGiGLE
- GpsDrive
- Alternatives

☑ Summary

☑ Solutions Fast Track

Introduction

Kismet's data formats are well-suited to allow integration of this data into other tools and programs. In terms of Kismet, the tools that are often most helpful or useful are mapping programs. The focus of this chapter will be on the use of mapping programs (both native and third-party) to enhance Kismet's ability.

GPSMap/KisMap

Kismet's native mapping tool is known as GPSMap. GPSMap is designed to download maps from online repositories and overlay Kismet networks onto them. GPSMap's features include:

- Travel path/track

- Approximate network circular range

- Approximate network center

- Convex hull of all network sample points

- Interpolated (weathermap-style) graphing of power and range

- Labeling of network centers

- Scatterplot of all detected packets

- Legend showing total sample networks, visible networks, colors, power ranges, network center, and so forth

NOTE

Unfortunately, the current incarnation of GPSMap is hobbled by the fact that most of the source data for the maps is no longer available. GPSMap has been patched to use Expedia data, but this is only available for Europe. To remedy this situation, you can patch GPSMap to work with Google Maps (see below).

Patching GPSMap

You can patch GPSMap to work with Google Maps, but this also presumes that you have a place to display those maps (i.e., your own Web server).

First, download the patch (http://parknation.com/gmap/files/gpsmap-gmap-0.1.tgz). Then, uncompress and apply the patch to the source and compile the binary:

```
tar zxf gpsmap-gmap-0.1.tgz
cd /pentest/svn/kismet-devel
patch -p0 < /root/gpsmap-gmap-0.1/gpsmap-gmap-0.1.diff
./configure
make gpsmap
```

Next, copy *gpsmap* to your desired location. Then, copy *index.html* and the *mapfiles* folder from */root/gpsmap-gmap-0.1* (or wherever you uncompressed it) to your web server. Run *gpsmap* against one of your Kismet *.GPS* files:

```
gpsmap -j -o gpsdata.js -u -r Kismet.gps
```

Your output file, *gpsdata.js*, should be copied to your Web server. Finally, you'll require a Google Maps API (http://code.google.com/apis/maps/signup.html). When you get your key, paste it into the *index.html* file (conveniently, where it says "KEYHERE"). This process is a bit complicated, and it does require that you have a Web server, but the results speak for themselves.

KisMap

Due partially to the lack of map sources and the limitations of the patches, GPSMap is currently being re-written from the ground up as a new python-based tool (currently known as KisMap). KisMap works with Google Maps (something that was not originally supported in GPSMap), with other formats likely to come in the future.

WiGLE

As has been mentioned in the BackTrack chapter, WiGLE (Wireless Geographic Logging Engine) is an online database that includes in excess of 15 million recorded wireless networks, most with geographic coordinates. WiGLE gives you access to Service Set Identifier (SSID) and manufacturer statistics, octet and channel usage statistics, and a browsable Web map of the world (see Figure 9.1).

Figure 9.1 WiGLE Web Maps Display of the Baltimore-Washington, DC Corridor

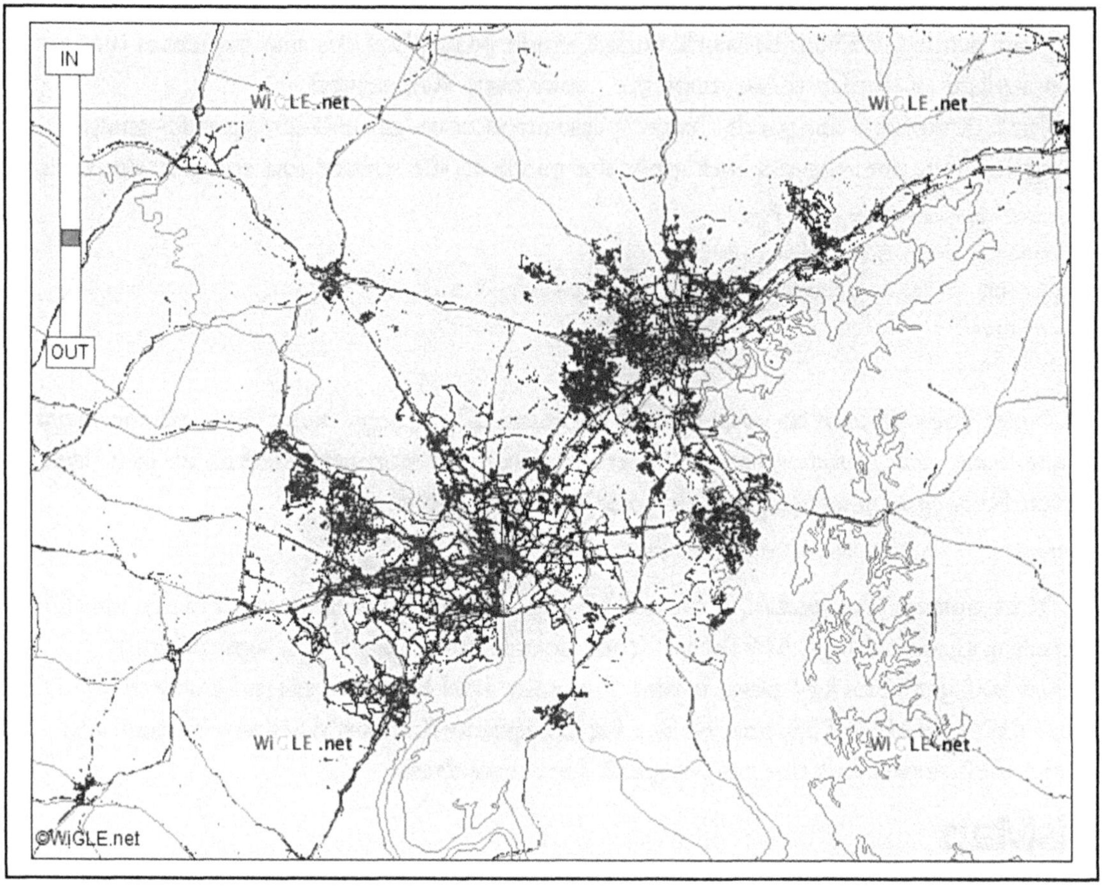

WiGLE Google Map

WiGLE Google Map (http://wigle.rustyredwagon.com/) is a Web-based tool that
displays WiGLE data on Google Maps. Simply enter an address, select the type of
networks you'd like to see, and WiGLE Google Map will query the WiGLE database
and display the appropriate network data on the map.

IGiGLE

IGiGLE (Irongeek's WiGLE WiFi Database to Google Earth Client for Wardrive Mapping) is a simple Windows-based interface between the WiGLE database and Google Earth (see Figure 9.2). You can query the WiGLE database by zip code or latitude/longitude, and IGiGLE will download the data and convert it to .KML format to display in Google Earth (see Figure 9.3). You can choose to download all data for all particular areas, or just your data. The latter is especially useful if you use the WiGLE database as your primary location to store your own Kismet-collected data. IGiGLE can be downloaded at http://www.irongeek.com/i.php?page=security/ igigle-wigle-wifi-to-google-earth-client-for-wardrive-mapping.

Figure 9.2 IGiGLE Interface

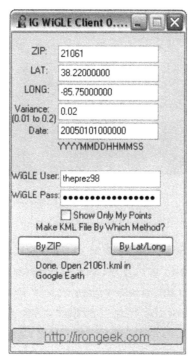

Figure 9.3 IGiGLE's .KML Output File is Displayed in Google Earth

GpsDrive

GpsDrive is a navigation system designed to display your GPS position on a zoom-able map (see Figure 9.4). While it can be used completely independently of Kismet as a standalone mapping program, it integrates nicely with Kismet (and MySQL) to display Kismet network data on the map. Furthermore, speech output through *festival* is supported (*flite* also works); so you can even have GpsDrive tell you when it finds new networks. If your GPS receiver works with *gpsd* (or *gpsdold*), it should work with GpsDrive.

Figure 9.4 GpsDrive Homepage

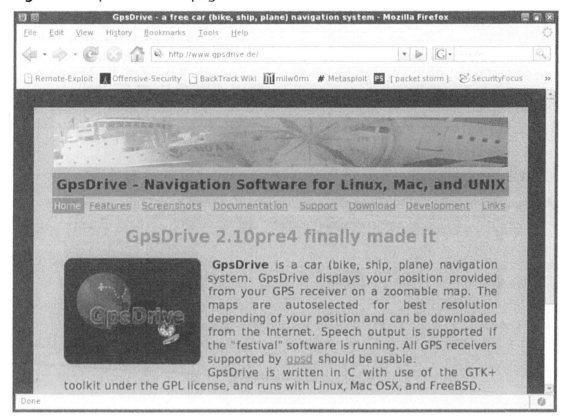

Installation

Installation of GpsDrive presumes that you have installed BackTrack 3 Beta (or another distribution of Linux) to your hard drive. You will also require the following packages: *gpsd, GTK-+2.x* (better *>=2.2.x*), *pango, atk, pcre, xdevel* (X11 development), *gettext, libcrypt, glibc, gcc >=3.x, and make.* In many cases, some or all of these packages will already have been installed. In any case, you ought to check beforehand to avoid any problems. Finally, GpsDrive requires Structured Query Language (SQL) support to interface with Kismet. In the case of BackTrack, MySQL is already installed; on other distributions, you may have to do it yourself.

WARNING

In Debian and Slackware distributions (including BackTrack), GpsDrive will not compile correctly without *gcc 3.x*. Unfortunately, *slapt-get* does not work correctly out of the box in BackTrack 3 Beta, so you'll have to do a manual upgrade of *gcc* (http://gcc.gnu.org/) and then compile GpsDrive. Alternatively, you could simply download a pre-compiled version of GpsDrive.

Install from Source

To install from source, download the source from the GpsDrive Web site (http://www.gpsdrive.de/). The current stable version (although old) is v2.09. Then:

```
tar -zxvf gpsdrive-2.09.tar.gz
cd gpsdrive-2.09
./configure
make
make install
```

NOTE

If you don't require support for Garmin's GPS protocol, configure with the *--disable-garmin* argument.

Install from Package

Alternatively, you may want to go with a GpsDrive package that is already compiled. Depending upon the distribution you're using, the package installation procedure may vary. You can find a Slackware-compatible (and BackTrack-compatible) Gps-Drive package at http://slackware-current.net/package.php?id=345 (note that this version has Garmin's GPS protocol already compiled into the package). To install (see Figure 9.5):

```
installpkg gpsdrive-2.09-i586-1.tgz
```

Figure 9.5 Installing GpsDrive from Package

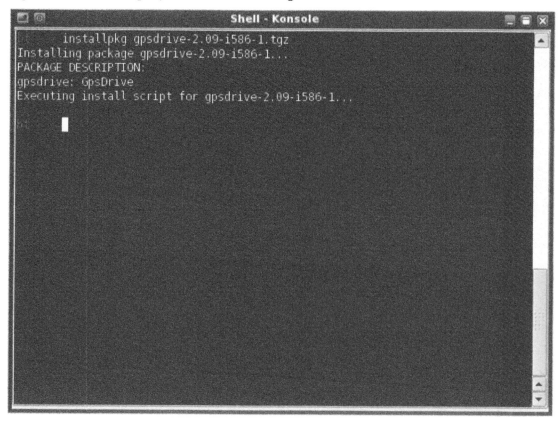

To start, type **gpsdrive**.

MySQL

While GpsDrive will work fine on its own, it does require SQL support to properly interface with Kismet. As previously noted, MySQL may or may not be installed on your particular version of Linux; we will be using BackTrack, which comes with MySQL already installed.

Even if MySQL is already installed, it may seem a little daunting if you haven't used it before. No fear! Remote-Exploit forums (http://forums.remote-exploit.org/) user Dr_GrEeN created a small script, which will do everything for you. Simply copy and paste the code into a new file (here we call it *start-mysql*):

```
#!/bin/sh
#
#### Backtrack Mysql Startup Script by Dr_Gr33n ####
#
option=6

echo "Welcome do the Dr_Gr33n's Backtrack 2 Mysql Startup Script"
#
echo "1) Start Small Server"
echo "2) Start Medium Server"
echo "3) Start Huge Server"
echo "4) Check Mysql is running"
echo "5) Stop Mysql"
echo "0) Exit"
read option
      case $option in
            1)echo "Starting Small Server"
              cp /etc/my-small.cnf /etc/my.cnf
              chown -R root .
              chown -R mysql /var
              chown -R mysql /var/lib/mysql
              /usr/bin/mysql_install_db --user=root
              /usr/bin/mysqld_safe --user=root &
              su
              mysql;;

            2)echo "Starting Medium Server"
              cp /etc/my-medium.cnf /etc/my.cnf
              chown -R root .
              chown -R mysql /var
              chown -R mysql /var/lib/mysql
              /usr/bin/mysql_install_db --user=root
              /usr/bin/mysqld_safe --user=root &
              su
              mysql;;

            3)echo "Starting Large Server"
              cp /etc/my-huge.cnf /etc/my.cnf
              chown -R root .
              chown -R mysql /var
              chown -R mysql /var/lib/mysql
```

```
            /usr/bin/mysql_install_db --user=root
            /usr/bin/mysqld_safe --user=root &
            su
            mysql;;
    4)echo "Checking Mysql is running"

            /usr/bin/mysqladmin -u root -p version
            cd /root;;
    5)echo "Stop Mysql Server"

            /usr/share/mysql/mysql.server stop
            cd /root;;

            0)echo "*** Bye ***"
            ;;
            *).  exit &;;

    esac
```

Save the file, and don't forget to *chmod 755.* When you run the file, it will give you three options: all of these (small, medium, large) options have been tested and appear to work fine.

Kismet + GpsDrive + MySQL

Once you have everything installed, it's time to get started. First, start MySQL manually, or by using Dr_GrEeN's script, which we have named *start-mysql.* This will start MySQL on port 3306 (its default port). Next, start the GPS daemon (for example, *gpsd –p /dev/tts/USB0*). Next, start Kismet. Finally, start GpsDrive (simply, *gpsdrive*). On the left-hand side of the GpsDrive interface, be sure to check "Use SQL." This is critical to ensuring that Kismet's networks are stored in MySQL and properly displayed in GpsDrive.

NOTE

Even though you already started *gpsd* earlier, you may have to click it to start within GpsDrive.

Maps

You'll note almost immediately that GpsDrive doesn't come with any (useful) maps, so you'll have to get them yourself. There are two methods of obtaining maps:

- Within GpsDrive, click the "Download map" button. This will open a dialog window (see Figure 9.6), which will allow you to specify the coordinates and scale. Keep in mind this downloads one map (at one scale) at a time, so it can be time-consuming if you are trying to get multiple scale maps of larger areas.

TIP

GpsDrive will color the map yellow to indicate the area that will be downloaded by a particular scale map. Changing the scale will quite obviously change the area to download; keep in mind that the larger the scale, the more detail, at the expense of less area, and vice versa.

Figure 9.6 Map Download Dialog Box

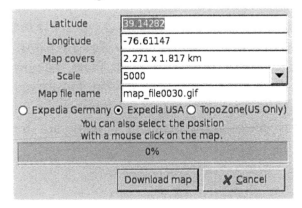

- GpsDrive comes with a perl script *gpsfetchmap.pl*, which automates the process of downloading multiple maps at a time (see Figure 9.7.) Type *gpsfetchmap.pl --help* for available options. You'll definitely want to read through all available options to ensure you get the right maps for the right location in the right scale!

Lastly, you can create your own maps (see the Maps section of the FAQ located at http://www.gpsdrive.de/documentation/faq.shtml for more details).

Figure 9.7 GpsDrive Interface

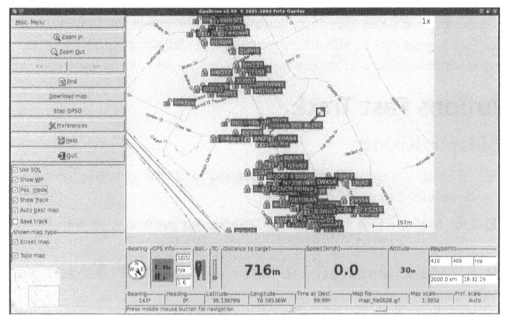

Alternatives

The previously mentioned tools are certainly not the only ones available to do mapping with Kismet data. In this section, we'll mention a few alternatives that you might want to consider. Even so, these alternatives are not the extent of available tools. Google is your friend!

Kismet Earth

Kismet Earth (http://www.niquille.com/kismet-earth/ is a tool to parse Kismet's . XML and .GPS files for display on Google Earth.

OpenStreetMap

While it is not directly related to Kismet, many Kismet users also like to share their GPS data beyond sites like WiGLE.net. One example is OpenStreetMap (http://www.openstreetmap.org/), which is an editable map of the world using user-contributed GPS data.

Summary

As we have seen, Kismet's data formats are well-suited to allow integration of this data into mapping-related tools and programs. As we have demonstrated in this chapter, obtaining, installing, and configuring these tools and programs is relatively easy; furthermore, it yields some very positive results. Whether you only want to upload your Kismet data to WIGLE, or configure an elaborate GpsDrive setup with voice announcements, it is all within your reach with a little bit of additional work.

Solutions Fast Track

GPSMap / KisMap

☑ GPSMap is a native Kismet tool designed to overlay networks on maps downloaded from online sources.

☑ Due to the lack of map sources, GPSMap was patched to include Expedia (Europe), and can be patched to use Google Maps.

☑ GPSMap is currently being re-written and replaced with KisMap.

WiGLE

☑ WiGLE is an online database that includes in excess of 15 million recorded wireless networks, most with geographic coordinates.

☑ WiGLE gives you access to SSID and manufacturer statistics, octet and channel usage statistics, and a browsable Web map of the world.

☑ You can query WiGLE for overall statistical information, or just information that you uploaded (provided you uploaded it with a personal account).

WiGLE Google Map

☑ WiGLE Google Map is a Web-based tool that displays WiGLE data on Google Maps.

IGiGLE

☑ IGiGLE is a Windows-based program that queries the WiGLE database, downloads the data, and then converts it to .KML for display in Google Earth.

☑ IGiGLE will download data by area (latitude/longitude) or zip code.

GpsDrive

☑ GpsDrive is a navigational system that displays Kismet data on maps.

☑ GpsDrive requires SQL support to store Kismet network data.

☑ GpsDrive has *festival* (and *flite*) support for voice announcements.

Alternatives

☑ Kismet Earth displays Kismet data on Google Earth.

☑ OpenStreetMap is an editable map of the world using user-contributed GPS data.

Chapter 10

Wardriving with Kismet and BackTrack

Solutions in this chapter:

- Obtaining BackTrack
- Configuring Kismet
- Wardriving with Kismet
- Managing your Results

Introduction

The goal of this chapter is to provide an explanation and demonstration of wardriving while using Kismet with BackTrack, a live Linux distribution. The focus will be on the fact that we'll be using a live CD, so no installation is required, and very little configuration is necessary. This is also useful for those who are running Windows and need to use Kismet but don't necessarily want to install an entire Linux distribution. It is also important to note that wardriving is just one example of why you might want to use Kismet from a live CD. Other possibilities are rogue access point (AP) detection or graphical mapping of networks.

Obtaining BackTrack

This section will focus on acquiring BackTrack by download (direct or torrent), and then burning it to CD.

Downloading BackTrack

If you don't already have BackTrack, it will be necessary for you to download it. Point your favorite browser to http://www.remote-exploit.org/backtrack_download. html to find the download page for BackTrack (see Figure 10.1).

Figure 10.1 Remote-Exploit.org Download Page for BackTrack

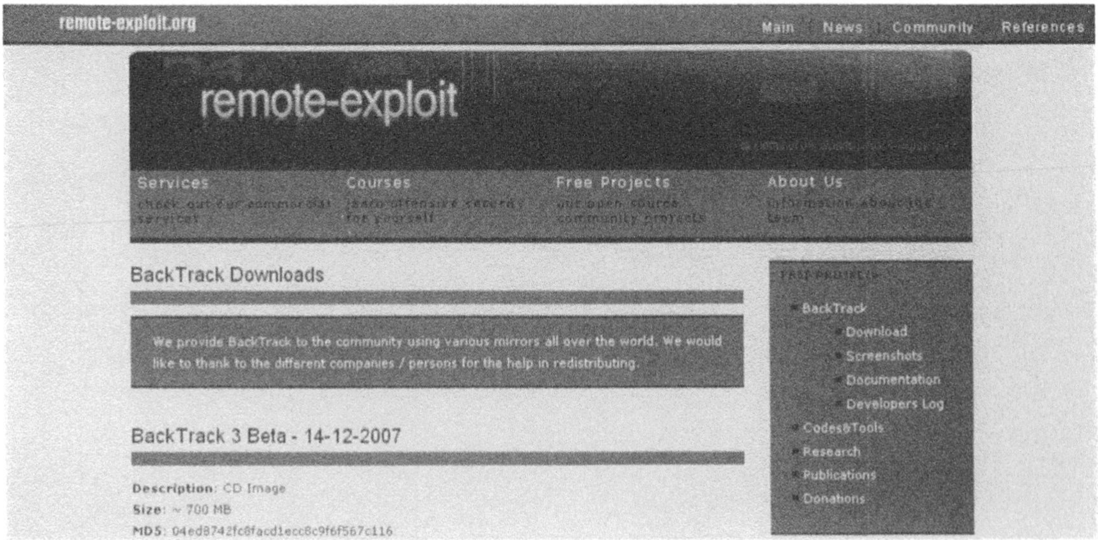

Both BackTrack 2 and BackTrack 3 Beta are available. Since BackTrack 3 Beta has very few bugs and is otherwise stable, this version is recommended (and will be the focus of this chapter). Furthermore, there are two versions of BackTrack 3 Beta: a ~700 MB CD image version (used in this chapter), and a larger (~1 GB) version for Universal Serial Bus (USB) thumb drives that includes some additional (but unnecessary for our purposes) modules.

You can download directly via Hypertext Transfer Protocol (HTTP) or File Transfer Protocol (FTP) from ten different mirrors, or by torrent. If you have the time, it is recommended (and more courteous) to use the torrent so that you can share some bandwidth. When you're finished downloading the ISO, be sure to check the MD5 hash of the file. This will save you some hassle later if the burned CD doesn't work correctly. You can find a simple Message Digest 5 (MD5) hash calculator at http://www.pc-tools.net/win32/md5sums/ (see Figure 10.2, with BT3b hash inset). Simply match the MD5 calculation with the hash posted at the Remote-Exploit download page, to confirm that your file is an authentic reproduction of the original, free from tampering or errors.

Figure 10.2 Confirming the MD5 Hash

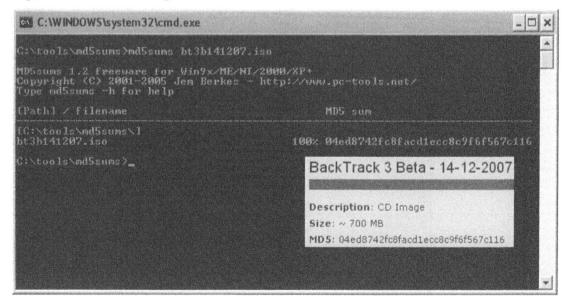

Burning BackTrack to CD

Your downloaded file is an ISO, or CD image file. To use BackTrack, you'll need to burn the ISO to a CD using any of the many available CD burning programs. A good and easy-to-use example is the program *DeepBurner*. A freeware version (DeepBurner Free) can be found at http://www.deepburner.com/.

While this chapter is not meant to be a tutorial on burning CDs, simply follow the wizard that starts when you open DeepBurner. Select a project type (Burn an ISO image), browse to and select your image file (bt3b141207.iso), select your CD write drive and write speed, and finally click Burn ISO (see Figure 10.3). It is that simple.

TIP

While your CD drive may be capable of burning at high speeds (40x and above), it is recommended that you burn BackTrack at slower speeds—preferably as slow as possible (4x or 8x). For whatever reason, more problems have occurred at higher burning speeds, and lower speeds have had better results.

Figure 10.3 DeepBurner Burns BackTrack to CD

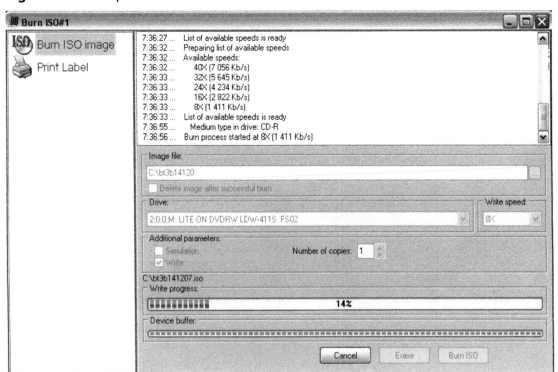

Configuring Kismet

This section will focus on booting into BackTrack and configuring Kismet.

Booting into BackTrack

To boot into BackTrack, insert the CD and restart your computer, taking care to ensure that your BIOS is set to boot from CD. BackTrack will run through the boot process. At the graphical boot menu, select the first option, which boots you into BackTrack using the KDE graphical desktop. The small, black terminal window icon on the left side of the taskbar will open up a console window.

Wireless Card Configuration

Perhaps the most important requirement is a wireless card that is supported by Kismet (see the Kismet documentation, section 12 "Capture Sources," located at http://www.kismetwireless.net/documentation.shtml for supported cards). This being said, if you start BackTrack and simply type **kismet** at the prompt, you will likely encounter the most common of all Kismet errors, which is the failure to configure a capture source (see Figure 10.4).

Figure 10.4 Kismet Fails; No Capture Source Enabled

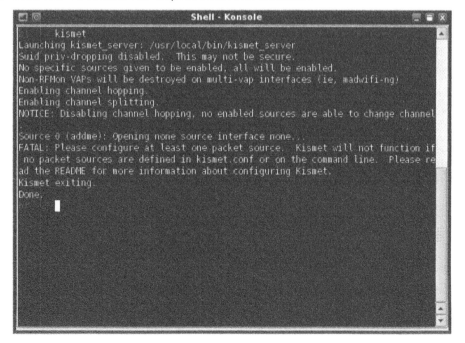

Before you decide to give up (and sadly, some people do), read the error message for an explanation of why Kismet failed to start. In this case, no capture source was enabled. As you might expect, this is a fatal error. We can also deduce from this error that we can correct this problem by specifying a capture source either via the *kismet.conf* file or the command line.

kismet.conf

To enable a capture source within the *kismet.conf* file, use your favorite text editor (in this example, we used nano) and edit */usr/local/etc/kismet.conf* (see Figure 10.5).

Figure 10.5 Editing kismet.conf

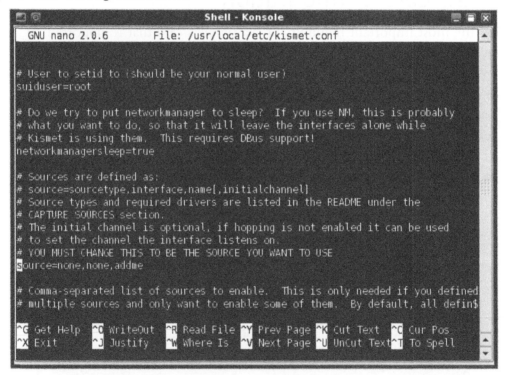

Scroll down approximately one page to the section that begins with:

```
# Sources are defined as:
```

Be sure to read through the notes within the section as to what is required: the source type, the interface, and the name. For source type and driver, refer to section 12, "Capture Sources," of the Kismet documentation. The interface is defined by Linux, and is dependent upon the particular card (in this example, we're using an Atheros card, which uses the *ath#/wifi#* interface). You can also find this information within the particular source type listing. Finally, the name is whatever you choose; it is only a label.

Command Line

To enable a capture source from the command line, start Kismet with the *–c* switch and follow it with the same syntax you used within the *kismet.conf* file: sourcetype, interface, and name:

```
bt ~ # kismet -c madwifi_g,wifi0,Atheros
```

Log File Configuration

By default, Kismet will save its log files to the location where you started Kismet. For example, if you start Kismet while in */root* (the default directory if you log on as the root user), the log files will be saved there. In a hard disk installation, this may be fine. However, when booting a live CD, these files are only stored in a temporary RAM disk and will be gone when you power off the system. In this case, you have two options: either copy the files to a thumb drive (or other device) before powering off; or better yet, start Kismet from the thumb drive so the files are automatically saved there. USB drives are typically mounted as *sda#*, so simply *cd* to */mnt/sda1* (or whatever the correct number is) and start Kismet from there.

Other Configuration Issues

While a Global Positioning System (GPS) receiver is not required to use Kismet, it is required if you want location data. If you're using Kismet to wardrive, it becomes a necessity. To configure Kismet to use GPS, you first need a GPS receiver that supports NMEA (virtually all of them do). Second, you'll need to start GPSD and point it to the path of your GPS receiver. To find the correct path of your receiver, plug in your GPS and look at the results of *dmesg* (you might try */dev/ttyUSB0* or */dev/tts/USB0* for a USB device):

```
bt ~ # gpsd -p /dev/tts/USB0
```

You won't get any feedback, but you can type *ps aux|grep gpsd* to ensure that the process started. To confirm that *GPSD* is working, Telnet to localhost port 2947 and type **R=1**; you should get scrolling NMEA strings with the current latitude and longitude.

TIP

For one reason or another, some people have had trouble running Kismet with the most recent version of *GPSD*. To fix some of those problems, a Kismet and Netstumbler forums user named Dutch, released an older, scaled down version of *GPSD*, appropriately titled *gpsdold*. Those who have used this version (including this author) have reported no problems. Dutch's version of *gpsdold* can be found at http://www.netstumbler.org/158973-post 1600.html. Download and install to */usr/bin*, and then use in the same way you'd use *GPSD*.

Wardriving with Kismet

If you've made it this far, congratulate yourself: you've downloaded BackTrack, burned it to a CD, booted up the live distro, and properly configured Kismet to work with your particular wireless card and GPS receiver. Now it's time to go wardriving.

Tools & Traps...

Optional but Useful Items for Your Wardriving Setup

In addition to your current setup, if your wireless card supports it, you may want to consider an external antenna. A simple 5 dBi omni-directional antenna designed for 2.4 GHz will significantly aid in the discovery of networks (an external antenna outside the car is eminently preferable to an internal antenna inside a wireless card sitting inside a metal car!). Most antennas will also require a pigtail, which is a short adapter cable that connects the antenna coaxial cable to the antenna jack on your wireless card. For special cases, you may want to consider a cantenna or other form of directional antenna. The folks at http://wardrivingworld.com and http://www.fab-corp.com are highly respected among wardrivers and will go out of their way to ensure you get the right equipment for your setup.

An additional consideration, especially for longer drives, is a power inverter. This device (which typically costs about $25–30) will plug into your cigarette lighter (or other vehicle power socket) and convert the vehicle's DC power to AC for your laptop.

Wardriving

We said that it was time to begin wardriving, but there are a few important tips to consider before you start (see also "Notes from the Underground"):

- Be sure that your wardriving setup does not physically impair your ability to drive, or block your line of sight. This may seem like common sense, but the more complex your wardriving setup, the more potential exists for exotic things that could get in your way of seeing. Don't let antennas, cables, or the laptop itself prevent you from being a responsible driver.

- Once you start Kismet and configure everything to run (see Figure 10.6), close your laptop lid. Again, this is a matter of common sense, because an open laptop is an invitation for distraction. Closing the lid removes the invitation to constantly peek at the screen. And believe me, if the screen is open, you'll peek at it.

Figure 10.6 Kismet is Started and Configured to Run

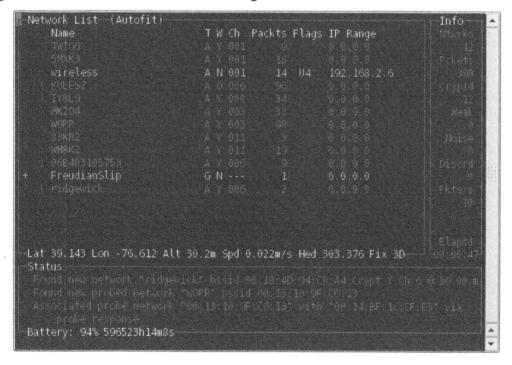

- Law enforcement officers will tell you that many more people talk themselves into tickets than the other way around. Should you be stopped by law enforcement, it is not necessary to fabricate some far-fetched story about what you're doing, or make false claims about the secret project you're working on and how they don't have a need to know. Wardriving is legal, so telling the truth is the easiest and simplest explanation.

Notes from the Underground...

RenderMan's Stumbler Ethics

1. Do Not Connect! At no time should you ever connect to any AP's that are not your own. Disable client managers and Transmission Control Protocol (TCP)/Internet Protocol (IP) stacks to be sure. Simply associating can be interpreted as computer trespass by law enforcement.

2. Obey traffic laws. It's your community too, and the traffic laws are there for everyone's safety including your own. Doing doughnuts at 3:00 A.M. gets unwanted attention from the authorities anyways.

3. Obey private property and no-trespassing signs. Don't trespass in order to scan an area. That's what the directional antenna is for. You wouldn't want people trespassing on your property would you?

4. Don't use your data for personal gain. Share the data with like-minded people, show it to people who can change things for the better, use it for education, but don't try and make any money or status off your data. It's just wrong to expect these people to reward you for pointing out their own stupidity.

5. Be like the hiker motto of "take only pictures, leave only footprints." Detecting SSID's and moving on is legal; anything else is irresponsible to yourself and your community.

6. Speak intelligently to others. When telling others about wardriving and wireless security, don't get sensationalistic. Horror stories and FUD are not very helpful to the acceptance of wardrivers. Speak factually and carefully. Point out problems, but also point out solutions.

7. If/when speaking to media, remember you are representing the community. Your words reflect on the rest of us. Do not do anything illegal no matter how much they ask. They may get pissed off, but at least you have demonstrated the integrity that this hobby requires. http://www.renderlab.net/projects/wardrive/ethics.html

You are wardriving to detect networks. Networks exist where people exist. While not absolute, it seems likely that the more people in a given area, the more networks. Office buildings, apartment complexes, and college campuses are locations that are ripe for wardriving. Furthermore, the closer you can get to buildings, the more likely it is that you'll detect more networks. If you can safely and legally drive through a parking lot to get closer to a particular building, by all means do so.

Do you have a goal in mind? Driving aimlessly in your pimped-out wardriving-mobile, especially given recent gas prices, can get mighty expensive. You ought to have a specific objective in mind when wardriving: cover a specific section of a particular neighborhood, or locate the APs of a particular location (perhaps as part of an authorized penetration test). Better yet, you might consider wardriving as a secondary effort of something else: while driving to work, visiting family in a different city, or on the way to a client's location. The final reason you ought to be wardriving is that it is fun. Wardriving is a hobby. If you're not enjoying yourself, you probably need to find a new hobby!

Tools & Traps...

GPS Location Data

Users are often confused about the GPS data that Kismet provides. A common question is: how does Kismet geo-locate an access point? Or, Are the GPS coordinates the actual location of the access point? While Kismet does take a number of signal readings at different locations, the real answer to the question is that it doesn't actually geo-locate anything; and the GPS coordinates are not the actual location of the AP.

The GPS receiver marks your location when you detect an AP. So while you're driving down the street and detect an AP in a house off the street, Kismet sees the AP as being in the street at the location where you were when you detected the AP (a quick look at street level maps at WiGLE.net will confirm this). When Kismet has more than one set of GPS coordinates, the displayed location is the set of coordinates where Kismet reported the strongest signal. In an ideal world, this would seem to provide you with a fairly accurate "abeam" location: as you detect an AP, the signal will be weak, and growing stronger until you pass abeam the AP, and then becoming weaker again until it is no longer detected. However, the harsh reality of obstructions and multi-path reflection will tend to skew these results. Still, all things considered, Kismet does a pretty darn good job.

Before you shut down your laptop, remember to save your log files to a USB thumb drive (or other external source) if you didn't already run Kismet from it. Remember, when running a live CD, the log files are saved to a temporary RAM disk, which will not be saved when you power off your laptop.

Managing Your Results

You've returned home from your first wardrive, and have collected hundreds (or perhaps even thousands) of networks. Now, what exactly are you going to do with this data? Hopefully, as we explained in the previous section, you had an objective in mind. If you were wardriving as part of a penetration test, you might want to parse out only those networks in the vicinity of your target location. Or, you might be interested in compiling statistics on the networks you collected: channel usage, encryption, and so forth. Either way, consider uploading your data to WiGLE.net.

WiGLE

WiGLE.net (Wireless Geographic Logging Engine) is an online database that holds in excess of 15 million logged wireless networks, most with geographic coordinates. WiGLE gives you access to Service Set Identifier (SSID) and manufacturer statistics, octet and channel usage statistics, and a browsable Web map of the world. By creating an account, you can upload and track your logged networks, and be credited with networks that you found first.

Obtaining BackTrack

☑ You can download directly or via torrent from http://www.remote-exploit. org/backtrack_download.html.

☑ Be sure to check the MD5 hash to ensure your download is free from tampering or errors.

☑ Burn the BackTrack ISO at slower speeds (4x–8x) for better results.

Configuring Kismet

☑ Be sure to use a supported card (see http://www.kismetwireless.net/ documentation.shtml for details).

☑ Make certain that you enable a capture source, either by editing the */usr/local/etc/kismet.conf* file or via the command line.

☑ Start Kismet from the location where you want the log files to be saved.

Wardriving with Kismet

☑ Don't let your wardriving interfere with safe driving. Close your laptop lid to resist the urge to peek at the laptop screen.

☑ Adhere to RenderMan's "Stumbler Ethics" when wardriving.

Index

A

Advance Packaging Tool (APT), 50
Airpcap Windows adapter, 175–177
apt-get command, 50
apt-get install command, 174
Asus eeePC installation
   Kismet installation, 172–173
   tools installation, 173–175
Asus WL–500g Premium router, 178
Atheros chipset, 53
Atheros mini PCI card, 178
Atmel chipset, 53
autofit, default sorting mode, 87

B

BackTrack
   booting, 243
   burning into CD, 242
   download page, 240
   MD5 hash calculation, 241
Backtrack, Live distros, 41
Basic Service Sent Identifier (BSSID),
   88, 105, 153, 167
Bluetooth, 13
buildroot tool, 205

C

Cacetech tool, 175–176
channel hopping, 196–198, 216
   fine-tune, 124
client_manuf file, 97–98
color-coding, Kismet interface, 91, 113
color scheme, 168
command-line switches, 168–169
cross-compiling process, 189
Cygwin library, 176

D

Darwin's speech functionality, 166
DeepBurner program, 242
Dr_GrEeN's script, 233
driver program, 50
drone, 188. *See also* Kismet drones
dumb kismet client interface, 110–111

E

Electronic Numerical Integrator and
   Computer (ENIAC), 6
Enhanced Specialized Mobile Radio
   (ESMR), 10
/etc/config/network file, 180, 199
/etc/init.d/S60kismet_drone file, 197
/etc/init.d/S70Wl_scan file, 196
/etc/kismet/kismet.conf file, 181
/etc/kismet/kismet_drone.conf file, 193, 200
Ethernet. *See* Local Area Network (LAN)
EXT3 file system, 182

F

firmware-based network discovery tools, 131
flags, 154

G

gkismet interface, 108
Global Positioning Systems (GPS), 92, 103,
   107, 165
   applications
      mapping and wireless, 12–13
      public safety, 10–11
   and kernel, 21
   receiver, in Kismet
      disadvantages, 74–77
      plug and null modem, 77–78

Global Positioning Systems (GPS)
(*Continued*)
signal measurement, 72
software used, 73–74
GPSD interfaces, 127
gpsd-p /dev/ttyS0 command, 74
gpsd-p /dev/ttyUSB1 command, 74
.gpsdrive/ directory, 138
Gpsdrive, navigation system, 137–138
homepage, 229
installation, 229–230
Kismet + GpsDrive + MySQL, 233
mapping, 234–235
MySQL support, 231–233
gpsd software, 72–74
GPSMap
features, 224
patching, 225
Graphical User Interface (GUI), 151

H
Hermes II chipsets, 53
hostap-compatible cards, 120

I
IGiGLE interface, 227
Irongeek's WiGLE WiFi Database to Google
Earth Client for Wardrive Mapping
(IGiGLE), 227–228

K
Kamikaze OpenWRT
allowedhosts parameter, 200
enable parameter, 202
LAN configuration, 199
start command, 202
wl command, 204
KisMap, python-based tool. *See* GPSMap
Kismet
complete setup, 78–80

configuration
booting BackTrack, 243
GPS receiver, 245
kismet.conf file, 56
log file configuration, 245
madwifi_g,wifi0,ProximBG source, 59
none.none.addme source, 58
suiduser and user root, 56–57
wireless card configuration, 244–245
and C++ program, 41–42
customizing panels interface
client list window, 96, 106
customizing colors, 107
modified network list window, 106
definition, 84
GPS receiver
disadvantages, 74–77
plug and null modem, 77–78
signal measurement, 72
software used, 73–74
graphical front end, 35–37
information panel, 86, 93
Linux installation, 23
APT, 50
card driver and chipsets, 50–54
configure command, 46–47
make dep, make, and *make install*
command, 47–49
server running, 60–61
source code, 43–45
log files, 27
monitor installation, 184
ncurses/panels interface, 84
network list panel
color-coding, 91, 113
column descriptions, 88
Global Positioning System (GPS),
92, 94, 103
Service Sent Identifier (SSID), 88–89, 92
sort options, 87–88

omni-directional antenna
    gain levels, 68–69
    with magnetic mount base, 67–68
panels interface, 84–85, 104
pigtails, 70–71
pop-up windows display
    client details window, 99
    client list window, 96, 106
    columns description, 105
    network details window, 95, 98, 105
    network location display, 104
    packet rate window, 99
    packet type display, 100
    statistics display, 102
    wireless card power display, 103
server connection, 36
source variable, 26
status panel, 93–94
third-party tools for, 111
user interface
    file type, 64
    play sound, 66
    splash screen, 65–66
wardriving
    client List, 34
    GPS data, 249
    hacking components, 178–179
    help Interface, 35
    ipkg command, 181–182
    LAN configuration, 181
    Law enforcement officers, 247–248
    network details, 33
    network detection, 249
    process ID file, 30
    router configuration, 179–180
    sort options, 32
    WiGLE.net online database, 250
in Windows system
    installation, 176–177
    troubleshooting, 177

kismet_client command, 143
kismet.conf file, 25, 27, 56, 174, 176, 194,
    204, 213
Kismet config file, 116–117
kismet-devel directory, 174
kismet_drone.conf file, 193–194,
    213–214
kismet_drone file, 120
Kismet drones
    buildroot installation
        Message Digest 5 (MD5), 210
        PKG_VERSION, 210
        target system and Makefile, 206
        troubleshooting, 211–212
    channel hopping, 196–198
    cross compiling process, 205
    Kamikaze OpenWRT, 198–200
    Linksys WRT54G, 188
    OpenWRT and buildroot tool, 205
    PC drone configuration
        channel hopping, 216
        command-line switches, 220
        defaultchannels parameter, 219
        hostap-compatible cards, 216
        kismet_drone.conf file, 214
        make install command, 212
        sourcechannels parameter,
            217–220
    server configuration
        hop channels and command line, 196
        run and config file, 194–195
        troubleshooting, 197–198
        wl commands, 196–197
    Whiterussian OpenWRT
        BOOT_WAIT parameter, 192
        ipkg command, 192–193
        jffs and *squashfs* file system, 191
        wl command, 193
Kismet Earth, mapping tool, 235
Kismet parameters. *See* Kismet server

Kismet-Sep-26-2006-1.gps, 141
Kismet server, 116–117
  airjack tools, 131
  alert patterns, 129
  allowedhosts= parameter, 152
  channel hopping, 120, 122–124
  client= line parameters, 161–164
  column= line parameters, 153–160
  command-line parameters, 117, 134,
      164–165
  command-line switches, 143, 146
  configdir parameter, 143
  decay= parameter, 152–153
  defaultchannels parameter, 124
  enablesources= parameter, 145
  festival= line parameters, 166
  fuzzycrypt= parameter, 141
  GPSD interfaces, 127
  .gpsdrive/ directory, 138
  hostap-compatible cards, 120
  limitations, 120
  logdefault parameter, 141, 144
  logexpiry= parameter, 133–134
  scripts
    /etc/init.d/gps, 183
    /etc/init.d/kismet, 183–184
  servername parameter, 117
  sourcechannels parameter, 125
  speech_encrypted and *speech_unencrypted*
      parameters, 167–168
  speech_unencrypted
      parameters, 137
  traffic decay, 152
  types of log files, 138, 145
Kismet's native mapping tool. *See*
    GPSMap
kismet_ui.conf file, 25, 64–65, 84, 89, 105,
    126, 134–135, 150, 168
Knoppix, Live distros, 41
KWrite, text editor, 56

L
Law enforcement officers,
    247–248
LibPcap package, 42
Linksys WRT54G, 178, 188
Linux-based Kismet front end, 108
Linux operating system
  GPSD installation, 24
  kernel configuration, 17–22
  Kismet installation, 23
listchan.pl script, 124, 218
"Live Distros," 41
Local Area Network (LAN), 6
lsmod command, 20

M
MAC addresses, 128–129, 137
Madwifi driver, 55–56
Madwifi-ng, 121–122
madwifi.org, 55
make command, 43
make dep command, 47–48
make install command, 47–49
make menuconfig command, 21
make suidinstall command, 48
mapping tools, 224, 228, 235
-max-packets switch, 145
Media Access Control (MAC)
    address, 97
Metasploit project, 132
MMCX connector, 70
MySQL, 231–233

N
National Marine Electronics Association
    (NMEA) protocol, 75
ndiswrapper driver, 53
network discovery tools, 131
North American datum of 1927
    (NAD27) data, 75

O

OpenStreetMap, mapping tool, 235
OpenWRT
  and buildroot tool, 205
  Kamikaze version, 178–179
  Wiki version, 179
Organizationally Unique Identifier (OUI),
    97–98
ORiNOCO Gold 11b/g Card, 52–53
Orinoco proprietary connector, 70

P

Passive sniffers, 130
PC Kismet drone configuration
  channel hopping, 216
  command-line switches, 220
  defaultchannels parameter, 219
  hostap-compatible cards, 216
  kismet_drone.conf file, 214
  make install command, 212
  sourcechannels parameter, 217–220
perl script *gpsfetchmap.pl*, 234
Personal communications
    services (PCS), 8
Pigtail cable, 70–71
probe networks group, 165

R

Radio Frequency Monitor mode
    (rfmon), 48
-retain-monitor switch, 146
RS-232 data protocol, 75

S

secure shell (SSH), 180
  Kismet drones, 192
Service Sent Identifier (SSID), 17, 32,
    88–89, 92, 225, 250
SETUID user, 118
Shortssis, 158

SOMElib package, 42
su command, 48, 50
sudo apt-get install gpsd command, 74
sudo command, 48, 50

T

tar-zxvf kismet-2007-10-R1.tar.gz
    command, 45
third-party front-end interfaces
  dumb kismet client, 110–111
  gkismet interface, 108
  KisWin interface, 109–110
Trivial File Transfer Protocol (TFTP),
    179, 192

U

uname–a command, 51
uname–r command, 51
Universal Serial Bus (USB) adapter, 175
USB memory stick, 178, 182
/usr/bin/festival, 135, 166
/usr/bin/play, 134, 164
/usr/local/etc, 84, 150
/usr/local/etc/kismet.conf, 244, 251
usually/usr/local/etc/, 137

V

virtual private network (VPN), 9

W

Wardriving
  definition, 14
  and hacker, 15–16
  Linux operating system
    GPSD installation, 24
    kernel configuration, 17–22
    Kismet installation, 23
Wellenreiter, network discovery
    tool, 130
WEP, 152, 154–155, 160, 164

Whiterussian OpenWRT
  BOOT_WAIT parameter, 192
  ipkg command, 192–193
  jffs and *squashfs* file system, 191
  wl command, 193
Wide Area Networks (WAN), 7
WiFi drivers, 121
WiFi mini PCI card, 180
WiFi Protected Access (WPA)
    network, 18
WiGLE Google Map, 226
Winpcap libraries, 176
Wireless card configuration
  command line sources, 244–245
  kismet.conf file, 245
Wireless card driver and chipset, 50–54
Wireless card power, 102–103, 113
Wireless Geographic Logging Engine
    (WiGLE), 225–226, 250
Wireless Local Area Networks (WLAN)
  omni-directional antenna, 68–69
  pigtails, 70–71

Wireless technology
  in airports and hotels, 9
  applications
    bluetooth devices, 13–14
    delivery and courier services, 10
    financial fileld, 11
    messaging and mapping, 12–13
    monitoring, 12
    point-of-sale (POS) applications, 11
    public safety applications, 10–11
    Web surfing, 13
  and cell phones, 7–8
  radio
    invention description, 4
    mobile radios, 5
wl command, 193, 196–197, 204
World geodetic system of 1984
    (WGS84) data, 75
www.kismetwireless.net, 43–44

X
XML log files, 139

Printed and bound by CPI Group (UK) Ltd, Croydon, CR0 4YY

03/10/2024

01040345-0003